MW00626141

Florida A&M University, Tallahassee
Florida Atlantic University, Boca Raton
Florida Gulf Coast University, Ft. Myers
Florida International University, Miami
Florida State University, Tallahassee
University of Central Florida, Orlando
University of Florida, Gainesville
University of North Florida, Jacksonville
University of South Florida, Tampa
University of West Florida, Pensacola

Other Books by William Logan

POETRY
Sad-faced Men
Difficulty
Sullen Weedy Lakes
Vain Empires
Night Battle
CRITICISM
All the Rage
Reputations of the Tongue

Gainesville · Tallahassee · Tampa · Boca Raton · Pensacola · Orlando · Miami · Jacksonville · Ft. Myers

Desperate Measures

William Logan

UNIVERSITY PRESS OF FLORIDA

Copyright 2002 by William Logan
Printed in the United States of America on recycled, acid-free paper
All rights reserved

07 06 05 04 03 02   6 5 4 3 2 1

Library of Congress Cataloging-in-Publication Data
Logan, William, 1950–
Desperate measures / William Logan
p. cm.
Includes bibliographical references.
ISBN 0-8130-2562-1 (acid-free paper)
1. American poetry—20th century—History and criticism.
2. English poetry—20th century—History and criticism. I. Title.
PS323.5.L643 2002
811'.509—dc21   2002027133

The University Press of Florida is the scholarly publishing agency
for the State University System of Florida, comprising Florida A&M
University, Florida Atlantic University, Florida Gulf Coast University,
Florida International University, Florida State University, University
of Central Florida, University of Florida, University of North Florida,
University of South Florida, and University of West Florida.

University Press of Florida
15 Northwest 15th Street
Gainesville, FL 32611–2079
http://www.upf.com

For Christopher Ricks

A man . . . is taken by surprise between the hedge and the ditch; he must tempt fortune against a hen roost; he must root out four paltry musketeers from a barn. . . . The least brilliant occasions happen to be the most dangerous; and . . . more good men have been lost on trivial and unimportant occasions and in fighting over some shack than in worthy and honorable places.

Montaigne, "Of Glory"

Contents

Acknowledgments   xi

1. The Other Other Frost   1
2. Abroad and at Home
   Ted Hughes, Eavan Boland, John Ashbery, Paul Muldoon   27
3. The Fallen World of Geoffrey Hill   37
4. Dreams of an Uncommon Tongue
   Gjertrud Schnackenberg, C. K. Williams, Thom Gunn   51
5. A Material World
   Jorie Graham, Richard Kenney, James Fenton   57
6. Old Faithfuls
   W. S. Merwin, Mona Van Duyn, John Ashbery   63
7. Pound at the Post Office   79
8. Eliot among the Metaphysicals   102
9. Classics and Commercials
   Christopher Logue and Alice Fulton   111
10. In the Lectureship of Verse
    Seamus Heaney, Helen Vendler, Anthony Hecht   117
11. The Bounty of Derek Walcott   123
12. Verse Chronicle: Martyrs to Language   127
13. Verse Chronicle: Gravel on the Tongue   141
14. The Unbearable Lightness of Elizabeth Bishop   155
15. Lowell in the Shadows   175
16. Verse Chronicle: Old Guys   187
17. Verse Chronicle: Hardscrabble Country   202
18. Richard Wilbur's Civil Tongue   217
19. Verse Chronicle: Betrayals of the Tongue   238
20. Verse Chronicle: Soiled Desires   254

21. Three Magi
    Charles Wright, Edward Hirsch, Henri Cole   269
22. Four or Five Motions toward a Poetics   274
23. Twentieth-Century American Poetry, Abbreviated   289

Books under Review   329
Credits   333

Acknowledgments

Poets do not need their occasions; but critics require theirs, and these pieces would not exist if editors had not asked for them. I am grateful to the editors of the *Chicago Tribune*, *Essays in Criticism*, the *New Criterion*, the *New York Times Book Review*, *Parnassus*, *Poetry*, *Sewanee Review*, *Southwest Review*, and the *Washington Post*.

chapter 1

The Other Other Frost

There have always been good reasons to ignore Robert Frost. The most traditional, the most metrically and morally conservative of modern poets, he was in a sense the last American poet of the nineteenth century (twelve at the death of Dickinson, he entered Dartmouth the year Whitman died). He could be hidebound and narrow and backward looking, his Yankee landscape the agrarian fantasy of a Southern Democrat—not John Crowe Ransom or Allen Tate, but Andrew Jackson. The land he celebrated (not just the physical landscape but the moral landscape) had already vanished, if it had ever existed. No American poet has created a more profound pastoral than Frost—profound because we believe it was a real place, not just the landscape of poetry.

Part of Frost's despair was his knowledge that his world was gone (when the terms of Frost's world were gone, the people remained). Many of his best poems take loss as their theme—sometimes loss as private and as crippling as anything in American literature. He was a ruined melancholic, and the dark gestures of his late Romanticism make him a moodier and far more difficult figure than Stevens, or Eliot, or Pound—compared to Frost they are shining untroubled aesthetes. They took America as a hypothesis; he took it for what it was—Frost told the stories that Whitman only suggested.

Frost was a poet of missed chance, of failed opportunity, of regret and cold disappointment. Of all the moderns he is the one we have not come to terms with, yet part of the problem has always been Frost himself. He did so much to emphasize, to publicize and receive honorary Ph.D.s for, his own worst instincts, to make himself the cracker-barrel Yankee sage that people were glad to take him for, a kind of Grandma Moses on the deck of the *Pequod*, that we shouldn't be surprised if now it is almost impossible to take him for anything else. More than forty years ago Randall Jarrell wrote two remarkable essays of rehabilitation, "The Other Frost" and "To the Laodiceans," arguing for the gloomy, hard, human Frost (*human* was a favorite Jarrell word), the Frost of "The Witch of Coös," "Provide, Provide," and "Home Burial." We have made Jarrell's other Frost part of our Frost—but now we have two Frosts, a farmer schizophrenic, half Vermont maple syrup and half raw granite, an old man of the mountains people can take home to dinner.

Each of these Frosts serves the idiom of our beliefs—we need the one to believe that poetry is good, the other to believe that poetry is true. Each version is a fact, but each is also a bias confirmed by the partiality of a reading. Frost was at times a bad philosopher, a man who wore his morals on his sleeve, and as he grew older he convinced himself he was a *philosophe* of masques and fables—he almost became a fable himself (or an apophthegm dreaming it was a fable). For sententious observation, homespun morals, for complacent sentiment and barn-idle philosophizing (the kind a cat does, tangled in a ball of yarn), you can't go much further than the later Frost. By the time John F. Kennedy invited him to read at the 1961 Inaugural, Frost was more a monument than half the equestrian statues in Washington—a brass-necked cold calculation, standing proudly on all fours. Has any major poet written a worse poem about America than "The Gift Outright"? It contains every part of Frost's terrible sentiment for the Land, America, the Past, for Ourselves, for the general myth that replaces the mangled event—even the best line, "To the land vaguely realizing westward," drowns in the horror of all that is left unsaid.

When "Home Burial" and "The Death of the Hired Man" can sit comfortably in high-school anthologies, no longer cruel rural dramas but complacent period pieces, perhaps it is time for a different Frost, one not so easily lost to high-mindedness. There is need for a Frost less dramatic and more demonic, a Frost of impermanent mood, whose own moods seemed a confusion to him (hence his reliance on, his attraction to, codes of behavior, morals, blind jurisprudence, the otherworldly forces that might set the world in order, or strip it to raw design).

Jarrell wanted people to read Frost, to suffer from his range and his terrors, and what is permanent in Frost now includes many of the poems Jarrell salvaged from neglect: "The Witch of Coös," "Neither Out Far Nor In Deep," "Home Burial," "Acquainted with the Night," "Design," "Provide, Provide," "An Old Man's Winter Night," and "Desert Places." (Even "After Apple-Picking" and "The Gift Outright," poems I can't imagine anyone liking. I must admit my taste is different from Jarrell's—I don't like "Directive"; I don't think "Provide, Provide" an "immortal masterpiece," though I like it well enough; and I despise "The Gift Outright." Every reader should have a list of the Frost poems he can't stand.)

If Jarrell's Frost was the Frost of interior and melancholy, of moral observation and metallic cunning, he was also the Frost whose monologues and scenes tended toward sentiment (a poet a lot like Jarrell, in other words). I would like to propose what might seem impossible after Jarrell, a list of a dozen or so of Frost's best poems rarely seen in anthologies and likely to be new to most readers. Here is the list: "The Code," "A Hundred Collars," "The Bearer of Evil Tidings," "Snow," "Place for a Third," "The Exposed Nest," "The Fear," "Spring Pools," "The Thatch," "Sand Dunes," "The Strong Are Saying Nothing," "The Draft Horse," "The Silken Tent," and "Willful Homing." This is a list of moral ambiguity and suspended grief, of stark horror and shy confusion—if Frost was a confusion to himself, we should, part of the time, be as confused and surprised by the Frost we read.

"The Code" starts with three men haying a field under an advancing thundercloud:

There were three in the meadow by the brook
Gathering up windrows, piling cocks of hay,
With an eye always lifted toward the west
Where an irregular sun-bordered cloud
Darkly advanced with a perpetual dagger

Flickering across its bosom. Suddenly
One helper, thrusting pitchfork in the ground,
Marched himself off the field and home. One stayed.
The town-bred farmer failed to understand.

The farmhand's mysterious act is abrupt as a scrawl of lightning, and the rest of the poem sets out to explain it. Silence has the force of speech in Frost, but this is one of the few places where silence is interpreted. The opening lines might seem just an excuse for a story, the story the remaining farmhand goes on to tell about another haying, another farmer who offended the code—in a more straightforward mood (even a rambling storyteller like Frost generally got on with things), the prologue could have been dispensed with. But the action is not just about the code, it is in code—a tale is required to explain the tale. The poem's lovely, lopsided organization is rougher and more accidental than in Frost's conservative dramas—the reader almost requires doubt about the form, as an imitative action. Only gradually is it clear that the second tale is in code as well—that the second farmhand is delivering a genial threat.

"But the old fool seizes his fork in both hands,
And looking up bewhiskered out of the pit,
Shouts like an army captain, 'Let her come!'
Thinks I, D'ye mean it? 'What was that you said?'
I asked out loud, so's there'd be no mistake,
'Did you say, Let her come?' 'Yes, let her come.'
He said it over, but he said it softer.
Never you say a thing like that to a man,
Not if he values what he is. God, I'd as soon
Murdered him as left out his middle name.
I'd built the load and knew right where to find it.
Two or three forkfuls I picked lightly round for
Like meditating, and then I just dug in
And dumped the rackful on him in ten lots.
I looked over the side once in the dust
And caught sight of him treading-water-like,
Keeping his head above. 'Damn ye,' I says,

'That gets ye!' He squeaked like a squeezed rat.
That was the last I saw or heard of him.
I cleaned the rack and drove out to cool off."

"I went about to kill him fair enough," the hand says later—he can afford to be so casual (death is often casual in Frost) because he knows his actions were understood, part of the code, never written down, by which men get along with each other. The farmer didn't die, but he earned his life at the cost of a lesson. The force of the poem is in the implicating conduct of different stories: the squall of violence when the farmhand throws down his pitchfork, the patient explanation of the second farmhand (a code of courtesy here), the town-bred farmer's incomplete understanding of what he's been told (he had been guilty of an unintentional insult), the silent courtesy of the threat the remaining farmhand delivers. The farmer has been warned—that is part of the code, too. Frost lets each of these stories rustle over the others (he knows something about literary codes as well); but the poem would never be effective without his warm feeling for the way men work, their stiff prides and dishonors, the lies they tell themselves.

The texture of those prides is in the texture of the details, the force that starts as invention and ends as a kind of second life: that "bewhiskered" farmer, about to be whiskered in hay; the ominous way the farmer "said it over, but he said it softer"; the almost meditative construction (*more* codes), "I'd as soon / Murdered him as left out his middle name"; the further meditative gesture of the farmhand picking "lightly round" the hay (how lovely to describe it as a kind of meditation); and that terrible sound, that terrible image, of the farmer squeaking "like a squeezed rat" (there is danger throughout—recall that "perpetual dagger" in the storm cloud). Running through the poem, as in the best of Frost, is the haunted echo of men's speech. Frost's pentameter is always too dependent on monosyllables, like the speech of most men. Here and there the lines are posed or stilted; but most of a century later these sound like men talking, not like a man writing.

"A Hundred Collars" starts in a similar offhand way—a man misses a train, is forced to lodge at a local hotel, but the hotel is full. He doesn't want to share a room—he doesn't *want* to, and Frost conveys with typical economy the apprehension that rises in such a man on such a night. He'd like to know who's in the room already:

> *"Who is it?"*

> *"A man."*

> *"So I should hope. What kind of man?"*

> *"I know him: he's all right. A man's a man.*
> *Separate beds, of course, you understand."*
> *The night clerk blinked his eyes and dared him on.*

> *"Who's that man sleeping in the office chair?*
> *Has he had the refusal of my chance?"*

> *"He was afraid of being robbed or murdered.*
> *What do you say?"*

> *"I'll have to have a bed."*

His resistance collapses, but not before he endures the delicious malice of the night clerk (the whole point of "A man's a man" is that it isn't true—a man's a man until he's a murderer). It's an old traveler's fear. Frost has to specify the separate beds—that should remind us not only of the close quarters earlier travelers had to tolerate, but of the scene in the third chapter of *Moby-Dick*, where Ishmael has to share a bed with Queequeg at the Spouter-Inn (when Ishmael is reluctant, the landlord there is more considerate—he starts to plane down a rough bench). It's one of the most gripping scenes in American fiction—the exhausted young man, reconciled to sleeping with the strange harpooner (who's off somewhere selling a shrunken head), then abed in the freezing room, on a mattress that seems "stuffed with corn-cobs or broken crockery," finally awoken by the entry of Queequeg (tattooed like a checkerboard, still holding the unsold head), who gets into bed smoking his tomahawk (the weapon doubled as a pipe) and then wildly threatens the young man he finds there. When Ishmael wakes the next morning, Queequeg's arm is thrown over him "in the most loving and affectionate manner."

Melville's scene turns maternal and comic there, and the trust between Ishmael and Queequeg is sealed by their night together. Frost has only a scholar and a subscriptions agent to work with, and he toys longer with the dread. The agent is named Lafe.

> *The Doctor looked at Lafe and looked away.*
> *A man? A brute. Naked above the waist,*
> *He sat there creased and shining in the light,*
> *Fumbling the buttons in a well-starched shirt.*
> *"I'm moving into a size-larger shirt.*
> *I've felt mean lately; mean's no name for it.*
> *I just found what the matter was tonight:*
> *I've been a-choking like a nursery tree*
> *When it outgrows the wire band of its name tag.*
> *I blamed it on the hot spell we've been having.*
> *'Twas nothing but my foolish hanging back,*
> *Not liking to own up I'd grown a size.*
> *Number eighteen this is. What size do you wear?"*
>
> *The Doctor caught his throat convulsively.*
> *"Oh—ah—fourteen—fourteen."*

Every gesture is alive with threat—the half-naked man talks of being "mean lately," talks of choking (a scholar the least sensitive to language would flinch at the latent violence). We're delighted with the unease that Frost so easily manufactures—but we're uneasy too. Frost sets the reader even with the characters—we're given no more information than the Doctor, and we must feel our way as clumsily. Lafe wants to know his collar size because . . . because he wants to give the Doctor a hundred old collars. But we're frightened to take anything from those we fear—what would be generosity seems only a further threat, perhaps even a trick. Frost has taken his character into the worst of fear—and then Lafe offers to take off the Doctor's shoes! Each clumsy action allows a new misinterpretation. The Doctor is poised to run away—but Lafe's worried only about the landlord's sheets. (Who but Frost, his eye on the meanness and misgivings, would pause for the beautiful line where Lafe, though half-naked, seems to *be* his shirt, all "creased and shining"?)

Eventually they find themselves in hobbled conversation ("Now we are getting on together," says Lafe), which leads to one of Frost's typical passages of observation, plain and circumstantial, but with the consuming conscience of character:

> *"It's business, but I can't say it's not fun.*
> *What I like best's the lay of different farms,*
> *Coming out on them from a stretch of woods,*
> *Or over a hill or round a sudden corner.*
> *I like to find folks getting out in spring,*
> *Raking the dooryard, working near the house.*
> *Later they get out further in the fields.*
> *Everything's shut sometimes except the barn;*
> *The family's all away in some back meadow.*
> *There's a hay load a-coming—when it comes.*
> *And later still they all get driven in:*
> *The fields are stripped to lawn, the garden patches*
> *Stripped to bare ground, the maple trees*
> *To whips and poles. There's nobody about.*
> *The chimney, though, keeps up a good brisk smoking.*
> *And I lie back and ride."*

How calmly and warmly and suggestively this is rendered, like harvest scenes from a medieval calendar—or like Wordsworth's first view of London in *The Prelude*. There's that beautiful surveyor's phrase, "the lay of different farms"; the simplicity of feeling in "I like to find folks getting out in spring"; the long patience of "There's a hay load a-coming—when it comes," even if we now think "a-coming" a bit corny (corny, but country); the visual fable of "The fields are stripped to lawn"; and then Brueghel's barren landscape of winter. It's not important to the poem—it's just there, like the landscape, the way that the characters are just there, accidentally thrown together and forced to make something like peace. So many of Frost's effects are almost negligent, as if they just happened. The scholar remains wary even at the last—that is *his* character. All his knowledge is no use in judging men—even when Frost disliked men like the Doctor, it was with fondness and understanding. That was what they were—and Frost's poetry is about the way men are. It would take so little for the Doctor just to accept the collars, yet all he can say is, "But really I—I have so many collars." (This is one of many times that Frost's meter allows a trembling hesitation of emphasis.) "There's nothing I'm afraid of like scared people," says Lafe.

Frost knew when to let a poem go—in his best poems the ending comes as a slight shock, as if the poem *couldn't* be over (in his worst the reader feels the poem shouldn't have begun). The actions seem to move beyond the end of the lines—this is an old trick in fiction, but how many poets other than Browning have used it well? Fiction wouldn't have served Frost's temper (if he'd been a novelist he might have written something awfully like *Ethan Frome*); but when we place him it must be alongside those moody gothics Hawthorne and Melville, the New England geniuses of guilt and redemption, and failures to redeem. Something of the violent fate that moves their fiction moves through his verse, but it is a fate blinder and more callous. Here is "The Draft Horse":

With a lantern that wouldn't burn
In too frail a buggy we drove
Behind too heavy a horse
Through a pitch-dark limitless grove.

And a man came out of the trees
And took our horse by the head
And reaching back to his ribs
Deliberately stabbed him dead.

The ponderous beast went down
With a crack of a broken shaft.
And the night drew through the trees
In one long invidious draft.

The most unquestioning pair
That ever accepted fate

And the least disposed to ascribe
Any more than we had to to hate,

We assumed that the man himself
Or someone he had to obey
Wanted us to get down
And walk the rest of the way.

This is the Frost who makes readers uncomfortable. We ought to be able to call it an allegory—but no allegory suggests itself (or, rather, the allegories are too simple for the savagery). The murder of the horse is so abrupt, so unforeseen, that the murderer seems more than just part of that unknowable agency that makes life harder (no memory "keeps the end from being hard," Frost wrote in "Provide, Provide"). The couple, with their faulty lantern and fragile buggy, with the wrong horse, are destined for trouble—and how Frost loved those scary old woods. (One critic asked—this is the sort of question critics *should* ask—why the couple had hitched a draft horse to a buggy. The answer should have been obvious— because they had to.) Frost knew more about depravity than any American writer after Melville and before Faulkner, and he had a cellar knowledge of our irrational fears (Frost tells us the man stabbed the horse *deliberately;* but first, in the way he grips the horse's head, Frost shows us deliberation). This is the Frost people don't *want* to care for, and yet look how compellingly the poem ends. The couple don't curse their fate; they're so unquestioning they seem slightly stupid. Yet isn't this a philosophy, a kind of clear religion, not "to ascribe / Any more than we had to to hate"? As readers we know we wouldn't act this way, and we're not finally sure that we *should* act this way—but we're not sure we *shouldn't*, either. That makes Frost strange, and us, in our settled, suspicious natures, ill at ease.

Frost's simplicity is deceptive, because it deepens so pitilessly into complication. When we say a man is complex, we mean we're not sure of his responses; and in Frost we're often measured by the way we read. Consider "Sand Dunes," a poem that starts so plainly it hardly starts at all:

Sea waves are green and wet,
But up from where they die,
Rise others vaster yet,
And those are brown and dry.

They are the sea made land
To come at the fisher town
And bury in solid sand
The men she could not drown.

She may know cove and cape,
But she does not know mankind
If by any change of shape,
She hopes to cut off mind.

Men left her a ship to sink:
They can leave her a hut as well;
And be but more free to think
For the one more cast-off shell.

Without the title, the first stanza might be opaque; but the shore is where waves die, and the dunes rise from the tide line. "They are the sea made land"—this might be mere ingenuity, a metaphor of sand, but Frost's idea is more peculiar: the dunes are the macabre way the sea will conquer the fishermen it hasn't been able to drown. (Dunes *could* bury a village—I saw them bury a cemetery once.) Even here, when Death and Fate and the Sea all seem inexorable, the poem hasn't finished. The sea isn't clever enough! If Frost were a worse poet, he'd linger here, and tell us that men can abandon a philosophy or an idea—but he doesn't. His men are like hermit crabs—he *says* they'll be freer to think, but we remember that for hermit crabs life is just one abandoned shell after another.

"Sand Dunes" is a trial piece for a poem more poignant (Frost is one of the few poets of whom one can, sometimes, use *poignant* without embarrassment) and more Stygian, "Neither Out Far Nor In Deep"—think of the syntactic organization of the last stanzas. It shows how good Frost can be when he isn't great, and how disturbing and not quite settled even his settled endings are. Frost is always catching his readers out—he is a poet disastrous to underestimate (even in his late poems, which are very hard to underestimate, there are words, lines, sometimes a stanza or two, that have the old rough homemade truth in them).

No one thinks the sea really has designs on the land—or no one would think it, if Frost hadn't said so. His fantasies have a primitive agency, a primitive terror—and don't men act at times *as if* they believed what Frost is only whimsical about? His poems require not that we believe them, but that we know we could believe them if we were different—that is, if we were Frost. This slight offness or strangeness lets his readers take as pleasant fictions what would otherwise be unpleasant truths, though that doesn't make the truths less unpleasant. "The Bearer of Evil Tidings" might have been written by Kipling—it is no more than a fantasy about a cliché:

> *The bearer of evil tidings,*
> *When he was halfway there,*
> *Remembered that evil tidings*
> *Were a dangerous thing to bear.*
>
> *So when he came to the parting*
> *Where one road led to the throne*
> *And one went off to the mountains*
> *And into the wild unknown,*
>
> *He took the one to the mountains.*
> *He ran through the Vale of Cashmere,*
> *He ran through the rhododendrons*
> *Till he came to the land of Pamir.*

This seems to be a poem about cowardice; but, by one of those reversals that drive Frost's poems into the blackness of our psychologies, it is really about prudence.

> *She taught him her tribe's religion:*
> *How ages and ages since*
> *A princess en route from China*
> *To marry a Persian prince*

Had been found with child; and her army
Had come to a troubled halt.
And though a god was the father
And nobody else at fault,

It had seemed discreet to remain there
And neither go on nor back.
So they stayed and declared a village
There in the land of the Yak.

Frost is good about religion—his distrust is wolfish and cagy. The Christian religion *has* to say that its god was the father of Jesus—otherwise there would be no religion. The oriental army advances under a similar suspension of disbelief; but it acts in just that bothersome human way Frost loves, accepting enough to believe, doubting enough not to go on and not to go back. (As readers we know that Frost is still thinking Christian thoughts.)

And that was why there were people
On one Himalayan shelf;
And the bearer of evil tidings
Decided to stay there himself.

At least he had this in common
With the race he chose to adopt:
They had both of them had their reasons
For stopping where they had stopped.

As for his evil tidings,
Belshazzar's overthrow,
Why hurry to tell Belshazzar
What soon enough he would know?

Few things escape Frost's brutal wryness here (though look at how delicately he suggests that other shelves might have other stories). *They had both of them had their reasons*—this doesn't mean that the reasons are good or honorable. The reasons for sacrifice (honor, integrity, loyalty to country or king) are never argued here—Frost knows all about them already. It is the small salvation of the slightly disreputable case that interests him. After all, the news would have had no effect on the outcome—Belshazzar was already overthrown. The poem might have stopped just before the last, throwaway stanza; but then it wouldn't have drifted beyond our expectations. A reader almost forgets that those evil tidings had somewhere to get to. That is the cold form of Frost's genius, and genius allows no pity for Belshazzar.

Frost's poems often find something human but distasteful in knowledge and belief—not just religion's set beliefs, but the beliefs men have to accept to get from one day to another. He recognizes that belief can be a weakness, that strength often requires a restraint. "The Strong Are Saying Nothing" ends there, but it starts in a casual, causal, haphazard way.

> The soil now gets a rumpling soft and damp,
> And small regard to the future of any weed.
> The final flat of the hoe's approval stamp
> Is reserved for the bed of a few selected seed.
>
> There is seldom more than a man to a harrowed piece.
> Men work alone, their lots plowed far apart,
> One stringing a chain of seed in an open crease,
> And another stumbling after a halting cart.
>
> To the fresh and black of the squares of early mold
> The leafless bloom of a plum is fresh and white;
> Though there's more than a doubt if the weather is not too cold
> For the bees to come and serve its beauty aright.
>
> Wind goes from farm to farm in wave on wave,
> But carries no cry of what is hoped to be.
> There may be little or much beyond the grave,
> But the strong are saying nothing until they see.

How lovely that *rumpling* in the first line is, and how ambiguous that *harrowed* later on. There is much in the loneliness of the way these men work, in that farmer *stumbling after a halting cart*. The brilliance of Frost's poems is often in these small acts of noticing, in the contrast between the harrowed soil (retaining the decay in that other sense of *mold*) and the white plum blossoms. Frost isn't a poet for mere beauty. The beauty of the plum tree comes ripe with disaster: if the weather is too cold for the bees, the beauty will not be served with plums. It's as if to say, "Beauty is all very well, in its place, but what's really important is the homely old plum." This isn't the point of the poem, but it leads to the point by a round-about way. Farming is the faith and hope of seeds, the religion of what comes after—suddenly we're in a poem about death. Frost's farmers don't trust anything they can't see. It might be tempting to predict a crop, and for many men it's tempting to predict what lies beyond the grave. It takes a kind of strength, Frost is saying, to resist from hope—those harrowed fields are bleak and Old Testament.

Frost could barely think of beauty without thinking of death. At times it made him arch and melodramatic, those two sins of Romantic character (there's a self-congratulatory cruelty to the end of the mawkish "'Out, Out—'"—the boy probably died from bad doctoring and an overdose of ether); but usually he just suffered his understandings, half sad and half stoic. He knew how much death cost the people who survived, how much even the prospect of death cost them. The odd little poem "Not to Keep" is about a wounded soldier, sent home to his wife. She thinks that they've escaped, that the war is over for them; but she cannot see his wound. Finally she has to ask, and he has to tell her—the wound is severe enough to send him home, but not to keep him home. He has to go back to war.

Frost is a master of what people have to endure for each other. The visual arts have never been much good at showing what people say without saying, but in "Not to Keep" it's all there in a line or two. (The movies cheat and use music, and perhaps you could say that de la Tour cheated with light and with significant glances.) It is easy to forget how much Frost does not say in his poems, how much power lies in his reticence.

Frost was unashamed of writing as a man (not *for* other men, but *about* other men), in a way that would be almost impossible now. The women in Frost's poetry usually stand apart from the action, like a Greek chorus—and yet we've had few poets who understood women better. How many wonderful women he created as characters: the wife in "The Death of the Hired Man" and the wife in "Home Burial," The Witch of Coös and the Pauper Witch of Grafton, the wife in "The Fear" and the depressed wife in "A Servant to Servants," the mother in "The Housekeeper," the wife of "In the Home Stretch." There's a fine anthology to be made merely from Frost's women, merely from Frost's wives (Frost must have been a bit afraid of women—in the dialogues, the women usually come off better than the men). Frost wasn't ashamed of being a man, and that gave him an understanding of women—not *the* understanding, but an understanding that can come only from liking what women are. It shows in poems like "The Silken Tent."

> *She is as in a field a silken tent*
> *At midday when a sunny summer breeze*
> *Has dried the dew and all its ropes relent,*
> *So that in guys it gently sways at ease,*
> *And its supporting central cedar pole,*
> *That is its pinnacle to heavenward*
> *And signifies the sureness of the soul,*
> *Seems to owe naught to any single cord,*
> *But strictly held by none, is loosely bound*
> *By countless silken ties of love and thought*
> *To everything on earth the compass round,*
> *And only by one's going slightly taut*
> *In the capriciousness of summer air*
> *Is of the slightest bondage made aware.*

The language here (that *sunny summer breeze*, that *gently sways at ease*) doesn't have the considered simplicity of the best of Frost—Frost hovered around clichés so often that sometimes he just lit on them. From the middle of the poem onward, however, this metaphysical conceit (how rarely that plain old lover-of-metaphysics Robert Frost chose to be metaphysical) gains from the force of its slightly self-conscious, off-the-shelf poetic language; and the concentration of the final three lines can scarcely be equalled. Reading those lines, the reader finds something pulling taut in him, too. The awkwardness is a homage to feeling, as it was in Hardy.

This doesn't mean that Frost understood all women, or even specific women. Many of his best poems recognize the mystery between women and men—the mystery that is misunderstanding. The insignificant incident of "The Exposed Nest" starts in that kind of misunderstanding:

> *You were forever finding some new play.*
> *So when I saw you down on hands and knees*
> *In the meadow, busy with the new-cut hay,*
> *Trying, I thought, to set it up on end,*
> *I went to show you how to make it stay,*
> *If that was your idea, against the breeze,*
> *And, if you asked me, even help pretend*
> *To make it root again and grow afresh.*
> *But 'twas no make-believe with you today,*
> *Nor was the grass itself your real concern,*
> *Though I found your hand full of wilted fern,*
> *Steel-bright June-grass, and blackening heads of clover.*
> *'Twas a nest full of young birds on the ground*
> *The cutter-bar had just gone champing over.*

The woman wants to make it right, somehow (how many opportunities this poem gives to modern critics, those proud descendants of Freud). Few passages in Frost are as rich with the inevitability of death as "your hand full of wilted fern, / Steel-bright June-grass, and blackening heads of clover." The couple are trying to do the impossible, to restore the entire field so the mother bird won't abandon the nest. The field has a mortal beauty, like a Van Gogh; but Frost isn't interested in that. He sees "The way the nest-full every time we stirred / Stood up to us as to a mother-bird / Whose coming home has been too long deferred." There isn't much time for these nestlings—and the couple don't know if their meddling will make things worse. They work on anyway.

> *We saw the risk we took in doing good,*
> *But dared not spare to do the best we could*
> *Though harm should come of it; so built the screen*

You had begun, and gave them back their shade.
All this to prove we cared. Why is there then
No more to tell? We turned to other things.
I haven't any memory—have you?—
Of ever coming to the place again
To see if the birds lived the first night through,
And so at last to learn to use their wings.

The poem abandons the nestlings, as the couple did, when every-thing that could be done had been done—even if they'd done the wrong thing. Without quite saying so (Frost's poems are expert in not quite saying so), the poem has sketched the boundary of this couple's lives: the way the man assumes the woman is playing; the way he wants to show her how to do what she's doing (*just like a man*, we might think now); the way the end acknowledges not just that there are other matters, but that some matters must be abandoned. That such things, some things, need to be left alone insinu-ates darkly into these lives—there is a risk to what kindness can do, a risk and a limit. But sometimes you have to be kind anyway.

The men and women in Frost often stare bleakly past each other. It's not that they have too little to say, but that they have too much. Those birds, or birds very much like them, disturb the com-placent rage of the speaker in "The Thatch." He has stormed out of his thatched cottage, into the winter rain, and won't come back until his wife puts out the bedroom light. She won't put out the light until he comes in. Their cast-iron mulishness might last for-ever—it has the inevitability of myth (Frost is good about the mean things that make us mulish—however leathery the moral quality in his souls, he sees their weakness, too). But:

> *as I passed along the eaves,*
> *So low I brushed the straw with my sleeves,*
> *I flushed birds out of hole after hole,*
> *Into the darkness. It grieved my soul,*
> *It started a grief within a grief,*
> *To think their case was beyond relief—*
> *They could not go flying about in search*

Of their nest again, nor find a perch.
They must brood where they fell in mulch and mire,
Trusting feathers and inward fire
Till daylight made it safe for a flyer.
My greater grief was by so much reduced
As I thought of them without nest or roost.
That was how that grief started to melt.

He didn't mean to bother those birds, didn't mean to add their hardship to his; but that's the way anger is (it's no use arguing with Frost that anger isn't always this way). The innocent suffer, sometimes without knowing the cause of suffering. The man can do nothing to repair the injury; and there's a naked recognition in that remarkable line "It started a grief within a grief" (a line that echoes in the scarring ambiguity of *brood*). Frost tended to jingle in couplets (his ear grew unsure when his rhymes were too close together), but here the jingling underlines the absurdity of a man standing out in the rain to prove a point. And some of those rhymes are canny—that hollow, eaten-out *soul* is rhymed with *hole;* the *grief* is intimately bound, not with *relief,* but with *beyond relief.*

Those tangles of grief and regret between men and women, regret and sometimes the kindness of regret, unravel in odd directions. In "Place for a Third" (what an awful maker of titles Frost could be—sometimes they're slapped on like gummed labels), a man wants to respect his wife's dying wishes. She's had three husbands, he's had three wives; and she doesn't want to lie with the other women.

One man's three women in a burial row
Somehow made her impatient with the man.
And so she said to Laban, "You have done
A good deal right; don't do the last thing wrong.
Don't make me lie with those two other women."

Laban said, No, he would not make her lie
With anyone but that she had a mind to,
If that was how she felt, of course, he said.
She went her way. But Laban having caught

This glimpse of lingering person in Eliza,
And anxious to make all he could of it
With something he remembered in himself,
Tried to think how he could exceed his promise,
And give good measure to the dead, though thankless.

It's a surprise to him, *This glimpse of lingering person* (what a judicious, delighting phrase); but he wants to give to the dead just measure, or measure more than just (how loyal Frost's characters are—our poetry has almost forgotten the homiletic portion of character). He thinks of buying her a plot of her own:

He'd sell a yoke of steers to pay for it.
And weren't there special cemetery flowers,
That, once grief sets to growing, grief may rest;
The flowers will go on with grief awhile,
And no one seem neglecting or neglected?
A prudent grief will not despise such aids.

This is typical of Frost. Laban will grieve, but he'll be practical, too. How can we not admire a character whose complications come so coiled in pathos, whose trivial economies lie next to absurd generosities? (That yoke of steers is a sacrifice—they had to be trained to the yoke.) He thinks of a better way of satisfying his duty, and his love: he'll bury her next to the boy she first loved, who lived in a neighboring town. He finds the grave (it's marked *John, Beloved Husband,* but we're never told where John's wife lies—that may be another story), and Laban goes to plead his case before the dead man's sister.

                              The sister's face
Fell all in wrinkles of responsibility.
She wanted to do right. She'd have to think.
Laban was old and poor, yet seemed to care;
And she was old and poor—but she cared, too.
They sat. She cast one dull, old look at him,
Then turned him out to go on other errands
She said he might attend to in the village,

While she made up her mind how much she cared—
And how much Laban cared—and why he cared.
(She made shrewd eyes to see where he came in.)

Here the run of shortened sentences follows the short reversals of a mind at odds. She's shrewd, but not heartless. Finally she can't consent; and she tells Laban through a closed screen door (how good Frost was at paltry details). The reason's so funny it's almost sad: "There wouldn't be no sense. / Eliza's had too many other men." The poem might have ended there, but it can't—it would *be* a bad joke. Laban goes back to his first plan, to buy Eliza her own plot: it "gives him for himself a choice of lots / When his time comes to die and settle down." That *settle down* is terrifying. Frost's disquiet about the afterlife usually revealed a disquiet about our arrangements in this one; and death here is "settling down" in a way we usually don't like to think of (earlier, death is made almost willful—"She went her way"). We understand too little of people if we don't appreciate how they can be canny and caring at the same time—and the abyss that remains between.

Frost's poetry is one long exploitation of a fairly limited notion about character, and yet to the limitations what a rare and brush-fine rendering he brings. There is more truth in Frost's simplicities, his love of morals and homilies and examples, than in all the dry chaff of autobiography on which our poetry now subsists (*This was my life*, our poems protest, as if having a life were the same as having art). How interested Frost seems in other people—and yet how interesting that makes *him* seem. The problem is not that Frost is too simple for us; it's that we are too simple for him.

"Snow" is another of Frost's wretched claustrophobic dramas. There's a blizzard. The Coles have been wakened by a visitor, a preacher trying to get home after a prayer meeting. He's named Meserve, one of those cross-grained backcountry names, and he's a preacher in some backcountry Christian sect. He calls his wife to tell her he's still on the way. The couple want him to stay the night, but they can't make themselves make him stay; and he's stubborn enough to go on (stubborn enough to have gone to town to preach on such a night). Much of the poem consists of the couple squabbling, in a half-fond, half-irritated marital way—the poem is almost as long as *The Waste Land*. Meserve goes out to the barn to check his horses, and when he comes back they plead with him to stay.

> *Meserve seemed to heed nothing but the lamp*
> *Or something not far from it on the table.*
> *By straightening out and lifting a forefinger,*
> *He pointed with his hand from where it lay*
> *Like a white crumpled spider on his knee:*
> *"That leaf there in your open book! It moved*
> *Just then, I thought. It's stood erect like that,*
> *There on the table, ever since I came,*
> *Trying to turn itself backward or forward,*
> *I've had my eye on it to make out which;*
> *If forward, then it's with a friend's impatience—*
> *You see I know—to get you on to things*
> *It wants to see how you will take, if backward*
> *It's from regret for something you have passed*
> *And failed to see the good of. Never mind,*
> *Things must expect to come in front of us*
> *A many times—I don't say just how many—*
> *That varies with the things—before we see them.*
> *One of the lies would make it out that nothing*
> *Ever presents itself before us twice.*
> *Where would we be at last if that were so?*
> *Our very life depends on everything's*
> *Recurring till we answer from within."*

The symbol is too available here—the book is no doubt the Bible. (What other book, likely to lie open in a farmhouse, has pages so thin they might stir in the lightest breeze—and what else does Meserve "heed"? And yet why doesn't he name it?) The preacher's hesitation makes the moment less certain; he can't say when we'll see the way things are, and there's more than a shiver of apocalypse in his speech—a preacher who thinks about what comes again (which our lives depend on, when we will "answer from within") is half thinking of the Second Coming. The couple don't much like Meserve, and they're angry with him because they're afraid for him (if he dies in the blizzard, they'll feel responsible). There's something else, something not quite said in the poem—the wife and Meserve were apparently friendly as children. The couple go back and forth with him, and she makes one last attempt:

> *"But why when no one wants you to go on?*
> *Your wife—she doesn't want you to. We don't,*
> *And you yourself don't want to. Who else is there?"*

> *"Save us from being cornered by a woman.*
> *Well, there's—" She told Fred afterward that in*
> *The pause right there, she thought the dreaded word*
> *Was coming, "God." But no, he only said,*
> *"Well, there's—the storm. That says I must go on.*
> *That wants me as a war might if it came.*
> *Ask any man."*

How crafty Frost is. He wants Meserve to surprise us, but it's more of a surprise if we know the *expected* answer—making sure causes a delay, and delay heightens the expectation.

Meserve goes off into the blizzard. "It's quiet as an empty church without him," the husband says. He means to say only that the storm of Meserve's presence having passed, they are left in a strange silence. But Meserve *is* a preacher, and they are left in the church a preacher has abandoned. They are still *inside* a church— the church of their wintry home, their narrow tight religion of each other. And yet that church feels forsaken—as if the god (the word Meserve hasn't said) has passed out of it, too. We know that when a church is empty, the god's still there; and yet an empty church can feel less than spiritual, just an empty warehouse. What devastating resonances this simple line lets loose, and how long it takes to explain poems that so simply explain themselves.

Hours later Meserve's wife calls—he still hasn't returned. The couple descend to new guilt; they admire and despise Meserve for being what he is. They try to ring her back, but she's left the phone off the hook. (This is an early village party-line system—her number's 21, just two digits, and when her phone's off the hook they can hear the sounds in her house without ringing her.) Then Meserve calls—he's come home. The couple should be relieved, but they're not, quite. A tremor has gone through their lives. Perhaps they'll just forget it. The nearness of death; the icy white desolation of the night (Meserve remembers something he heard a boy say: "You can't get too much winter in the winter"); the runty and nearly repulsive Meserve, down to the lovely, horrible description of his hand, "like a white crumpled spider"—it's a winter nightmare, all below-freezing anxiety. Frost knows not to let the couple subside into forgiveness, or rise to pure irritation. Frost used dialogue as well as Eliot or Joyce—he may be nineteenth century in his philosophy (early Frost sounds as if it were written before Darwin), but he's modern in his voices. Eliot caught something of the twenties when his characters spoke, but Frost's characters are almost our contemporaries.

I don't have space—though I wish I had space—to discuss that wintry companion piece, "Willful Homing"; or the mysterious poem "The Fear" (with that wonderful line, "I saw it just as plain as a white plate"); or the ending of "A Brook in the City," where the hidden won't stay hidden (Freud might have written such a poem, if he hadn't *been* a poem). Let me end, since I've lingered so long in the bleaker regions of Frost, with something almost springlike, "Spring Pools":

> *These pools that, though in forests, still reflect*
> *The total sky almost without defect,*
> *And like the flowers beside them, chill and shiver,*
> *Will like the flowers beside them soon be gone,*
> *And yet not out by any brook or river,*
> *But up by roots to bring dark foliage on.*
>
> *The trees that have it in their pent-up buds*
> *To darken nature and be summer woods—*
> *Let them think twice before they use their powers*
> *To blot out and drink up and sweep away*
> *These flowery waters and these watery flowers*
> *From snow that melted only yesterday.*

The pools reflect the whole sky because the forest leaves haven't come on (the *defect* would be the thin high branches). Their nearly faultless reflections, like barely scratched mirrors, must give way to a darker nature. The darkness in the forest means only the leaves; but we know what Frost *really* means. He was such a plain poet in his words (he so rarely tried for those "poetic" effects of sound and usage that most poets live on like the air—a plant that does that is an epiphyte), but such a devious man in his lines. This doesn't mean that he couldn't be ornamental when he chose—there's that beautiful chiasmus here, "These flowery waters and these watery flowers," and think of the ornate line from "The Black Cottage," "A buttoned hair-cloth lounge spread scrolling arms." But think also how later in that poem the minister rises briefly into "poetry," and then stops, as if embarrassed. Few poets have ever caught such power in plain speech; Frost's lines bear their ideas without the distraction of ornament, or with the least ornament necessary for the democracy of argument (how tangled the notions in the simple "pent-up" buds here—they're all raw DNA, with empires to build).

The complications are in the shrewdness of the said. How could the summer woods have that kind of fairy-tale darkness? There is no evil, and yet the loss of the pools is a minor kind of evil, just because it is a loss. "Let them think twice," Frost asks, but we know they won't, and can't. The snow has melted into pools, the pools melt away into foliage—the competing forces are just a long chain of sources, of dying supersessions. And yet something remains to be mourned, if we remember how transient our lives are, about to vanish with the silence of the pools. It takes a hard nature to be grateful for the use our lives are to others. Frost knew that necessity as a form of regret.

Frost was a vain and arrogant man, and some of his humility is merely vanity. But some of it is humility, too. He knew his poems might not always be of use—he knew his life had not been much use to those he loved. When we tire of "Birches" and "Mending Wall," of "After Apple-Picking" and "The Road Not Taken" and "Stopping by Woods on a Snowy Evening," of "Nothing Gold Can Stay" and "Fire and Ice" and all the other poems anthologized into the thick crust of our memories—after we have tired of these, there is another Frost, and another. The good in Frost often lies so close to the sentimental and bad, it is difficult to remember that some of the best-loved poems *are* the best, just as some are the worst and most trivial.

I've wanted here to be like Frost, to be a noticer of common things, of the uncommon in the common. Many of the poems in this other other Frost have caught the eyes of scholars (occasionally only to be dismissed—one weighty critic thought "The Code" and "A Hundred Collars" were "fatuously obvious"), but that has not saved them from general neglect. A reader who hasn't gone beyond the white picket fence of the poems everyone knows by heart will find in Jarrell's essays a remarkable unknown Frost (not quite as unknown now as then), and I hope another unknown Frost here. And I haven't had a word for the grim poverty of "The Housekeeper," for the chilling anecdote of "The Vanishing Red," for "The Ax-Helve" or the strange fable of "Paul's Wife" or the rough comedy of "Brown's Descent," for all the secret bitterness and knowledge in "Fireflies in the Garden," for "The Mountain" (I might as well nominate all of *North of Boston*) or the brilliantly handled monologue of "The Black Cottage" (which Jarrell likes and then calls "lesser") or "On Going Unnoticed."

Frost is a Vermont-granite original. He is strange in the way that Whitman is strange: inconsistent, knowing and yet unknowable, likely to go off on goose chases, self-satisfied and yet raging against self-satisfaction, moral and honest (even when a little immoral and dishonest), his bad jumbled with his good, and yet finally and unconsciously and proof-bright American, representative of even the striving, sentimental, blank and blinkered parts of being American. An art like Frost's is not just the residue of the country he inhabited, it is the factual prelude to that country's imaginative acts. If we want those strange citizens of the next millennium to know what it was to be American in the last centuries of this one, we could do worse than to bury, in Camden or Keokuk or Fresno, in Tie Siding or Pensacola or Hanover or Fort Smith, a lead box with the collected poems of Walt Whitman and Robert Frost.

chapter 2

Abroad and at Home

Ted Hughes

The current poet laureate of Britain has always written as if poetry required not just theology but pathology. Since the publication of *The Hawk in the Rain* in 1957, Ted Hughes has forced a medium of great suppleness and electric charge from a style impatient, wrenched, violent, almost Anglo-Saxon in its guttural address. His poems, at first all muscle and masculine shorthand, served the darker, bestial strain of English poetry that runs from Wyatt and Marlowe through Coleridge, finally draining into the sexual murkiness of D. H. Lawrence. In two or three of the poems in *Wolfwatching*, there is still that wary, lean wolfishness:

He knows how to lie, with his head,
The Asiatic eyes, the gunsights
Aligned effortless in the beam of his power.
He closes his pale eyes and is easy,
Bored easy.

Such poetry survives in the tension between passion and humorlessness; though humorlessness is a quality relatively easy to sustain as one ages (even born comedians like Auden get a little arthritic after forty), passion must be present in the movement of a poem as well as the dramatic architecture. It is no use borrowing the great themes if mere lines do not convince.

Hughes has been considered a poet of nature so long—and he can be a poet of almost animal instinct and cunning (the Bard of Beasts, as A. Alvarez once called him)—it is perhaps useless to suggest that his bestiary, that zoo of the poet's imagination, is now good for nothing but little exercises in a peculiar Hughesian diction. His portrait of a macaw, for example, "The Punishment of Iago, Re-incarnated as Malvolio in the Form of a Macaw," has a handsome title for a poem in which neither Iago nor Malvolio figures. Even if we dimly perceive them in the evil, gimlet-eyed comedy of the macaw, transformed by Hughesian bombast ("Gomorrah! Sodom! Your eye squirms on its pin / In its socket of ashes"), Hughes has announced this Armageddon of animals too often. Some years ago the inner necessity went out of such language, as happens when a poet mantles himself in a diction and forgets, or mislays, the psychological pressures that formed it. A reader has to return to *Wodwo* or *Lupercal* to find that language used as if it mattered—in the incantatory, apocalyptic poems of *Crow*, portentousness had already become self-parody.

In his meditations—and his lyrics are often just excuses for meditation—Hughes presents a figure of powerfully lonely and attractive burden, for whom nature provides the only adequate suffering and purity. His late style, however, seems to demand bushels of rhetorical questions and a lot of shouting, as if the reader had gone slightly deaf ("And the paced-out length / Of his leash! The limit of human strength!"). Hughes has never been much of a prophet—his temperament suits a more mystic attention—but he has become a little desperate and wild-eyed. Worse, when he chooses to write with Serious Purpose, as in "The Black Rhino," composed to raise funds to protect an endangered species, he takes tragedy into the music hall:

The Black Rhino is vanishing.
Horribly sick, without knowing,

She is vanishing. She is infected
With the delusions of man. She has become a delusion.

Every cell of her body is ruptured with human delusion.
She is vanishing

Into a hallucination. She has blundered somehow into man's
phantasmagoria, and cannot get out.

Hughes is still a poet of raw phrase and raw reserve, more by fits than by starts. Individual lines have a sculptural or textural gravity, even if too often the elements of power are present without the animation. His most attractive new poems derive from family—as if the family were his bestiary now—and have some of the offhand logic and dynamic shift of Lowell's *Life Studies*. In portraits of a muscular, devil-may-care uncle or a silent, war-hero father (a poem marred only by its mawkish last lines), his mannerisms find a substance, and the substance is the beast beneath the skin:

After some uncle's
Virtuoso tale of survival
That made me marvel and laugh—
I looked at your face, your cigarette
Like a dial-finger. And my mind
Stopped with numbness.

Your day-silence was the coma
Out of which your night-dreams rose shouting.

Such poems about memory, the very meanness of memory, have a ghostly, transfiguring presence in a book where many of the animals, and much of the style, are on steroids.

Eavan Boland

Eavan Boland is a domestic but not domesticated animal. Like other Irish poets, she has been formed by a national culture that has become national myth, however riven and violently marked that culture has been. *Outside History*, her third book to appear in America, is devoted to women, whose lives have rarely figured in the national accounts. When she writes about Daphne, Daphne is trapped in the kitchen.

New mythologies are rarely less sentimental than old ones, and Boland avoids few of the obvious risks. She is expert in the passionless household poem, its subject the incident reminiscent, its tone the retrospect melancholy, its diction the vernacular significant. She likes to start with a hard fact ("It is Easter in the suburb" . . . "My mother kept a stockpot" . . . "The chimneys have been swept"), but she tends to drift off into the abstract language of *fluencies, patterns, complexities, densities.* Every object is a little too neatly or symbolically in order. When a mug breaks, a love affair is over.

For Boland, the kitchen is a mortuary, but in poem after poem kitchen and garden provide scenes for her bloodless anger. When a poet is so self-divided, so drawn to the realms she despises, her poetry suffers division too, here between prose and the poetic. That division affects many poets, whose very inheritance may be division; but rarely does it do so as forcefully. The featureless prose and aimless, airless philosophizing of Boland's work are transformed only by a love of pure detail, of the incandescence of the visual. A poem moony with memory is hardened into "the arc of the salmon after sudden capture— / its glitter a larceny of daylight on slate." She has a gift for the graven phrase ("this rephrasing of the air") or the poetic tremor of a single word ("midges freighting the clear space between / the privet and the hedge"), though she uses it sparingly, as if too much might be a bad thing.

Boland seems to wish to be, even to believe herself to be, a poet of some mystic immanence, for whom the natural powers are landscape, garden, memory, and children. She attempts to write by force of personality, which is difficult even when a poet has a striking personality and is almost impossible when she is a set of attitudes. Whenever she nears the gravitational pull of the past, however, she becomes a darling of the sure particular:

The German girls who came to us that winter and
the winter after and who helped my mother fuel
the iron stove and arranged our clothes in wet
thicknesses on the wooden rail after tea was over,

spoke no English, understood no French.

. . . To me they were the sounds
of evening only, of the cold, of the Irish dark and

continuous with all such recurrences: the drizzle in
the lilac, the dusk always at the back door, like
the tinkers I was threatened with, the cat inching
closer to the fire with its screen of clothes, where

I am standing in the stone-flagged kitchen; there are
bleached rags, perhaps, and a pot of tea on the stove.
And I see myself, four years of age and looking up,
storing such music—guttural, hurt to the quick.

This is prose, pure prose, but it has the eloquence of a remembered world. For all her virtuous, even virtuoso details (the best of them with the sharp sting of ammonia), too many of Boland's poems lack definition; they fade into the reverie of revered objects, without the pressure to make of disparate events more than desperate complacencies. Poems of quiet desperation in the kitchen are not worth writing home about. Only when subjects impose design upon her do they have the bad manners of emotion:

It was a school where all the children wore darned worsted,
where they cried—or almost all—when the Reverend Mother
announced at lunchtime that the King had died

peacefully in his sleep. I dressed in wool as well,
ate rationed food, played English games and learned
how wise the Magna Carta was, how hard the Hanoverians

had tried, the measure and complexity of verse,
the hum and score of the whole orchestra.
At three o'clock I caught two buses home

where sometimes in the late afternoon
at a piano pushed into a corner of the playroom
my father would sit down and play the slow

lilts of Tom Moore while I stood there trying
not to weep at the cigarette smoke stinging up
from between his fingers and—as much as I could think—

I thought this is my country, was, will be again,
this upward-straining song made to be
our safe inventory of pain. And I was wrong.

Here mere retrospection darkens past introspection. The po-
ems of emigration, of the wear and tear between two cultures,
make the dainty melancholies of her other poems seem crewel
work. When she stops being the bard of fabric (in one stretch of
ten pages we find silk, lace, crepe de Chine, cotton, linen, damask,
gabardine, synthetics, calico, and dimity, some of them two or
three times), she is truest to her own culture and most deeply
nestled in its falseness.

John Ashbery

The long poem, in our fallen postmodernist world, is often an an-
nouncement of exhaustion cast in the form of an attack against it.
The armature of religious belief will no longer carry the weight of
a poem as long as *Paradise Lost*. The few attempts at poetic narra-
tive in the past century have revealed, by their conscious submis-
sion to the forms of the novel, the subsidiary status of a poetry that
attempts to carry the burdens of fiction.

The most demanding long poems of our century—Pound's *The
Cantos*, Eliot's *Four Quartets*, Geoffrey Hill's *The Mystery of the
Charity of Charles Péguy*—have been poems of fragmentation and
ruptured design, where the horizon of attention can be kept very
close. The problem of attention is solved at the cost of coher-
ence and integration, though incoherence and disintegration have
sometimes been felt to be an advantage, and even an aspiration, in
our poetry. It is in such a context that the new long poems of John
Ashbery and Paul Muldoon must be measured.

John Ashbery has been a prickly figure in American poetry for
more than thirty years. He has passed through a bewildering suc-
cession of radical experiments, though his loyalty to mild surreal-
ism, extreme self-consciousness, indeterminacy, and ungovernable
silliness has been constant. His most significant achievement, the
long poem "Self-Portrait in a Convex Mirror," was unusual in its

seriousness and its flirtation with sustained argument; the error of that success has not been repeated, and through the eighties Ashbery was content to publish reproductions of his familiar late manner, masterful largely in their resemblance to one another. *Flow Chart* is an ambitious departure from the settled understandings of a poet who has rarely been settled.

Ashbery's poetry is an endless tease, promising meanings that never arrive, sorting itself into sentences that never quite compromise their hidden intents, that perhaps have no intents at all. It is the appearance rather than the force of meaning that troubles a passage like this:

> *the while sinkholes open up, and K Marts fall into them,*
> *as icebergs are delivered up to the whims of oceans. It wasn't bad*
> *while one stood,*
> *but as soon as you sat down you appeared vulnerable; issues were*
> *raised; and from feeling*
> *it all a mild annoyance but a mere formality, as when a stranger*
> *stops you to ask directions*
> *and begins asking pointed questions about your religion, it quickly*
> *escalated*
> *into a nightmare that waking would not heal. Retreat, retreat!*

The lines have a sense, even a direction—the attempt to describe the faltering of the usual certainties. But the difficulty with Ashbery is never the particular sentence, which is often attractively composed, with just enough oddity to catch at the reader's inner sense of logic and arrangement. The problem—what some would call the real genius—is the way in which a passage seems to lure meaning toward it, only to veer off in a sort of Brownian motion or drunk man's walk, oblivious to all that has gone before.

Flow Chart is two hundred pages of such frustrating and infuriating circumambulation. To a disabling degree it is a poem about the acts and enactions of reading. The most striking lines frame just the criticisms composing themselves in the reader's mind ("There must have been some purpose to this, / some idea hiding in the vacuity"). Ashbery's refusal to permit the reader a shred of story or coherence, or any satisfaction of the impulse toward compression and substance, has proved attractive to postmodern critics suspicious of ground on which the reader might stand. But Ashbery's nihilism is darker and more despairing, because carried off with such an air of insouciance, armchair wit, bland charm. His control and subversion of the conventional poetic strategies have made him a master of imbalance, able to keep the reader always at the edge of surprise—the weaknesses being, first, that the surprises are all roughly equal in value, so the law of diminishing returns soon comes into play; and, second, that the strategies responsible for the surprise are also responsible for the blinding tedium.

Flow Chart reads like a poem composed on a word processor by a word processor. Like Melville's confidence man, Ashbery cheats his victims in a way ironically just—the reader who searches for meaning will be persuaded that meaning doesn't exist, is not just unnecessary in poetry but tainted. What we might have thought our strength proves the point of greatest vulnerability. That is why reactions to him have been so overwrought. The dissonance he creates in a reader's faith in literature can be resolved only by violent rejection or violent embrace.

Future generations may laugh at the idea that Ashbery was taken seriously. He can be the most boring poet imaginable—no poet who actually set out to be boring could succeed half as well as Ashbery does. On the other hand, his lines are dizzy with apprehension, or the illusion of apprehension, and he has an inexhaustible appetite for language. He has mastered, more fully than any contemporary, the range of dictions and vocabulary, the dreck and linguistic junk of the modern, that make up the civilized and not-so-civilized commitments of our culture.

Ashbery has restored to our poetry a sense of imaginative play, and his poems have been unusual and occult. There is nevertheless something wrong with an art that leaves so little trace in the reader beyond mild annoyance. Those who loathe John Ashbery have most to learn from his frivolousness, but those who admire him often do so for the wrong reasons.

Paul Muldoon

Paul Muldoon's *Madoc: A Mystery* is a more dangerous and raucous affair. The most influential Irish poet of his generation, Muldoon in recent years has lived in America. Though his earlier work was clever to the point of glibness, or giddiness, beneath the surface were signs of the poetic intelligence fully on display in this long poem. Borrowing some of Ashbery's capriciousness, his distrust of linear narrative and the correspondence between word and meaning, Muldoon has fashioned a poem as disquieting and ambitious as a postmodern novel.

The numerous short sections of *Madoc* follow the adventures of Robert Southey and S. T. Coleridge, who as young poets with radical sympathies dreamed up a utopian democratic community, a "pantisocracy" they would found on the banks of the Susquehanna (they were steered there by an American real-estate agent). The scheme collapsed before they could leave England; but in Muldoon's alternate history they set sail and become minor attendants to the American past, entangling themselves with Lewis and Clark, Aaron Burr, George Catlin, and the Indian chief Joseph Brant.

The poem is a vast jigsaw, each lyrical fragment contributing its nugget of information and mystification. Each section is titled with the bracketed name of a philosopher, from Thales to Stephen Hawking, and in a broader sense that includes scientists like Darwin, critics like Coleridge. The relation between philosopher and poem is often obscure, sometimes baffling, usually sidling: Machiavelli's deals with plots, Kant's with reason, Descartes' with skepticism. Fibonacci's mentions the number 233, a number in the Fibonacci sequence and, not coincidentally, also the number of sections in the poem.

The bracketed names become a ghostly commentary on, a partial naming of, the actions in the text—as if culture were a matrix of action, a web of responses, radiating from the thought of the past and preparing that of the future. Such philosophers have affected our understanding of certain words, have invented the modern faculty of those words, and are thus the inventors of the language we use so smugly and transparently. By using their names in such a mordant and mocking relation, Muldoon has troubled the surface of that language and provided in those brackets a partial etymology of his narrative.

It is a narrative enforced through a language of puns, slippery rhymes, Joycean play, and light-footed improvisation. At times it seems over-rich, like a chocolate torte; but it attends continually to the possibilities, the unseen connections, of language and history. A sample of the style suggests the sort of wordplay Muldoon uses to such purpose:

> *From behind a freshly-scraped, buffalo-hide arras*
> *on which hangs an elk-horn*
>
> *bow and a brangle of blood-stained arrows*
> *a woman begins to keen:*
>
> *"Now your snouterumpater is a connoisorrow*
> *who has lost her raspectabilberry."*
>
> *An elk-horn bow. A brangle of blood-stained arrows*
> *tipped with chalcedony and jasper.*

The fanciful turns and contrivances, the crisscross and double cross of fiction and history, are too elaborate for a brief review. The poem is founded on one of those historical whimsies that might have provided the mythic penetration of a Thomas Pynchon novel: that a tribe of Indians were the descendants of a twelfth-century Welsh warrior named Madoc. The tale, which haunted Lewis and Clark, was written up by Southey in one of his interminable blank-verse epics, also called "Madoc." Muldoon's act of homage to the radical Romantics, to their understanding of the bearings of personality on language, is a triumphant and sometimes irritating re-invention of the methods of the long poem. Few poems of our moment have been as darkly dyed in language, as daring, as extravagant, as bizarre.

chapter 3

The Fallen World of Geoffrey Hill

The poet's dilemma in a fallen world is not how far he has fallen, but how little ground he has regained. Crabbed, clenched, intransigent, the words plain but the language tangled: the inconvenience of a poetry as difficult as Geoffrey Hill's is that it demands more than readers are usually willing to lose, at least to the trivial "art" of reading. If Hill's work makes most contemporary poetry appear trivial, contemporary poetry makes Hill's appear stilted, clotted (even gelatinous), deep in confusion and the calculus of decay.

Our poetry has long been at the mercy of its prose. Hill argues for a poetry secure in its doubts, wretched in its responsibilities, devilish or bedeviled in its labors. His works, previously published in five books and now gathered in his *New and Collected Poems*, form an achievement remarkably fertile but narrow in its numbers: two longish poems and some seventy short poems and sequences. He might be compared to Eliot, a poet of more complex despairs and more common joys, in the asperity of his production (when poets' lives were shorter their works were longer). As with other poets of rapture and self-loathing, the case against Hill has little to do with the dislike his poetry arouses, though that dislike has often schooled his critics in intemperance ("kitsch feudalism. . . . a grisly historical voyeurism . . . both insular and complacent"). It is a case intimate with the difficulty of the poetry itself.

Consider the telling grandeurs and tolling gradations of a poem as early as "Requiem for the Plantagenet Kings":

For whom the possessed sea littered, on both shores,
Ruinous arms; being fired, and for good,
To sound the constitution of just wars,
Men, in their eloquent fashion, understood.

Hardly a phrase fails to quarrel with its colloquial fiction, hardly a noun or adjective or verb steels itself against the infection of double meaning. The war is the Hundred Years' War, whose staggering cost in men and materiel gave no profit to England or France. The sea may be a king's mere property, his possession by force of arms; but the tides are never subject to noblesse oblige, and the sea may rise and destroy as if demonically possessed. "Ruinous" is a famously mirrored word, silvering now toward the destructive and disastrous, now toward what has fallen to ruin. Those arms, both ruined and ruining (we should perhaps remember the etymological root in fall and collapse), may be steel helmets and swords littering the beaches, or the hacked limbs of fallen soldiers. What is done "for good" is not always "done for good."

The compression of such language answers no intensity of circumstance—this is, after all, a requiem. It responds to anger at the futility of such loss, for which language, however compacted, can offer no gain. But the angers must still scruple at the difficulties of language, of *interpretation*, on which wars are founded: words may mean quite different things "on both shores," and the poem disturbs by its troubled compression our easy compassion for one side or another, or for soldier against king. Whether these are *just* wars or just *wars*, the dead are just as dead.

Knowing the dead, and how some are disposed:
Subdued under rubble, water, in sand graves,
In clenched cinders not yielding their abused
Bodies and bonds to those whom war's chance saves
Without the law: we grasp, roughly, the song.
    ("Two Formal Elegies")

The dead are the common property of Hill's early verse; his first book, *For the Unfallen* (1959), is a dark sounding of the teary inversions and lying solemnities of Laurence Binyon's anthology piece,

"For the Fallen" ("They went with songs to the battle, they were young, / Straight of limb, true of eye"). Under Hill's hard scrutiny, poems for the dead are always for the living. Such recognition may recommend no ease or pleasure in the condition of speech, and the harshness and marmoreal coldness of Hill's early work may be plundered by the critic in a way that seems chilling to the reader: Hill seems gripped by a mortuary lust. The first book, within its sweetly bitter ironies, has a number of thwarted love poems worked out in terms scarcely different from the battles and alarums:

> *By such rites they saved love's face, and such laws*
> *As prescribe mutual tolerance, charity*
> *To neighbours, strangers, those by nature*
> *Subdued among famines and difficult wars.*

This was called "The Troublesome Reign." Thereafter love, unless sanctioned as "divine," unless sainted in religious trapping, almost never returns to his work (except in deadly guise: "An owl plunges to its tryst / With a field-mouse").

The complex guilts of Hill's poetry are keenly judicial; the judgments in language are also the judgments of history and religion, of the gas chamber and the cross. His poetry, the most narrowly formed and most thinly and invariantly proposed of the major work of our late century, might be construed as a search for adequate authority, a search deviled by a skeptical mistrust of the common palliations of government, of religious practice, of language. The poetry attempts, in lonely and resistant fashion, to oppose their emollient nature, without being immune to their lure or unaware of the self-deceptions that afflict such a venture. The fable that informs his second book, *King Log* (1968), warns not just against the wish for such authority, but against the divine spirit who treats lowly creation with such cruel mockery. Dissatisfied with the log Zeus sent them when they asked for a king, Aesop's frogs were even more unhappy with the ravenous stork that replaced it. A poet who both desires and distrusts authority, a poet of uncertain belief, should be wary of such morals.

I love my work and my children. God
Is distant, difficult. Things happen.
Too near the ancient troughs of blood
Innocence is no earthly weapon.

I have learned one thing: not to look down
So much upon the damned. They, in their sphere,
Harmonize strangely with the divine
Love. I, in mine, celebrate the love-choir.

Apart from an epigraph from the *Amores,* that is the whole of "Ovid in the Third Reich." We do not know what Ovid saw or did at the court of Augustus that required his banishment to the Black Sea, nor do we know what he might have observed at the court of Hitler. His terrible punishment (to be removed from the sources of pleasure in his life, to be removed from his own language) and his abject and fruitless apologies make him a compelling symbol of the bitter fate that awaits poetic witness, however "innocent." Those "ancient troughs of blood" recall the blood that gutters after battle, the blood guttering from ritual sacrifice, but also the blood-filled trench at which the hungry ghosts came to feed in the *Odyssey.* The sacrificial in Hill's poetry summons the dead in like fashion. (The gods also want "gobbets of the sweetest sacrifice," and surprisingly often in Hill's work flesh is rendered disturbingly in terms of food.)

King Log is haunted by civil and uncivil wars, and most terribly by the War of the Roses. "Funeral Music," the sonnet sequence dedicated to three of the noble and ignoble dead of those wars, is central to an achievement where blood sacrifices are never far from failures of government (both civil and personal) and are often potent in the misplaced faiths religion sets one against another. Hill has registered his ambition in this sequence for "a florid grim music broken by grunts and shrieks," which might serve as a satanic description of the liturgy.

They bespoke doomsday and they meant it by
God, their curved metal rimming the low ridge.
But few appearances are like this. Once
Every five hundred years a comet's

> *Over-riding stillness might reveal men*
> *In such array, livid and featureless,*
> *With England crouched beastwise beneath it all.*
> *"Oh, that old northern business . . ." A field*
> *After battle utters its own sound*
> *Which is like nothing on earth, but is earth.*
> *Blindly the questing snail, vulnerable*
> *Mole emerge, blindly we lie down, blindly*
> *Among carnage the most delicate souls*
> *Tup in their marriage-blood, gasping "Jesus."*

This is the Battle of Towton, Palm Sunday, 1461, and Hill is minding fatalities more than facts. The sonnets have been hacked clean of rhyme, metrical favor, anything but the beastlike music of noun and adjective, two-faced ambiguity (*bespoke* also means *custommade*) and cunning enjambment. The blood of battle and the blood of the marriage bed are set at one; the gasp of the death throes is one with the gasp of orgasm, both taking in vain (and taking vainly) the name of the Lord, from whom descends all possibility of resurrection.

Critics who would pigeonhole Hill all too conveniently as a conservative fail to understand the radical nature of his mistrusts, from which no complacent sentence is safe. All speech is unfaithful in its faiths. These early books are perhaps too greedily satisfied with the demands of rhetoric (a rhetoric calculated to make the reader feel unworthy of it), the forced phrases and hot solemnities all too reminiscent of the religiose high-mindedness of Allen Tate. Hill's childhood Christianity finds an austere outlet in his monkish faith in the phrase, the squalor of the said, the poet having fled the trappings, but never the traumas, of the religious urge. The thickened lines of Tate and the young Robert Lowell have the same soaked intensity that Hill labored to achieve (by influence, not indenture); having secured such brooding morality, he might have continued to offer, like his older contemporary Anthony Hecht (for whom the moral sources were Jewish, not Church of England), darker and darker variations in the secular shudder of religious guilt.

The discordant prose musics of *King Log* were shortly followed, however, by a sequence of prose poems at times agleam with wit. (Hill would have made a ghoulish song-and-dance man—who would have thought he could be funny?) Without sacrificing the fastidiousness or ore-bearing density of his language, the thirty poems of *Mercian Hymns* (1971) put that language in service to an idea beyond moody requiem. The hymns are sung for, by, on behalf of Offa, the eighth-century ruler of the kingdom of Mercia, a figure whose achievements in coinage and brutal political union continue to preside over notions of Britain as a nation-state. Hill's Offa, however, lives into the present, a king of such gravity that time distorts around him: as Hill noted, this Offa "might . . . be regarded as the presiding genius of the West Midlands, his dominion enduring from the middle of the eighth century until the middle of the twentieth."

> *King of the perennial holly-groves, the riven sandstone: overlord of the M5: architect of the historic rampart and ditch, the citadel at Tamworth, the summer hermitage in Holy Cross: guardian of the Welsh Bridge and the Iron Bridge: contractor to the desirable new estates: saltmaster: money-changer: commissioner for oaths: martyrologist: the friend of Charlemagne.*

> *"I liked that," said Offa, "sing it again."*

The sudden, baffled displacements of this history betray the narrow respect for force and influence found in mere chronology. History is no neat laying down of sediments: we fail to understand the deep or abiding authority of an Offa if we do not see where the past still afflicts the present, not least in the perennial holly-groves (symbol of winter rebirth for pagan and Christian both). Offa has his thumb in every pie (the editors of the *Norton Anthology of Modern Poetry* further swelled his powers by annotating the M5, not as the main highway through the Midlands, but as a branch of British Intelligence—they were thinking of MI5). The complicities of the past with the present are not always immune to a downward spiral into sentiment and vulgarity, and the remains of the past often produce a mere fiction of the flesh.

*On the morning of the crowning we chorused our remission from
school. It was like Easter: hankies and gift-mugs approved by his
foreign gaze, the village-lintels curlered with paper flags.*

*We gaped at the car-park of "The Stag's Head" where a bonfire of
beer-crates and holly-boughs whistled above the tar. And the chef
stood there, a king in his new-risen hat, sealing his brisk largesse
with "any mustard?"*

The chef in his silly "new-risen hat" (white like risen dough, but
also new-risen like Christ at Easter) reminds us that any man
might be king, if the domain is small enough, though his kingly
largesse may be reduced to sausages. Hill is keenly aware that in
their fallen graces these "hymns" are to a lord secular, not spiritual.
The wryness of this impiety, and the attendant commercial kitsch
of "hankies and gift-mugs," honor the throne they impoverish.
Majesty is also outward show, and without inner substance only a
tarnished show. The bloated pomp and circumstance of royal in-
vestiture in Britain is a late Victorian invention: as the throne con-
tracts, the need for empty display expands.

Into this welter, whose vulgarities are still heir to the richness of
the past, is inserted the hobbled autobiography of the child Hill:
"Dreamy, smug-faced, sick on outings—I who was taken to be a
king of some kind, a prodigy, a maimed one." The child acts out
dreams of kingship (dreams alluring to a child later tormented by
rituals and sacrifices, and ritual sacrifice), and often retreats, "calm
and alone, in his private derelict sandlorry named *Albion*." The
childhood loneliness is at once ripe and wretched ("my rich and
desolate childhood"), a shadow over the loneliness of the throne,
which reveals some of the complex sources of Hill's poetic lan-
guage. The wreckage of the truck bears, with a certain merciless-
ness, the ancient name of Britain, now derelict itself.

In *Mercian Hymns* Hill sacrificed the proud aloofness of his
verse, its pure and chilly witness, for a private recital of those be-
trayals with which history cooperates and toward which history
tends. It is difficult to understand modern England without know-
ing where it has been irrigated in ancient blood. The damaged
ghosts of his past violated the antique boundaries of his verse; and

if his poetry has never again risked such half-embarrassed, half-guilty intimacies, it has never again been as moving or appealing.

The sonnets and devotional songs of *Tenebrae* (1978) are a mysterious coda to the themes of national decay and private despair in *Mercian Hymns*. Hill has always been hesitant (even hedging) in declaring his religious conviction: the three religious sequences in *Tenebrae* are cast in idioms of the counterfeit antique, of chemical patina applied like paste. They are repellent alike in their self-lacerating unworthiness and their eyes-lifted piety. Our laggard century has not discovered its religious idiom; neither is it likely to embrace one formed like this:

> *As he is wounded*
> *I am hurt*
> *he bleeds from pride*
> *I from my heart*
>
> *as he is dying*
> *I shall live*
> *in grief desiring*
> *still to grieve*
> ("The Pentecost Castle")

Hill's sources, in Spanish lyrics of the Counter-Reformation, mix the sexual and the spiritual; but not even a church that has given its choirs up for guitars would find these the lyrics of its dogma or its doubt.

Even in the seven sonnets of "Lachrimae," where Hill's language returns to its cold depths and contortions, the religious despair is curiously hollow and unconvincing (the multiplication of the loaves and the abstractions), as if spurred to intensities beyond the idiom's belief in itself:

> *Crucified Lord, however much I burn*
> *to be enamoured of your paradise,*
> *knowing what ceases and what will not cease,*
> *frightened of hell, not knowing where to turn,*
>
> *I fall between harsh grace and hurtful scorn.*
> *You are the crucified who crucifies,*

self-withdrawn even from your own device,
your trim-plugged body, wreath of rakish thorn.

The "rakish thorn" and "trim-plugged body" restore, however briefly, a language of sardonic observation; but the rest sounds like a corpse trying to stuff its mouth with the religious canticles of Eliot.

What salvages a book of despairing secrecy and incontinent satisfactions is a series of sonnets on the underkingdom of English landscape, "An Apology for the Revival of Christian Architecture in England." The title is grotesque and disfiguring, a further sign of the decline into pomposity; but not since the overripeness of Tennyson has anyone rendered so feverishly the doomed grandeurs of English nature.

The pigeon purrs in the wood; the wood has gone;
dark leaves that flick to silver in the gust,
and the marsh-orchids and the heron's nest,
goldgrimy shafts and pillars of the sun.

Weightless magnificence upholds the past.
Cement recesses smell of fur and bone
and berries wrinkle in the badger-run
and wiry heath-fern scatters its fresh rust.

"O clap your hands" so that the dove takes flight,
bursts through the leaves with an untidy sound,
plunges its wings into the green twilight

above this long-sought and forsaken ground,
the half-built ruins of the new estate,
warheads of mushrooms round the filter-pond.

Hill has been roundly reproved for nostalgic complacency in these poems. The English landscape inspires something like the religious passion missing elsewhere, and the longing is so rich in its returns that it is easy to miss the quarrels and doubts that hedge such lushness. If he has partially succumbed to the hypnotizing glory of the past, he has provided warning against such temptations and the meat of a criticism (he posts his warnings by subjecting the reader to his temptations). The mushrooms are not necessarily dangerous, but our nuclear world has given Hill a dangerous image; to the extent that we must think of the former in terms of the latter we have forever lost our innocence.

One may be of two minds about Hill, but then one may be of two minds about paradise. He has the valor of his limitations, though some might call it the cowardice of his securities. Hill's themes have been constant (the infection of ancient bloods, abiding afflictions in the affections of landscape, the moral responsibilities of language, unworthiness before grace), but his attentions unpredictable. He has forced the marginal into our modes of attention, at the risk of seeming bizarre or merely idiosyncratic, and therefore a figure of margins himself. The subject of *The Mystery of the Charity of Charles Péguy* (1983) is a French Catholic socialist, deeply (and perhaps bloodily) embroiled in Parisian politics before the First World War. He was a beetroot nationalist, poet and magazine editor, the intellectual son of peasants, and died leading troops through a beetroot field in the Battle of the Marne. Here and elsewhere this new edition has destructively discarded many of Hill's original notes, without which his poems are even more inscrutable; there he disclosed the attractions in this lonely and unattractive figure, "self-excommunicate but adoring," who despite his estrangement from the Church made two pilgrimages to Chartres. Hill has made such pilgrimages himself.

Péguy begins with the assassination of Jean Jaurès, the socialist deputy who had been subject to Péguy's admiration, then his attack. Péguy had called for his blood in metaphorical terms, and a young madman had obliged by shooting Jaurès through the head.

Crack of a starting-pistol. Jean Jaurès
dies in a wine-puddle. Who or what stares
through the café-window crêped in powder-smoke?
The bill for the new farce reads Sleepers Awake.

History commands the stage wielding a toy gun,
rehearsing another scene. It has raged so before,
countless times; and will do, countless times more,
in the guise of supreme clown, dire tragedian.

In Brutus' name martyr and mountebank
ghost Caesar's ghost, his wounds of air and ink
painlessly spouting. Jaurès' blood lies stiff
on menu-card, shirt-front and handkerchief.

Did Péguy kill Jaurès? Did he incite
the assassin? Must men stand by what they write
as by their camp-beds or their weaponry
or shell-shocked comrades while they sag and cry?

Such questions afflict a poet anxious that his words be more than gestures, worrying the responsibilities a poet takes on when he descends to the word. The language here responds to the cunning and stealth by which words keep their promises: the war has its aspect of farce—an ironically named *Sleepers Awake*, a matter of stage blood and stage villainy. The deaths are real, nevertheless, and the poetry keeps faith by breaking faith with the simply plainspoken: matters spoken are never so plain.

The hundred quatrains of *Péguy*, in the brilliant, battered guile of half-rhyme and harsh pentameter, wind through questions of honor and repentance, and the root nationalisms of "militant-pastoral" France, in a profound meditation on faith and the artist's responsibility. The most striking and demanding long poem in English after *Four Quartets*, it suffers its unsympathetic subject (in its droning repetitions even Péguy's poetry was absurd) with a duty bordering on complacent nobility. A style so guilty of chilling ironies and cast-iron wit (what would Hill's light verse be like?) is not likely to be accorded praise equal to its brilliance. That is itself an irony that would not escape a poet who often courts dislike with his despair. In such a book his varying powers have been drawn into new kinship, instead of being cousins squabbling over an old patch of ground.

Hill has an intelligence mortified by religious passion and goaded by lack of faith toward greater ecstasies in the only medium that can serve as the conduit of his trust: his language. I'm surprised not to find him drawn to the mysticism and misanthropy of some of the Counter-Enlightenment figures studied by Isaiah Berlin: Hamann, Herder, Vico, de Maistre. The British critics—most of them—have always admired Hill, though the admiration has sometimes been molded in terms of disapproval (the disapproval of other critics has been molded in outright rage). Good poetry is rarely so unremittingly serious, and the style has usually broken (the lapses into self-parody are like smashed china) when it could not be bent. The great English love affair with Larkin (a silver cup only a little dented by the slanders and self-hatreds of the letters, the pornography of the life) is almost entirely a love of style, and of the character that style creates. The secret sharings of these otherwise antagonistic talents and opposing spirits include the love of English landscape, the hauntings of religion and religious places, the abiding in tradition, the self-loathing, the loneliness, the fear of death. They are used by their materials to different ends (and with different impurities), but not with different integrities. Had Hill been more affectionately regarded in Britain, he might not have spent the last half-dozen years teaching in the Department of Religion at Boston University. For a poet of such wary religious instincts, this is one further irony the age has demanded. The age is not yet ready to understand Hill in religious terms, and perhaps will not be until religion has been understood in Hill's terms.

The thirteen new poems included in this *New and Collected* are ghostly, even ghastly reminders of former themes, elegiac in tone, many of them memorials for figures public and private. Hill's muscled lines have been wasted with diet, and a few of the poems are inconsequential or indistinct (though the otherwise unmemorable "To the Nieuport Scout" may illuminate the incident of the lost biplane in *Mercian Hymns*). In "Cycle," for William Arrowsmith, the words have been splashed on the page like paint, or spilled like fallen leaves:

> *So there   there it is   past*
> *reason and measure*
> *   sustaining*
> *the constancy of mischance*
> *its occlusion*
> *   a spasm*
> *a psalm*

Something imaginative has been foreclosed in such poems: they reek of a locked church.

A poet must be allowed something for his wintry beauty, and Hill's sequences for Aleksandr Blok and Churchill have a frozen reverence, moving in its damnations as well as in the pinched salvations of its language:

> *The brazed city*
> *reorders its own*
> *destruction, admits*
> *the strutting lords*
>
> *to the temple,*
> *vandals of sprayed blood*
> *and oblivion*
> *to make their mark.*
>
> *The spouting head*
> *spiked as prophetic*
> *is ancient news.*
> *Once more the keeper*
>
> *of the dung-gate*
> *tells his own story;*
> *so too the harlot*
> *of many tears.*
>   ("Churchill's Funeral")

Here the poet has glimpsed savage possibility in the short line, tense with its clattering ambiguities ("The spouting head / spiked" might be a headline or a newspaper columnist, as well as the head of the prophet). No poet since Pound in *Mauberley* has packed short lines with such guarded weight or intonation. Nevertheless, the implication of these brief or broken lines is that the weight of speech has become an almost intolerable burden, that the words have begun to collapse in upon themselves. The poet of such broodings must feel the kinship with Beckett that these expressive inexpressions morosely claim.

Hill has been an uncomfortable figure for contemporary poetry, resistant to the blandishments of "emotion" or appeal, proud in his lonely dignities as well as his reserves. His two books of criticism, *The Lords of Limit* (1984) and *The Enemy's Country* (1991), are among the most painstaking, brilliant, and claustrophobic analyses of literature in our century, elaborate in their concern for the guilts and guiles of language and the moral recognitions of the word. Hill's proud solitude and self-contempt have been subject to the poetry rather than subject of the poetry, in the current fashion (poets with standards make poets without them profoundly nervous). His style has been an outrage upon the glib decencies of recent verse. For this he has risked condemnation for a cold-blooded, reptilian manner—a style like "fatted marble," to use one of his phrases—and the suspicion that he has aggrandized his guilts, that (like the reactionary poseur Mishima) he has poked the arrows of St. Sebastian into his own flesh. He is the last man in poetry to wear wig and breeches.

Poets have so lost the respect of the audience they once labored to please—the ordinary half-educated reader (most poets are themselves half-educated, and not unappealingly so)—that it is worth asking, not whether poets are any longer worthy of their audience, but whether that audience is any longer worthy of poets like Hill. Should poets continue to stumble down the levels of prose until they are speaking the language of the worm (or, to be fair, a language not even worthy of worms), or should they bear a language in the burden of its saying, a language where the force of words is the trust that language demands? Asking this, in his skepticism, eloquence, and power, Hill is as good as his word.

chapter 4

Dreams of an Uncommon Tongue

Gjertrud Schnackenberg

Gjertrud Schnackenberg is the most talented American poet under forty. In her two previous books, *Portraits and Elegies* (1982) and *The Lamplit Answer* (1985), she was drawn to extremities of feeling through an enriched and image-drenched language. *A Gilded Lapse of Time*, her bleakest and yet most radiant book, is divided into three poetic sequences so enraptured, so lost in annunciations and resurrections, they might be called visions instead.

The title sequence is shadowed by a renunciation of poetry. Despairing at the end of a love affair, the poet is cast into a private Inferno during a trip to Ravenna, where Dante died. Dante's guide Virgil is reincarnated as the tour guides or guards who lead this lost traveler through the ancient churches and tombs, remnants of vanished Byzantine civilization.

> *Now in a gilded apse the celestial globe*
> *Has rolled to the end of an invisible rope*
> *And come to rest on a cliff in a blue-green garden.*
> *I look up, as if nothing had killed my hope,*
> *At a blue sphere, buoyant in the sixth-century tides*
> *Still surging and dying away through San Vitale,*
> *Where a spring has glinted in the numinous*
> *Fresh-cut grass for more than a millennium.*

In the thicket of historical incident and artistic illusion, the reader may feel lost as mosaic follows mosaic, angel follows angel. (Are we still in Ravenna? Is this the church, or are we in Dante's tomb now?) The final section, however, beautifully gathers up these shattered images in a dream, where the mute poet is offered a teaspoon of boiling honey, and awakes. The dream would be ambiguous if the poem were not evidence of her restoration to poetic language.

Schnackenberg's poems offer emotional power without coercive force: her lines unfold from terror to beauty to terror. "Crux of Radiance," the second sequence, follows Christ through paintings and historical tableaux into what might be called the still unsettled grief of Christianity. The poet seems beyond the consolation of religion, but not the consolation of the art that religion has inspired or extorted. The biblical imagery, classical allusions, and stray philosophy from which the poems are composed might be airless bookishness in another poet, but Schnackenberg can spin straw into gold (I wish sometimes she would *start* with gold—there's no telling what she might spin it into).

In a mock-Rome, built with bird cages,
The swallow was arrested for spying,
The pelican's beak was sawn off
For fishing a governor's pond without permission,

And a parrot, which made its entrance
In a covered basket, like a puppet-king
Carried in a litter who had recited
Upon his first glimpse of Rome

The lamentation of captivity
On behalf of those he had betrayed,
Now ignites into a dazzling green torch,
Crawling headfirst down

The wires against which, unfurling,
It momentarily crucifies itself,
Then folds into silence.

Haunted by the paintings of della Francesca and Mantegna, these poems take their tone from Auden's "Musée des Beaux Arts," where the amazing happens at a distance or the martyrdom in "some untidy spot / Where the dogs go on with their doggy life." The last poem, a meditation on the death of Osip Mandelstam in one of Stalin's labor camps, faces the thin salvations of art and the thinner salvations of culture, its "masterpieces ground down for ballast."

Schnackenberg's new poems have a leisurely grandeur—they are written in a melodic free verse, unfolding phrase by phrase into long, barely sustainable sentences. Less marked by form than her earlier work, they show an unusual concern with the market of mind and religion, the movement of mind and philosophy. In her seriousness and glamor she is reminiscent of Geoffrey Hill, a poet more repressed and less passionate. These dream visions, where one image shimmers over the next like water over water, glass over glass, sound like the voice of history—accusing, condemning, and rarely forgiving. *A Gilded Lapse of Time* is as difficult and moving a book as our poetry has recently produced.

C. K. Williams

Few poets since Whitman have written lines as eerily demotic, as gripped by coarse observation, or simply as long or furiously exhausting as C. K. Williams. His poems usually start or end as stories, or have stories leaking somewhere behind them—and they are always stories out of *The Psychopathology of Everyday Life*.

Williams has stolen from prose part of its poetic inheritance and returned to poetry the subtly altered rhythms of the long line. He has also taken on what might be called a prose sensibility—in other words he natters, and natters incessantly. Since his characters are often ruminant obsessives, this is not precisely a disadvantage; but his poetry has some of the grinding of gossip.

In his last book, *Flesh and Blood* (1987), what had earlier seemed an imaginative freedom became an imprisonment. In *A Dream of Mind* the decay of style has gone further (he refers to "That dedication, or obsession, or semblance of obsession"—we are now in the semblance). His poems are subject to continual repetition, pointless variation, and the automatic cloning of phrases. They are little Xerox machines of technique.

You can tell Williams likes to write about himself, he comes to it so eagerly after writing about others. His poems are most successful—surely this is the precinct of psychology—when purely voyeuristic, less when confessional, least when meditative: his achievement is roughly in inverse proportion to his moral seriousness. He has a genius, however, for creating extreme discomfort in the reader. His long poem "Helen," about a woman dying, is an unbearable anatomy of observation, of the mutilations of observation, prurient in its isolation of feeling, in its painstaking fidelity to the infidelities of love, the minute waverings and doubts, the mute disloyalties and betrayals. Though weaker in its later sections, this picture of a husband and wife caught in the simple weariness of love is an almost Jamesian labyrinth of thought and self-deception.

In such a poem, rather than in the poems of shock for which he has received attention, Williams finds the moral tension of his art, the possessiveness of the voyeur disguised as the self-righteous detachment of the reporter. He has the virtues of his idiosyncrasies—there is no poet at all like him—but there is something unsettling about his love for those moments when "you are supposed not to look or look and glance quickly away" [*sic*]. In one poem he meets a child horribly maimed by fire:

> *As though the skin had been stripped and pulled back onto the*
> * skull like a stocking and soldered*
> *too tightly so that it mottled to yellow and ocher, the pores and fol-*
> * licles thumbed out of the clay*
> *by the furious slash of flame that must have leapt on her and by*
> * the healing that hurt her—*
>
> *if it is healing that leaves her, age three, in a lassitude lax on her*
> * mother's broad lap,*
> *bleak, weary, becalmed, what's left of her chin leaned heavily onto*
> * what's left of her fingers.*

He likes looking, likes knowing he isn't supposed to look, and likes best reporting his ambivalence to the reader, who may dislike being made complicit. The poem ends, unfortunately, in a fireworks of self-pity ("forgive me"). Williams wants "Lascivious pity, luxurious pity," even where pity is inappropriate, even where pity is obscene. His poems suggest there is nothing in the service of others that can't be self-serving, too.

Thom Gunn

The aloofness of Thom Gunn's poetry has never served the warming emotions. His departure from England almost forty years ago stranded him between two cultures, and within his insulating privacy he has written of America without being of America. The new poems in *The Man with Night Sweats* are wry, self-consumed, a little eaten up with their advantages, charmingly stiff in an Old World way. A few are contingent, unlovely affairs *about* contingent, unlovely affairs—his poems of homosexual desire seem staged in their seductive bravado, like porno movies shot on home video. He often tries to be with it without being of it—his slighter poems have an irritating, smug triviality. A poem of empty-headed couplets (an invitation to a visit) drags in San Francisco's homeless and hungry as if they were part of a Cook's tour, the local flora and fauna, and then smugly turns to praise the cooks in the poet's household ("Each cooks one night, and each cooks well").

In many poems his aversion to the serious seems a pocket-sized pathology, but his allegorical or classical poems ("Odysseus on Hermes") are cruel as marble—if they were to come to life, like the Commendatore in *Don Giovanni*, the reader would die of shock. Gunn's best poetry is a resistance to the beautiful, a withholding or withdrawing in the formality of the verse movement, where his slightly elevated phrasing is that of a man who must be won over.

A poet of such withdrawing instincts often suffers failures of sympathy. He is therefore most attractive when being unpleasant, and neither requiring sympathy nor soliciting it. "Looks," about a poet uglier in mind than in body, is a pitiless, fin de siècle portrait of decadent desire, of the failure of art to rescue the artist from his moral ugliness. The more inhuman Gunn's poems, the richer and more fretful the imaginative resources. The more difficult the fabric of observation, the more textured the fabric of implication.

Revulsion is an emotion more organizing than desire, at least in a poet not complacent in his revulsions. Gunn's grimmest and most guarded poems are witness to the death of his friends from AIDS, a plague that has risen into metaphors of plague. Here his formal distances, his comforts in literary detachment, give him a purchase not available to poets more weakly personal. The poems are written in a voice of measured despair, every word a vain effort of memory, memory that is the only memorial to these abbreviated lives.

> *Your dying was a difficult enterprise.*
> *First, petty things took up your energies,*
> *The small but clustering duties of the sick,*
> *Irritant as the cough's dry rhetoric.*
> *Those hours of waiting for pills, shot, X-ray*
> *Or test (while you read novels two a day)*
> *Already with a kind of clumsy stealth*
> *Distanced you from the habits of your health.*

The tired and scarcely managed rhythms become part of the weary tone. It has taken great effort to compose the feeling in these elegies, especially for a poet uncomfortable with feeling. No one could fail to be troubled by them, even when they are not convincing as poetry—at some level even Gunn's imagination has flinched in its melancholy offices.

chapter 5

A Material World

Jorie Graham

The poems in Jorie Graham's new book, *Materialism*, come in a little fog of philosophy, their themes painted on ragged banners: EXISTENCE AND PRESENCE, SUBJECTIVITY, THE REALITY OF THE SELF. She has gone from a leaning toward philosophical language, a sort of Stevensian itch, to placing lengthy passages, even pages, of Plato, and Bacon, and Jonathan Edwards, and somewhat less philosophical writers like Audubon and Whitman cheek by jowl with her poems. This has her characteristic bravura, her passion for changing the way poems are put together; but the result is a little like Pound publishing not just *The Cantos*, but all the passages relevant to their composition. You have to be awfully confident of your poetry to pit its descriptive powers against five pages of Audubon's men shooting birds and buffaloes.

Appropriation and collage are of course high fashion in academia these days, and Graham's earlier work showed great cunning in domesticating the devices of writers more avant-garde. Her new poems commonly begin with a small domestic crisis (removing the stain on a dress, picking up a dead monarch butterfly) and attend with an almost nightmarish intensity to the flux of mental phenomena that follows—the poems slow down perception until the self becomes the character of its own fictions:

Whir. The invisible sponsored again by white
walls—a joining in them and then (dark spot)
(like the start of a thought)
a corner, fertilized by shadow, hooked, dotted,
here demurring, there—up there—
almost hot with black. . . . What time is it?
The annihilation. The chaste middle of things.

Graham wants to crawl back inside the experience, heavy with the burden of consciousness. But deeper nightmares afflict her, and the longer poems often leap from the perils of the household to perils of history, from delivering a leotard to the landing of Columbus, from the shooting of her dog to the Holocaust. Such ambitions are hostile to the present form of her talent. Her language lives in its imprecisions; but she hasn't half her old gift for metaphor, and she tends to write with the coat-tugging insistence of the quietly deranged ("*Meaning? meaning?* shrieked the small facts," "yes yes yes yes says the mechanism of the underneath tick tock") or a slightly feverish religious wonder ("and the minutes the sons of god shouted for joy, tick tock," "Lord, / I want to see this leaf"). In this version of Gresham's Law, bad writing drives the good writing out.

In our lost century there is perhaps a telling need for a poetry vulnerable to philosophy; but Graham is not above rewriting Whitman or Brecht, or misconstruing Plato, to make her point. She alters (and thereby misunderstands the point of) a passage in Plato, changes Brecht's mention of *producing* to *reproducing* (throwing out Marx and dragging in the fashionable Walter Benjamin), and chops up Whitman so that he says, not

Expand, being than which none else is perhaps more spiritual,
Keep your places, objects than which none else is more lasting,

but "Expand, being; keep your places objects." This is a fine method, if you wish to make your Whitman a William Carlos Williams. There is an artist who takes photographs of other photographers' photographs and signs her name. I'd like to think Graham is being false to her sources in order to be true to her poetry, but she has changed the words of the dead and signed their names.

I open each new book by Graham with a sense of potential enchantment—she has Rapunzel's character, and a splashy, faintly vulgar intellectual charm. Her fine eye for irony is rarely apparent here, but her poem about the Holocaust is savage and harrowing (although framing a concentration-camp diary with the shooting of her pet dog is the sort of mistake to which she is particularly prone). Grotesquely overmanaged, glutted on rare ambition and the vanities of ambition, *Materialism* steals its mysteries from the mouths of the dead.

Richard Kenney

Anyone who likes French pastry ought to like Richard Kenney's deft, delicately layered, fanciful poetry, all double cream and icing. Words like *rococo* and *Byzantine* (and *napoleon*) occur to you when reading his work, along with less flattering ones like *overwrought* and *self-indulgent*. He has taken the verbal richness of early Wilbur and Merrill about as far as it can go, and then a great deal farther. His first book, *The Evolution of the Flightless Bird* (1984), was one of the few distinguished books in the Yale Series of Younger Poets in recent years. It was written with great and youthful flair, but his third is the labored work of a decade or more.

At the heart of *The Invention of the Zero* are four military memoirs, rescued scenes of World War II and the Cold War: an atomic bomb explosion; life in the Galápagos with a chess-mad group of army officers; a typhoon in the western Pacific that destroys part of the Third Fleet; a navy Seal tangled in his parachute cords. Around these static tales, each with its gassy, orotund narrator (the tales represent fire, earth, water, air—the narrators sound exactly like each other and exactly like Kenney), is a preposterously elaborate scaffolding—astronomical and alchemical symbols; lyric passages of what the poet calls "machine conversation" (some of the book seems to have been composed by a computer); a "colloquy" of intertwined and tangled remnants of Einstein, Oppenheimer, Conrad, Newton, and others; an epilogue in which these shreds seem to have gone through a Waring Blendor.

It's no use trying to describe such poetry, and even a quotation can't quite represent its particular unhappy mixture of fake solemnity, pomposity, brilliance, and clotted gobbledegook:

> Date-
> line-like, itself, in point of fact, as wasn't
> that the real news? Space-time, for God's sake?—all past-
> time's tight curve's jack-in-the-pulpit boxed [T Y
> X Z] and no more circle squared: the first, dim, tempest-
> eyed instant's snowy contrail struck sunwise
> through a sea's horizon, sunk and rising.

The reader will find it hard to believe that passages like this aren't just common—they're the rule. Kenney never finds one metaphor when half a dozen will do, never simplifies when there's a way to complicate, never denies himself a bad pun ("a symbol's / crash," "the atom's / eve"—a pun he used in his last book) or a metaphor that lurches into absurdity—at one point he has Sherpas climbing up the Great Rift Valley of Kenya. This book has more oddly phrased, clumsily constructed, tongue-twisting lines than any I can think of ("scrawlings limn damned chromosomes" is my favorite). On such lines even Hart Crane would have choked.

At a time when most verse is too simple, it hardly seems fair to criticize an intelligence that lusts so after complexity. Kenney's great verbal sorcery (his verbal gifts are all surface values) has been grubbed toward erudition—he has obviously read shelves of science and philosophy, and spun more complications than DNA (in one or two places the science seems shaky, but perhaps these are just errors in the book's genetic code). None of the poets of his generation has command of such linguistic alchemy, but I'd be willing to trade most of his brilliance for something homely and unvarnished: he trivializes his grand matter by his own cleverness. By the time the poor reader gets to the campy, overwritten notes and acknowledgments, he wants to put on a rope of garlic and drive a stake through the poet's heart. Verse like Kenney's knows so much about the beautiful it has fallen into ugliness: it's all dressed up with no place to go.

James Fenton

James Fenton, the recently elected Professor of Poetry at Oxford, has had a wonderfully Byronic patchwork life as a foreign correspondent with a taste for trouble spots, a comically inept explorer in Borneo, a theater critic, an opera librettist, a columnist. As a poet he is half a grubby public-school boy (with a dog-eared paperback of *Das Kapital* in his pocket) and half an Archie Rice song-and-dance man. His poems are so direct, so entertaining, even so artless (in their artful ways), he has few of the problems that tie the hands and feet of poets more self-conscious. His poems are so raw he seems almost real.

Out of Danger is a ragbag of a book, full of love songs, political ballads, even a manifesto. It has little of the sustained melancholy, the moody strangeness, that sharpened the lines of *Children in Exile*, his book of a decade ago, and few poems to compare with his pieces on Cambodia and Germany, some of the most haunted and haunting (and yet occasionally comic) political poems of the Cold War. His poems often start with a rhythm now, rather than an idea—too often they seem to end there, too. The fall of communism does not seem wholly at fault.

Fenton's love poems are weightless as spun sugar. A British reviewer compared them to Johnny Mercer's lyrics, but they'd embarrass even Burt Bacharach ("Stay near to me and I'll stay near to you— / As near as you are dear to me will do, / Near as the rainbow to the rain, / The west wind to the windowpane"). Some of them have an intelligence not usually associated with cotton candy, however, and the reader may be prepared to forgive quite a few bad poems for one where every time the poet wants to say *in love* he says *in Paris* instead.

Fenton lives increasingly in the discords of his work, where the isolations of war have given him a rough compassion for the lies of language. The ballad of "Cut-Throat Christ," where Jesus is a gangster in Manila, has all of Fenton's comic sourness and local effect and moral force (so close to moral farce):

Well Jesus was a drinker as you might expect.
We got through plenty stainless and a few long necks
And then Jesus got mad as mad can be.
He said: One of you punks is gonna squeal on me.

Now that General Ching has put a price on my head
With disciples like you I'm as good as dead—
There's one who will betray me to the EPD.
We said: Tell me boss, tell me boss, is it me?

The simplicity of rhythm is itself a political form. Fenton's earlier work was written under the shadow of Auden, but his recent poems owe more to Kipling and the music hall. Their jingly rhythms, bald effects, and fondness for repetition have not been roughened against a political coercion or verse collusion (some of the poems were produced as a "pocket musical" in Paris). Even when he goes wrong, as he does in many of these sidewalk performances, he does so with élan. Fenton has already written four or five of the poems future anthologists will squabble over. *Out of Danger* has a few moments of Villon, but mostly it's Gilbert and Sullivan trying to overthrow Queen Victoria.

chapter 6

Old Faithfuls

W. S. Merwin

In his recent books, W. S. Merwin's poetry has been folded up like a fetus. His work has abandoned most of the techniques by which poetry measures its distance from prose, has gone further and discharged punctuation: the poems in *Travels* exist in their own inner exile, a stream of consciousness without barrier or limit, except the arbitrary limits of beginning and ending.

> *In a cold May travelling alone across*
> *stony uplands all afternoon the echoes*
> *lengthening with the light and the tattered*
> *crows exploding from their voices above*
> *bare scrub oaks and jagged sloes each clutching*
> *its fissured rock the wandering ruins*
> *of pasture walls orchard enclosures rooms*
> ("Barn")

Such a poetry suffers an extreme attenuation of vocal gesture and a corresponding expansion of vatic, dreamlike utterance (Merwin often sounds like a voice from beyond). The world in such poems has shrunk to its weary abstractions: not Platonic images but the mummified remains of ideals.

The "assumed authority" that drew W. H. Auden to Merwin's first book, *A Mask for Janus* (chosen by Auden for the Yale Series of Younger Poets and published in 1952), was the authority of a tradition with recognized limits, but without antagonism toward those limits. The gifts Merwin showed in apprenticeship to that tradition produced, for example, the memorably sullen rhythms of "Ballad of John Cable and Three Gentlemen." An apprentice is allowed to use (as well as abuse) the tools of the master, but the ballad's force derives from an uncanny impersonation of John Crowe Ransom, not mere imitation of his manner. Of the many apprentices to the style, few could out-Ransom Ransom.

R. P. Blackmur said of Emily Dickinson that the "cultural predicament of her time drove her to poetry instead of antimacassars," and Merwin's poetry has often seemed the cultural equivalent of crocheting antimacassars. The fecundity of his work, late and early (the poetry conducted in parallel to significant careers in translation and prose memoir), has been subject to a compulsive repetition of means: many of his poems have been indistinguishable and of negligible ambition.

The authority of tradition is largely an authority of circumstance, and without circumstance authority is entirely lost. (A critic might argue that Merwin's restless search for new styles is part of a fruitless attempt to recreate authority.) Merwin's first four books, from *A Mask for Janus* (a telling title for a poet of uncertain identity) to *The Drunk in the Furnace* (1960), were stuffed with odd notions, the forms barely containing the exuberance of invention. They were highly formed poems in a time devoted to rhyme and meter, yet the poems rarely seemed entire or complete. They were restricted expressions of an urgency that could be exhausted only by writing another poem, and another.

Most of Merwin's influence and virtually all of his standing derive from the starved Romantic diction of *The Moving Target* (1963), *The Lice* (1967), and *The Carrier of Ladders* (1970), a diction that became the favored medium of younger poets, even when they were unwilling to adopt his skeletal arrangements. The elemental language of *dark* and *stone* and *stars* and *water* and *silence*, the mythopoeic mythopoetry so characteristic of the period, was ludicrous except in a poetry capable of Merwin's hollow-voiced command.

The funeral procession swinging empty belts
Walks on the road on the black rain
Though the one who is dead was not ready

In the casket lid the nails are still turning

Behind it come the bearers
Of tires and wet pillows and the charred ladder
And the unrollers of torn music and a picture of smoke
    ("The Next")

Such lines are harsher and more allusive than virtually anything he has written since.

Having abandoned the surreal imagery but not the surreal juxtapositions or his hostility to form, Merwin's most recent idiom has worked a depleted vein, its narrow vocabulary perhaps requiring a narrowness of argument and articulation. The poems in *Travels*, like the poems of his last three or four books, have a similar ligature of feeling and lack of specific intonation, a bemused bearing, a love of nature confused with a slavishness toward it, a tendency toward the abstract (his poems rarely have the tang of the specific), as well as his distinctive sweetness, tentativeness, and modest scale. They are cartoons of poems rather than poems. His little shocks or derangements of the poetic line seem designed more to distract from the sentimental character of his subjects than to acknowledge an emotional difficulty or respond to an imaginative demand.

When years without number
like days of another summer
had turned into air there
once more was a street that had never
forgotten the eyes of its child
    ("Another Place")

    between files of pointed trees
on the empty road into the air small children
are running with arms raised toward the clouds

running and falling and I am running
like a small child running with arms raised
falling getting to my feet running on
after all having decided that
I am going to tell the whole story
  ("Mirage")

From the lazy syntax (are those small children running *into the air*?) to the bored accumulation of indifferent phrases, the poems are whimsical in their lack of attention to design and stifling in their sentimental embrace. Merwin is like a man obsessed with the divination of clouds.

Travels marks a further diminuendo of identity, the latest revenge of the present tense. In the design of the poems as well as in his refusal of technical restraint, lyric techniques now seem suffocating impositions. Even when they existed only in the faint penumbra of his free verse, those formal orders provided adequate antagonism to such constraints.

Merwin is now most himself when not himself at all. In half a dozen historical monologues, giving voice to some of the great naturalists, he has partially redeemed an unpromising style by escaping from the composures of his familiar, irritating mythology of self.

All day
the father said we rode
through swamps
seeing tupelo

cypress standing in deep water
and on higher ground palmettos
mingling with pine
deer

and turkeys moving under
the boughs
and we dined by a swamp on bread
and a pomegranate
  ("The Lost Camelia of the Bartrams")

The matter-of-fact detail isolates a nature at the time treated matter-of-factly, but already subject to the grinding curiosity of civilization. These poems about Rumphius, Marín, Douglas, and the Bartrams dissect the motivations of men responsible for the salvage of "living things / with no value that we know." Such men were not necessarily pure heroes of the scientific method and were governed by forms of acquisition little different from greed. Honoring the innocence of their confusions, Merwin's run-on manner captures the style of early notebooks and correspondence, of voices that can't be stopped.

Elsewhere, however, the poems lack such focus and adjustment. In most of Merwin's work, nature is not the medium in which we find ourselves, or a relentless and unforgiving condition, but the warm and nurturing substitute for vanished religion, repeating its claims while absolved of its guilts. The incantatory spell of the phrasing cannot disguise its damp philosophy: the poems using the poet's life are of weaker interest and weaker intent than any meager narrative, not because Merwin's experience is hobbled by a lyric measure but because the experience is never pursued as thoroughly, as subtly, or as defiantly as the smallest entry in a naturalist's journal. Merwin has been productive, and genuine within the restraint of his means and his ambition; but for two decades the poetic means have been the determining form of the ambition, rather than in service to it. His poems have lost the very terms most crucial to their shape as properties of a subject. At a certain point it is more difficult to be ambitious than to make antimacassars.

Mona Van Duyn

However disorganized or haphazard our habits, we read poetry in the sequence of an expectation. The original order of a poet's books is not what a later reader is likely to experience. The afterlife of most poets is in the crowded halls of the anthology (where a poet has position but little place), and once a poet is confined there no one but the moral scholar or tormented reader will begin his acquaintance with a poet's works in their written order. We read the living in expectation rather than elegy.

It is, however, a divided privilege to follow the work of our contemporaries as it is published. What we lose by not being able to comprehend the whole—the whole not being complete—is only partly recovered in our immediate, helpless intimacy with the smaller concentrations of the art: the labored progress, the inturnings, the abandoned passages and dead ends, the sudden and unexpected release into a larger climate. The volumes maintain their own version of an argument in which *High Windows* could no more precede *The Less Deceived* than *The Mills of the Kavanaughs* follow *Life Studies*. Our faith in the private reading of that argument lets us misread poets who deceive our expectations.

After the age of sixty, poets often write in the prison of prior understandings and in diplomacy toward the future, tacitly accepting the decline in invention that comes after long engagement with an art (or the distractions of recognition and regard—it was Eliot who said the Nobel Prize was a ticket to your own funeral, and he might as well have meant a funeral for the art as well as the life). But a poet may violently reject his old comprehensions, even when he has no idea how to replace them. It is hard to win any advantage over such conditions—the condition of paralyzed continuation or equally paralyzed revolt. The rare successes are a triumph not merely over time's debility but over the debility of a long habitation in the self.

Mona Van Duyn's best poems in *If It Be Not I: Collected Poems, 1959–1982* are a little clumsy in their casual charms: their honesty eases the slight roughness of their craft. She could make poems from table scraps and newspaper cuttings, as Auden used to do; and, like his, her poems are often just intelligent talk: sociable and even chatty, never accidentally revealing, fond-hearted if somewhat prickly, and inclined to tug on your lapels. She lacks his intelligent ear—her poems slouch off toward prose without some formal obligation to attend to, and her early experiments with rhyme sound like half-deaf doggerel:

Now, in this evening land of fire and shadow,
a swallow world, a fallow world, of lake and meadow,

where the mud turtle flops from his log, flat as our fate,
but the green-headed flies swarm up, so furious is our delight.
("From Yellow Lake: An Interval")

In such vacant painterly descriptions, you see her peculiar marriage of the mundane (perhaps the muddy) and the metaphysical ("when the world's slippery, solemn arrangements / slide to a comic pratfall"). Van Duyn's poems have been lessons in how to conduct a poetry not of philosophical density (the Symbolists were more acquainted with the unmeaning densities of philosophy) but of philosophical texture. Few poets have found inspiration in the ordinary domestic guilts—if there were no suburbs to feel guilty in, Mona Van Duyn would have had to invent them (a newspaper buried under a sycamore's fallen bark has inspired *two* poems, one of them a sestina). Even in the suburbs, however, the contracts of the everyday are unforgiving:

When she died last winter, several relatives wrote to say
a kidney stone "as big as a peach pit" took her away.
Reading the letters, I thought, first of all, of the irony,

then, that I myself, though prepared to a certain degree,
will undoubtedly feel, when I lie there, as lonesome in death as she
and just as surprised at its trivial, domestic imagery.
("A Relative and an Absolute")

When Van Duyn writes that she has "sucked the dark particular," it is out of recognition that her poetry is more than usually dependent on the small breakages or vantages of daily affairs, that the darkness of the world, its inevitable falling toward loss, is redeemed by the transient comedy of particulars: "we . . . pulled up over our heads / a comforter filled with batts of piney dark, / tied with crickets' chirretings and the *bork* / of frogs; we hid in a sleep of strangeness from / the human humdrum."

Her brisk, slightly wacky sense of language is the fitful and intimate counterpart of a grace achieved through awkwardness. In the beauty of their ungainliness, her poems have some of the lightness—the longing beneath the lightness—of Elizabeth Bishop. Van Duyn's poems are doughier, more thorough and thoughtful, less injured, and finally less moving because not open to being moved without the intercession of language. Van Duyn is a poet who can't think until she writes (in her worst poems she forgets to think even then) and can't feel until she thinks. This is not unusual for poets living through language—a poet's deliberate intentions often exist only in the dream-life of critics.

Van Duyn had a long apprenticeship—her first book was not published until she was thirty-eight. All the emphasis in her early work on what a poem is or does ("A poem can stay formally seated / till its person-to-person call, centuries later, is completed") was sly and unencumbered, the equivalent of what philosophers do when noodling around with their dead-cat-in-a-box conundrums. Her poems sidled toward their real subjects as if slightly intimidated by them: Van Duyn seemed surprised into tragedy or comedy by the domestic routine.

A poet so careless and beguiling could not believe in "working through otherness to recognition" if love were not the middle ground of tragedy and comedy (love may be the idea the suburbs were constructed to forget). In a life of common pursuits, love becomes an absorbing emotion not for its manners but its movement, its allowance of change, of the commerce of bodies: its passport out of the familiar into a "strange and willful country."

> *I still see the mother I wanted, that I called to come,*
> *coming. From the dark she rushes to my bedroom,*
>
> *switching the lamp on, armed with pills, oils, drops,*
> *gargles, liniments, flannels, salves, syrups,*
>
> *waterbag, icebag. Bending over me,*
> *giant, ferocious, she drives my Enemy,*
>
> *in steamy, hot-packed, camphorated nights,*
> *from every sickening place where he hides and waits.*
>
> *Do you think I don't know how love hallucinates?*
>   ("Remedies, Maladies, Reasons")

In the beautiful pregnancies of her half-rhymes, Van Duyn is our great, stinging poet of the adequacies of love, even of the worn or threadbare desires of the newspaper personals. A poet so haphazard rarely achieves such formal control, but in the rhymed poems of her middle period Van Duyn found a way to sharpen what she elsewhere calls "My capriciousness and downright perversity." All the casual losses could not conceal her mordant heart.

> *Against intention, the feelings raise*
> *a whole heavy self, panting and clumsy, into these*
> *contortions. We live in waste. I don't know about you,*
> *but I live in the feelings, they direct the contortions of the day,*
>
> *and that is to live in waste. What we must do, we do,*
> *don't we, and learn, in love and art, to see*
> *that the peony stalks are red, and learn to say this*
> *in the calm voice of our famous helplessness.*
> ("Peony Stalks")

Van Duyn is a poet more at ease in resolution than premise, but no matter where her poems begin (and they often seem to begin with dogs) they end in the mute regards of love: even a poem that starts with the invention of horseradish finishes in "married love." The subject so infuses her work, lurking so eagerly around every corner, that its appearance comes to seem a faded punchline; yet her endings have such forbearance, such wary gratitude, the poems have more dignity than they deserve.

Van Duyn has an unusual poetic intelligence—not pristine like Yeats's or Merwin's or Stevens's, not an intelligence that might have been perfectly content had the world never existed, acting as if the world doesn't exist outside poems (as if the world were the idea of the poem). It is an intelligence not corrupted by the everyday, only a little soiled by it: intimate with disappointment, with sultry and sour detachment, with the failing garden and the poisoned dog, full of minor joys and partial surrenders.

Her poems have faltered whenever they have strayed far from her themes or telling forms—her weakest work refuses the sophistication of voice and tone her subtleties elsewhere demand. The artlessly plainspoken *Bedtime Stories* (1972), tales told in dialect by a maundering grandmother, did not pander to the sentimental impulse so much as surrender to it. Her recent poetry has been more than occasionally occasional, though you expect that later in life a poet will write more than her share of elegies.

Van Duyn's new book, *Firefall*, is a book of elegy and farewell, a catalogue of the ills and complaints of age, the losses endured and those still to be faced. She has discarded much of her irony and bitter self-regard, and with them the technical fashioning that once created a metaphysical register beneath the headlong suburban crises. Her new poems seem more desperately contrived by their occasions: a poem about a painting by Chagall, a poem about ads for lost children, a villanelle for the Duc d'Orleans' fifteenth-century villanelle contest, a poem about winning the Pulitzer, a poem about writers and their dogs, a poem about not being Richard Wilbur. A poem of apology for having given a friend a hideously ugly shirt (black with yellow stripes) attempts some eighteen goofy rhymes on "hornet," including "highernote," "hernit- / wit," "keep even the whoreneat," "undo a hueorknot," "blow a hornat," "no matter howornate," and some even worse. There are two dozen "minimalist sonnets" and "extended minimalist sonnets" of this sort: "The Young plot / each glance / but know chance / will allot // a moonshot / of romance, / a slowdance / of pot, // not hearing / life's handcuffs / unlock // till wearing / their earmuffs / of Rock." Some translate famous anthology poems into Van Duynese. So, "The Circus Animals' Desertion": "Linking / starts / in stinking / hearts. // Dung / clings, / but rung / sings. // Then / rust. / Again / one must // think / stink." So, "Dover Beach": "Sweetness / seems. / Mess / screams. // Be / clone. / We / are alone // in unfaith / armed, / wrath / uncharmed, // an ungirled / world."

It is dispiriting to say that the charms and shrewd material intelligence of Van Duyn's poetry are almost entirely absent in this book. We are instead witness to what remains when the charms are stripped away: a scaffolding of artifice, forced reminiscence, labored jokes, and poems designed to do badly everything this poet once did so idiosyncratically and so well. Only a few passages remind the reader that she can be a poet of delicious, exotic language and difficult feeling:

On the table rolled to ours a flat pan holds
the posed trio under a fiery arbor
of crabs, tails to a blue-black coil of conger.
On either side, like bridesmaids, the symmetry,
grace, sea-molded curves of mullet and loup;
in the center, the bride ("a first-class bouillabaisse
owes its quality to the rascasse, *which is*
essential"), rascasse *the hog-fish, known to folk*
and fishermen as the ugliest fish in the world.
Round, lovely eyes of her finny attendants
are blind to the rope of grotesque neck
that lifts a snouted face to her clan of lovers.
("Rascasse")

To praise such passages (has anyone other than Anthony Hecht written with such furtive appetite?) is not to ignore the limitations of a poet more honored than anthologized: a world of enforced mildness has its tragedies, even if it has trouble naming them. Van Duyn has been—and still occasionally is—a rueful, darkly witty poet of odd emotional cadence and fine cautious rapture.

John Ashbery

It is hard to think of John Ashbery in twilight, near the end of a career weighted down with honors, because the poetry in *Hotel Lautréamont* is as preposterous and irritating as ever. He has been the major antiphonal voice in American poetry for more than thirty years, though his poems have long since lost their ability to shock, and have gradually subsided into a genteel form of nervous mockery and self-mockery. The critic who wishes to distinguish the good from the bad in Ashbery will need to invent a criticism outside our present orders, if criticism is not to embrace or abandon him whole (as it has embraced, for example, the unwieldy girth of Wallace Stevens).

Ashbery still makes more sense just before dawn, when the missed connections and jumpy ellipses seem signs of meaning on the edge of revelation, when the poems shimmer in the subconscious. A reader forgets, at such moments, the narrow intent of Ashbery's winks and shrugs, or the shallow reservoir of his technique: the offhand prose sentences; the wise-guy tone and adolescent jokiness; the logic that veers and darts like a water-strider over the surface of sense; the smart talk, so icy and self-referential, full of puns and pop culture and portly allusion. He has the comic beatitude of Magritte or Chaplin:

> *Let's make a bureaucracy.*
> *First, we can have long lists of old things,*
> *and new things repackaged as old ones.*
> *We can have turrets, a guiding wall.*
> *Soon the whole country will come to look over it.*
>
> *Let us, by all means, have things in night light:*
> *partly visible. The rudeness that poetry often brings*
> *after decades of silence will help. Many*
> *will be called to account. This means that laundries*
> *in their age-old way will go on foundering.*
>
> ("On the Empress's Mind")

These fizzy concoctions never have the courage of their misdemeanors: their mild provocations never place the reader's complacence under serious attack, though they pretend that to satisfy the reader's desire for sense would be an action nearly criminal. Where anything might burst in unexpectedly (this could be called Ashbery's ontology, even his theology), nothing can ever be amazing. "And then, unexpectedly, I am shown a dog." Ho-hum.

The only guarantor of Ashbery's art is his sensibility, and sensibility is peculiarly susceptible to a collapse of confidence. Ashbery has shuffled the deck of dictions so often that he perhaps hasn't noticed that many of his mannerisms now lack conviction:

> *Hell, it's only a ladder: structure*
> *brought us here, and will be here when we're*

honeycombs emptied of bees, and can say
that's all there is to say, babe; make it a good one
for me.
   ("Baked Alaska")

The exhaustion of means is an exhaustion by repetition, and a poet who will do anything to avoid repeating himself must, at last, repeat himself all the time. At his worst Ashbery rehearses all the forgotten exhibits of museum surrealism:

Night promontories can be sticky there is a whole other suite of
glabrous thingamabobs adhering to the minutes of my vacuum.
Then to get down and crawl it, into the unimagined spaces that
were, it's true, there. I still address it. Like a lost man.
The oldest sewer in captivity. I can shrink it too,
and desperately bawling you knows no man's coming to lick it,
be beside it, extrapolate us on the ledge. We're caring.
Shoo, that's all-important now. Under the legs
of this chair I can see into the runnels. Midnight's near.
   ("The Wind Talking")

Future generations may wheel out Ashbery's corpse once a year, like Jeremy Bentham's, just to see who wrote in this fashion. ("A yak is a prehistoric cabbage: of that, at least, we may be sure"— who wouldn't be curious?) His incoherence relies on the reader's suspicion that meaning, though frustrated and defeated, has only been withheld, that the frustration of meaning is indeed part of the meaning. But the daring leaps and deceptive intimacies that formed so much of Ashbery's patter are now an old song, and what once was intrepid now seems merely a lack of stamina. A poetry based on deceit must monitor its deceptions with far more rigor than mere organization would entail—deceit tends toward restriction and predictability, where organization moves toward the liberation of controlled energies.

Ashbery has the partial identity of a major poet: he writes abundantly and is abundantly inimitable. His league of minor followers has none of his lightness or sustained and transparent craft, and whatever they write seems in a minor key of the master. But the master himself prefers the minor keys these days; and when he concentrates on a subject, however briefly, he shows a deftness the aleatory or improvisational pieces never approach.

> *Something has got to stop,*
> *yet I tell you the enemies are for us, shouting in our ears.*
> *The leaves are too little at the top,*
> *and the years, well they come to seem little too, little and nifty,*
> *though I suppose not for long, and I seem to hear*
> *something will wring us, wrench us from the extremes*
> *of piety on the one hand and salacious diffidence on the other: just*
> *enough for the sing-song to get along, as we were,*
> *nice and easy for us, stone plinths with fringe of grass.*
> ("Wild Boys of the Road")

Such passages ought to remind us of the poet Ashbery chose not to become in the wake of his one acknowledged masterpiece, "Self-Portrait in a Convex Mirror." To turn away from the serious and philosophical poems he might have written required a lonely, monkish faith in his own peculiar aesthetic, an aesthetic that exists so easily on the edge of nonsense it can only rarely, and usually under the guise of comedy, make raids on sense:

> *My sister and I don't seem to get along too well anymore.*
> *She always has to have everything new in her house. Cherished*
>   *ideals*
> *don't suit her teal, rust and eggshell color scheme.*
> *Of course, I was a buyer when she was still on the street*
> *peddling the Communist Youth weekly. I have a degree*
> *in marketing. Her boyfriend thinks I'm old-fashioned.*
> *Well, I guess I do have an old-fashioned mentality.*
> ("Korean Soap Opera")

The title reveals how subtle and savage that old-fashioned mentality can be. If you didn't know better (who but the wolfish Ashbery has cried wolf more often?), you might think he was using the ambiguities of language to manage ambiguities of feeling, and that the dominance of the quotidian in his work is due not to some attention deficit but to his loyalty to the traditional form of comedy, the antic hay of everyday affairs.

The most subversive remarks by this most knowing of con artists have been the aesthetic manifestos smuggled into his work—their naked self-referentiality has disguised a droll looking-glass analysis of his art, neither thorough nor consistent, but comprehending as farce is comprehending:

> *Then I reached the field and I thought*
> *this is not a joke not a book*
> *but a poem about something—but what? Poems are such odd little*
> *   jiggers.*
> *This one scratches himself, gets up, then goes off to pee*
> *in a corner of the room. Later looking quite*
> *stylish in white jodhpurs against the winter*
> *snow, and in his reluctance to talk to the utterly*
> *discursive: "I will belove less than feared . . ."*
>
> ("Musica Reservata")

> *O my spirit shall be*
> *audited! and unknown readers*
> *grasp the weight of my words*
> *as their feathery hulls blow away*
> *leaving the crabbed and sullen seed*
> *behind. And how many of these shall grow?*
> *Really I thought it was autonomous*
> *as the birds' song, the vultures' sleep.*
>
> ("Le Mensonge de Nina Petrovna")

> *I've taken my stand and am pretty much prepared*
> *to let it wear me out. Nor does the crucible of what we said*
> *out of turn return to urge a new complacency, quiet*
> *between the paws of the sphinx, nor does anything electrical have*
> *   to interfere.*
>
> ("That You Tell")

Eliot might have written criticism in such a manner, had he given himself over to the vaudeville he admired. These fragments are the suggestive intimations of a severe (if absurdist) consideration of art. But that may be to import purpose to a career that has been carried on in fragments, or at least in fragmentary relations—Ashbery has won his audience in his waywardness, even if his later books have not been wayward at all. They are as alike as a line of Rockettes. He could write like this if he were asleep.

Ashbery can now alter at whim the formal terms through which his gift operates, the vessels into which the poetry is poured, but no longer the gift itself. In recent years he has written a book-length poem (*Flow Chart*), a sequence of sixteen-line poems (*Shadow Train*), a long poem in parallel columns ("Litany"), and much else. In his *Essays in Divinity*, John Donne wrote that "an enormous pretending Wit of our nation and age undertook to frame such a language, herein exceeding *Adam*, that whereas he named every thing by the most eminent and virtuall property, our man gave names, by the first naked enuntiation whereof, any understanding should comprehend the essence of the thing, better then by a definition." Ashbery's art cannot answer whether, in the naked enunciation of his naming, his talent has been continually renewed, ripening in its own ashes (as his own name puckishly suggests), or has simply succumbed to an endless fall down a flight of stairs.

chapter 7

Pound at the Post Office

Come we to full points here? And are etceteras nothing?
Pistol, 2 *Henry IV*

The seduction of force comes from below.
Simone Weil, *Notebooks*

Letters are our most private public act, and our most public private
act. I may write things to you I would never say aloud. I may write
things I wouldn't repeat, or would rather not have you repeat. You
may mouth these matters like a muezzin, broadcast like a bill col-
lector, gossip about them like geese, but if you do you will have
violated a confidence. You may hawk my letters in the market like
trousers or burn them like trash, may dole them as drawing paper
to your nieces and nephews, shave out my autograph and post it to
an admirer, ink out sentiments that horrify you, or cut my thoughts
to ribbons with your shears. You may die and leave my letters to a
library, where every scruffy scholar may paw through them and
bear away my secrets—or you may interdict their use for a year, or
fifty, or a hundred, may grant and grab back again, grip them like
an Indian giver, loan without license. I may marry and argue for
my billets-doux back by messenger—you may refuse, you may sell
them in secret to my new bride (but again you will have behaved
like a cad, again violated what once was inviolable between us). I
may die long before you, may claw at you horribly from my death-
bed, may plead in my will that you burn all trace of our life in let-
ters, that you turn our ancient ardors or cold conspiracies to ash
(whereas you want to exchange them for cold cash). You may

refuse, but in this you will generally *not* be felt to have put dishonor before death. The dead cannot be libeled, and there are certain rights the living abandon when they cease to breathe. The dead need accomplices to grub into the grave what they failed to destroy when outside it. We do not sympathize with Larkin's secretary for shredding and burning his diaries. And few owners of his letters, if any, heeded Auden's groan from the grave—*Burn them! Burn them!* Nor can the dead save from the flames what the living choose to incinerate. We curse Byron's friends and family for burning his memoirs. We curse Ted Hughes for his private fire. Here we sense the boundary between the public and the private, and the complication of realms in which letters uneasily exist. A recent book about biography was called *Keepers of the Flame.*

When I send you a letter I bind it into your possession. I may keep a copy, may hire an amanuensis to engrave what I say once for myself and once for you, may slip a sheet of carbon paper silently between your copy and my own, may sneak out to the Xerox shop before I fold your letter into its envelope, may ask my computer to print twice for every once I send. And you may treat my letter as you will, may long leave it sealed if you revile my hand or abhor its address. You may return to sender. You may take all these private actions with our private correspondence, may revere or ravage, save or savage my words as you wish, but you may not publish them. When I send you a letter, the paper belongs to you but the words belong to me; and I may hoard them, may refuse to release them to public gaze, may keep locked in my heart what my heart has already released. You may tell whom you like, but you may not set my words down in print—what I sent you in privacy may be known to everyone you meet, may be the story scholars tattle in the tea room; but my lawyers can prevent you from profit, can abort your charities before they are born. (If you sell them at Sotheby's, however, the auctioneer may publish extracts to advance the sale—this is the exception at law where commerce triumphs over privacy.)

For whom did I write my letters? If I keep copies I have written them partly for myself (or to protect myself from your callow misinterpretations). I may have written them with the public in mind, may have taken positions or feigned generosities (or genius) that would have people think well of me, would have me think well of myself. I may decide, in the doldrums of old age, to gather my lost letters into a book. And if you are kind enough to return them, since I am not the devious sort to keep duplicate accounts, I may find myself eager to edit, to introduce those puns by which I am now known, to polish the rough thoughts of a rougher time, to take advantage of *l'esprit d'escalier,* when for years I have been sitting on the stairs sulking over my rejoinders. I may take back what I said, may mangle my mind, and may then set a match to the evidence.

If I chance to die and a scholar salvages my stubby letters in eight volumes, he will usually bow to the pieties and blot any line offensive to the living. The living, as ever, take priority over the dead, may silence a statement or gag gossip, may tear my words from me without troubling to ask—their living is their legal writ, and by being conveniently dead I can say nothing against them. After we are dead, letters are the last fossils of our affections and our affectings, our hatreds and our private hells. I give you my word.

The Cantos were begun during September 1915, when the Allies were locked in trenches on the western front. Pound's wars were literary, and he took only desultory interest in the progress of fighting in France, except as it interfered with his friends: Lewis, Hulme, Ford, Gaudier-Brzeska. Throughout the war Pound offered his services to government, if in laggardly fashion—he favored interpretation or artillery, appropriately, and at one point considered serving with Theodore Roosevelt, who wanted to raise a new division of Rough Riders. Current events are an errant guide to the conditions that force a man to poetry, and particularly to a poetry of such guarded if grandiose design as *The Cantos*; but *The Cantos* is a poem founded in the vortex of war, in the effect on civilization of violence, and it is more than a curiosity that its muddy beginnings in London were parallel to the muck of trench warfare in France. The war was equally evident in *Cathay* and *Mauberley*, though Pound's poetry had warlike moments long before war was abroad.

The life is a menace to the literature, but there are flecks or traces the life throws out (or flak or tracers) that may prove clues to our later confusions. Pound's letters are a blueprint not just of the manifest style of *The Cantos*, but of the particular range of icon and image from which *The Cantos* was formed. We are not unaware of what we say in our letters, but we may be unconscious of the ways in which we *are* aware: we then inhabit the psychology of style. Kenneth Burke wrote that "if a man talks of *glory*, but employs the imagery of *desolation*, his *true subject* is desolation." My purpose is not to trace those fractures through the letters (though Pound in his letters is a man almost devoid of private feeling or private revelation, his public impersonations are personality enough), but to mark the liaisons or ligatures where the means of the letters reached ends in *The Cantos*. A man's letters, those documents so rarely troubled by literary intents (though their intentions may be as callously calculated or carelessly congealed), may sound the rough drafts of his poetry. At the least, we may look there for fair signs the foul papers conceal.

From the first Pound was a man for curious (even cryptic) schemes (just as in his letters he was a man for curious punctuation and cryptic spelling). In 1911 he wrote Dorothy Shakespear that his *Canzoni* was "supposed to be a sort of chronological table of emotions: Provence; Tuscany, the Renaissance, the XVIII, the XIX, centuries, external modernity (cut out)[,] subjective modernity. finis." The notion that lyric might sing the precise history of emotion would not have occurred to the older Pound, whose Cantos show so little awareness of emotion, even while their *melopoeia*, *phanopoeia*, and *logopoeia* affect the conduct of emotion. The argument of this synthesis, however, suggests that even in his twenties Pound was prepared to mount an assault on meaning beyond the minor saltings of his sub-Georgian lyrics. His poetry could not yet provide the substance of his ambition.

The ambition is scholarly (it might have appealed to Foucault), and it should be remembered that Pound and Eliot in their youth were serious academics in a way that would have seemed aberrant to most poets in the century before them—indeed, to most poets in the three centuries after Ben Jonson. Pound and Eliot studied for the Ph.D., Eliot in philosophy (but for the U-boats he might have received his degree) and Pound in Romance languages. Pound's anti-academicism took academic form in his early scheme for a College of Arts (1914) and his later Ezuversity. The manner of his later obsessions often mimicked crank scholarship, even when it was not crank scholarship; but the didactic proportions of *The Cantos* find earlier identity in the didactic imaginings of the letters.

> *I could however agree with Pico "animum sacra invadent" if he'd change the number of his verb—which would in consequence modify the interpretation of* sacra. *This whole renaissance affair seems quite pointless as it is quite certain the proceeds will not buy a house in Mayfair. . . .*
>
> *Of course nobody does* know *much about Etruscan gods and its hardly Etruscan gods that I mean—but nobody seems to know at all* what kind of gods did inhabit *"that section." Its my own belief that they matched up with a metallic architecture that Pater hints at . . . ; but this is a needless digression.*
>
> (to Dorothy Shakespear, August 24 or 31, 1911)

Eliot and Pound are two cases of reaction in exile (different in derivation and different in deceit). *The Cantos* might first be seen as an instance of the return of modes of scholarship repressed by circumstance: they are a crabbed and idiosyncratic outlet (art in its scholarship is almost immune to the criticism of scholars) at a time when the free strain of learning was dammed and embanked by war. In this they attempt to surpass Pound's real scholarship in *Cathay:* his use of Fenollosa's malformed cribs not just to revive and invigorate the translation of Chinese poetry but to reform the rhythms and the canons of imagery of English verse.

The condition of a poem's inception, and the abiding conditions of its composition, may introduce antagonistic and unhelpful tenors in our reading. The aubade written before battle is dignified not just by the poet's risk of death, but by his refusal to contemplate that death. *The Cantos* just as inevitably suffers when we judge its fortunes of war by the letters from the front Pound received in his snug apartment in Kensington. He began *The Cantos* only a few months after Gaudier-Brzeska was shot in the forehead at Neuville-Saint-Vaast, in June 1915. In September 1917, just after the last of the first three Cantos (in Pound's early versions and early arrangement—Ur-Cantos, as Hugh Kenner called them) had finally appeared in *Poetry*, Lewis wrote, "You meet plenty of dead men. I stumbled into one . . . with his head blown off so that his neck[,] level with the collar of his tunic, reminded you of sheep in butchers' shops, or a French Salon painting of a Moroccan headsman." In the same month T. E. Hulme was blown up by a shell near Nieuport. Pound's biographer Humphrey Carpenter is cool to the poet's reaction to these deaths, but a man might easily temper his grief (or indulge in black humor) in preference to easy displays. Pound wrote Harriet Monroe that all he had seen was "the ghost of a ghoul's article on Brzeska," which is a decent criticism. Reserve is not coldness, or contempt. Even a character as outspoken as Pound may have found certain things beyond expression. A few days after hearing of Gaudier-Brzeska's death, he had written Joyce, "I am very sick about it." And to his old teacher Felix Schelling, again within days: "The arts will incur no worse loss from the war than this is. One is rather obsessed with it."

The ambition of Pound's early Cantos was ambition without form, and we find the consequence not just in the need to revise and realign the early Cantos, but in their shuddering, juddering composition during and after the war. The composition halted in 1917 for almost two years, and once more in 1919, not to be kick-started again until early in 1922, after Pound had seen and edited *The Waste Land*. "Complimenti, you bitch," he had written Eliot, half in humor, or in half-humor. Had *The Waste Land* not been written, Pound might have abandoned a series of poems that had gained little interest from his peers and much hostility from his critics. Jealousy is a much underrated spur to writing. The odd episode of April 1922 may be relevant. On Good Friday, Pound announced his own death and had photos of a spurious death mask sent to the *Little Review*. He was furious when the editors refused to believe him. Such an incident, so soon after he had read *The Waste Land*, is suggestive: he intended to die like the Fisher King and rise again like Christ. This was at the least an attempt to avoid public contact and critical commitment, and return to poetry. It was also a shameless ploy for publicity. In the cruellest month.

The Ur-Cantos were inchoate, not because Pound lacked the burden of ideas, but because the ideas refused to organize that burden. "I have begun an endless poem," he wrote Joyce in 1917, "of no known category. Phanopoeia or something or other, all about everything." He may have meant panopoeia, as Carpenter notes, but neither his Greek nor his Latin always equalled the occasion. In his translations this weakness was transmuted to weird strengths—some of Pound's mistakes are mistakes of genius, if they are mistakes at all (it was bad memory, not bad Latin, that in one of his letters transformed Dante's *De Vulgari Eloquentia* into *De Volgari Eloquio*).

Pound's early Cantos are adequate signs of deracinated imagination (the discriminate knowledge of several literatures was severely impressionistic; the attraction to a poetry beyond lyric statement confused its means with its method). A man must in a strict sense be a megalomaniac to launch a long poem, and if not he must become a Bligh within his *Bounty*, willing to suffer for his breadfruit. A poet of less untroubled confidence would at the outset have been paralyzed by the hubris of modeling a poem after Dante's *Commedia*.

Nevertheless, exile often calls to exile. The attraction of the *Commedia*, the work of involuntary exile, lay not just in its synthesis of moral action and moral reward (*The Cantos* might be seen as an attempt to allow the judgments of art to usurp those of religion), but in its assumption of scattered acts, history's anecdotes and trace events, in a crucial underwriting of culture. Dante's interest in the troubadours and his standing in Renaissance politics, his devotion to the strengths of the demotic, and his confident belief in the artistic supplement of history are a perfected image of the young Pound.

Pound found ways of ignoring the differences (differences that provide his Cantos with their innovations as well as their irritations). *The Cantos* is an act of supreme artistic absorption and homage, even as it is a collapsing realm of arrogance and distemper—as Pound had written William Carlos Williams in 1908, "Why write what I can translate out of Renaissance Latin or crib from the sainted dead?" The remark anxiously rejects what later was furiously embraced (*The Cantos* is a repository of what was translated out of Renaissance Latin or cribbed from the sainted dead), and it is not the first virtue of *The Cantos* that is a virtue of necessity. Pound did not have an adequate synthetic mind—he habitually saw in glimpses (when he saw in wholes he was likely to seem paranoid or deranged). The fragmentary action of *The Cantos*, its conscious rejection of the Cartesian coordinates of narrative, answers a similar distrust of *ut pictura poesis*—there remain shards of the mirror of the visual, broken in cubist art. As the poem lumbered on (the Pisan Cantos always a partial exception—there, in a specific sense, he came to his senses), the fragmentations and displacements become symbolic actions of the poem's inner collapse of order, and its rages against order. The second half-century of Cantos is therefore twice as long as the first.

Consuming ambition required consuming form: *The Cantos* gave spurious unity to a man frayed in his interests, dissipating in his energies, shallower in his political than his artistic insights, yet capable of a poetry glaring with visual imagination and composed with an ear as subtle as Spenser's. In his need for such conspicuous consumption ("Give up th' intaglio method" [Ur-Canto I]), Pound naturally used what came to hand, and few poets have ever created a form so exactly congruent with their habits of mind—their prose habits of mind. Such exhaustion of means makes a poet jealous of the novelist or the essayist (the habits plain in the letters plot much of Pound's criticism). Pound removed himself from the confined lyric when it could not stretch to surrounding matters (*Mauberley* is a distinguished poem, but it is the end of a certain kind of imagination, not the beginning).

Pound's letters are variously intemperate, cajoling, didactic, advisory, equitable, irritable, generous, sly, adolescent. They present a more apprehensive and less specific intelligence than the capaciousness or capriciousness of *The Cantos;* but the specifications and technical organizations of that intelligence are largely the same, and we can see that however broad the factual catchment of the art, there lay beyond it the emotional bearing of a life not always available to the necessities of that art. The letters do not determine the stylistic or moral practice of *The Cantos;* they merely expose the reservoir of rhetorical fashion and prose concern from which Pound drew in creating a form that would hold material not always poetic. They offer the exercise of sensibility in a medium different from *The Cantos,* and so likely to show by its differences how the organizations were furnished, maintained, and executed.

A differential study would eat up a volume, and would guard the critic's descent through deepening circles of response, from stylistic tics and verbal twists; to mental habits or habituations (here not neglecting the psychology of imagery, in the manner of Caroline Spurgeon);* to the pursuit of particular interests, historical, economic, or literary; to the symbolic actions that the letters perform. For the last one might look first to the acts of patronage, the casual and complicated generosities, and then to Pound's relations with his own patron John Quinn, the series of letters between them providing the most haunting actions of the past in the present, as if the Renaissance patron who formed the moral model of so much

---

* Following Spurgeon's work on image clusters, poetry might productively be analyzed for syntactic and rhythmic clusters, where an image unconsciously accedes to a template of syntax or rhythm. Consider, in minor example, the repetitions in Cantos IV–V: "the green cool light," "the firm pale stone," "the black, soft water," "the bright pale sand," "the blanch-white stone," "the blue deep Nile" (in some editions), "the pale soft light." A study of such clusters would begin with Milman Parry's work on verbal formulae in the Homeric epic. The economy of such formulae, fitted to fixed parts of the hexameter line, conditioned the poet's vocabulary to the metrical scheme. One of Pound's characteristic terminal rhythms is (allowing for the transfer from quantity to accent) identical to the fragment of hexameter line following the "bucolic" diaeresis between the fourth and fifth foot ($|-\cup\cup|--$): "rose in the steel dust" (LXXIV); "wind in the beach grove" (LXXVI). Pound's ear may have been caught by the quantitative meter, transposed to an accentual measure.

of *The Cantos* had been incarnated as a New York lawyer. These consistencies of practice, though mutually modifying, would not much further our mastery of the particular metamorphoses that sustain a poem like *The Cantos*; and therefore a short study must concentrate not on the debts but the deviations.

The debts, however, have their own insistent order, and it might be well to establish one or two of the perfections of habit that the poem achieved. It was not Pound's practice, even in his earlier letters, to pursue a point, unless in service of a practicality (laying out the method of a new magazine or the madness of a manifesto). Even his arguments were disorganized, business out of hand before taken in hand, the mind loosed after half a dozen hares at once. Such antics of argument mimic the portraits of Pound in this period, his nervous energies more than nervous, his prose scarcely reined by his regard:

> *The public is still taken up, one half sentimentalizing over poor*
> *Brooke (which is all as it should be)*
>   *and the other half slopping over about Mestrovic, who is bull shit,*
> *six sorts of archaism, germany, Vienna secession, etc. true expression*
> *of Serbia, all right enough but damn poor sculpture. (Political slop,*
> *etc.) responsible for the exhibit (W.B.Y. (naturally) impressed) We*
> *hope to bring out a well illustrated memoir to Brzeska but god*
> *knows, John Lane is a shit, and publishers are timid, etc. etc.*
>   (to John Quinn, July 13, 1915)

Here the attention scarcely arrives before it has departed (in *The Cantos* that attention has sometimes departed before it has arrived); but we can measure in such a passage, in its asides, its angle of mental revision and attack (*which is all as it should be*), its telegraphese of historical and private reference, how the prose understudies the later poetry. *The Cantos* is littered with unstated etceteras. Even the dramatically dropped line, enacting the division of public reaction into concordant sentiment and discordant slop, shows the purpose of prose argument in a device Pound had used in his lyrics. Much of this would be no more interesting than mannerism if in *The Cantos* it had not been absorbed into the physiology of style.

Any review of *The Cantos'* visual form, intimately involved with Pound's acquisition of a typewriter during 1913 or 1914, cannot proceed without examining the letters in their library caches. In the interests of economy, the editors of his letters have "standardized" Pound's idiosyncratic spacings and indentations. Only a facsimile edition could indicate where the habits of expression accorded with habits of mind, where they had been tested in the letters before tried in *The Cantos*. Is it only in art that the appearance of the message is assumed to be part of the message? Pound was fortunate such editors did not "standardize" *The Cantos* as well.

The earliest Cantos, where the influence of Browning is strongest, and where the poem offers the prospect of different voices diverging into monologues (however difficult, however interpenetrated by historical period), are among the least susceptible to these private modes of disrepair, which displaced formal development with the impulse of intuition. A poet can too easily become helpless before his habits, in the belief that they are more than habits, that every seizure of mind is sacred. Wandering attention, like wandering Odysseus, was the only fixity of argument. Quinn, that shipshape lawyer, was so flummoxed by Pound's style of argument that he wanted Pound to write a separate letter on each topic, for the sake of the office filing system. Pound suggested he file one letter under "Ezra Pound, MESS!"

The great descants of *The Cantos*, the use of particular myths and historical periods in coordinated relation, are a mode of argument little different from stanzaic recurrence or a recrimination of theme. That these descants (like rhyme "in the old sense") have often been reduced to the rudest shorthand does not eliminate their resonant power; though it may place that power, not beyond the reach of formal interpretation, merely beyond the discipline of those who wish to read the poem without field guides or skeleton keys. Pound was worried by the obscurity of even the early Cantos (to Quinn in 1919: "I suspect my 'Cantos' are getting too too too abstruse and obscure for human consumption"), but the early obscurities are less intransigent, less internalized, and more obviously in service to certain responsibilities of argument.

The private codes that intimates allow, that appease the need for intimacy, can be unappeasable when everyone is assumed to be in on the joke. Pound's letters to Dorothy Shakespear can seem beyond the interpretation of anyone outside the group of two (one has to know, as a reader knows only from editorial notes, that CHARS, for example, were cats, cat spirits, and spirits of mischief "in the private mythology of the Shakespear family"), but elucidation often blunts the force of their initial effect.

> For the rest of your letter: I believe a mosseggg to be a small stone— one of a large number—so called from Mosegs having got the dekalogg on a large stone CHARS think, and thats why the café tables have marble tops.
>
> (to Dorothy Shakespear, April 21, 1913)

Dorothy had jauntily asked if he knew what "moseggs" were (mosaics, presumably), and Pound went off tilting at Moses. *The Cantos* has invited similar wrenching to less result; but the manner of allusion is more serious, if we take it on its own terms. To comprehend the vagrant work of history, the movements and countermovements, the indecipherable motives and illegible actions, the palimpsest of the past, requires a sensitivity to trace and suggestion, and to the possibility that trace and suggestion are all the archeologist of coherence is presented with. History coheres only inside the map of probabilities, the accord of fact and speculation where fact can merely be inferred: this is the only recourse for the fabric of poetry. But it is important to note how near such designs are to the immaculate coherence of conspiracy theories: the work of comprehension begins to master comprehension. The comic allusiveness of the early letters, their raw routine of dialect and familiarity, gradually overtakes the fondness of their purpose as a conduit of sensibility aside the normal channels of prose, and by the thirties reflects an increasing imaginative disorientation and mental diffusiveness.

Waaal ole SawBUKK
When a furriner looks at Baldwin's MOOG
in dh' wypers he SEES why you orter KILL J. Bull (and or Buhl)
This note is written is pure idleness/ between TEE/ruffic heaves
    (to Wyndham Lewis, December 5, 1936)

Rothschild/ vengeance running for 150 years/ Sas/ bloody/ shitten
soon; silver, and mass murder in China/ the cunt of all arseholes
Mond being nickel; the Times; Hamboro/ Manshitster Stinkereen/
60% interest; god save and so forth.
    (to Wyndham Lewis, February 7/8, [1940])

It is poetry (MOOG = mug, for example, wypers = papers, and Sas /
bloody / shitten soon = Sassoon), a poetry so angry with the plain
sense of the world, or the word, it compels the reader to submit to
the labor of understanding on the premise that only through rup-
tures of sense can sense emerge. What if understanding does not
repay the labor of understanding? Only those who do not go far
enough accuse the artist of going too far, but some of the disabili-
ties of *The Cantos* derive from the absorptions of a private style
incomprehensible at times even to his correspondents. (This did
not prevent correspondents from mimicking the style, just as the
blind indurations of *The Cantos* only encouraged imitation and
were more available to self-parody and parodic imitation than to
parody plain.)

My scrutiny, however, is directed toward the absorptions that
required alterations. The form of art exacts certain subsidies from
the artist's apprehension; and in a poet like Pound, where the art
became more and more the adaptation to a private idiom, it is sig-
nificant to know where the private idiom was found wanting. Only
by examining the poet's mental equipment can we venture some
notice of his predicament and calculate where his trust in his pow-
ers could not be simply reflexive.

Apart from rare passages of controlled translation or passionate
rhetoric (e.g., Cantos I and XLV), what most people remember in

The Cantos are its images; and when *The Cantos* is spoken of as great art it is often on the basis of scattered lines of description, the direct evidence of Pound's *phanopoeia*, his scattering of light: "Seal sports in the spray-whited circles of cliff-wash, / Sleek head, daughter of Lir, / eyes of Picasso / Under black fur-hood" (II), "Palace in smoky light, / Troy but a heap of smouldering boundary stones" (IV), "Boats drawn on the sand, red-orange sails in the creek's mouth" (VIII), "In the gloom, the gold gathers the light against it" (XI), "And the bees weighted with pollen / Move heavily in the vine-shoots" (XVII), "Wine in the smoke-faint throat, / Fire gleam under smoke of the mountain" (XXV), "Wind on the lagoon, the south wind breaking roses" (XXVI).

The manner of Pound's images changes little after his Imagist manifesto of 1913: they employ the same rich palette (like bold shades of lipstick) and dramatic gestures; they are gorgeous even when gloomy, classical in their isolated beauty and flattened in the visual realm (as if painted on vases or tomb walls). The lack of dimension is almost their drama, and they rarely violate the drama of the lines surrounding them: they are cool with contemplation. The demands on a writer of letters are different from those on a writer of poems; but in the speed of letter writing ("my letters done to save time are NOT model for print" [1930]) the poet will usually revert to his most basic or familiar repertoire of gestures, and in Pound's letters the signs of speed and reflex are everywhere apparent. The moods of his images, however, are strikingly changed. It is notable, first, that apart from his early letters to Margaret Cravens (1910–1912) Pound rarely records anything seen. His letters were practical, but this austerity seems unusual in a man whose recollections in poetry were so visually forced.

> *I sat on the Dogana's steps*
> *For the gondolas cost too much, that year,*
> *And there were not "those girls," there was one face,*
> *And the Buccentoro twenty yards off, howling "Stretti,"*
> *And the lit cross-beams, that year, in the Morosini,*
> *And peacocks in Koré's house, or there may have been.*
>   (Canto III)

(The visual memory here colludes with the tactile, the aural, and perhaps inevitably the financial.) Second, in the letters the modes of comparison are rarely modes of compassion: the visual is often invoked to secure a harshness or measure a contempt. It becomes a weapon of temper, and of metaphor rather than the picturesque.

To Dorothy Shakespear: "I'm trying to do an article on 'The Tradition,' hoping it will take *all* the bristles off all the dead pigs in Chicago." To John Quinn: "The author must know what he wants to say, and then he must say it without trying to wear a frock coat and black gloves in his mouth." To Louis Zukofsky, regarding *Poetry:* "the present staff of boiled vegetables." To Quinn again: "I put this money into [Eliot], as I wd. put it into a shoe factory if I wanted shoes. Better simile, into a shipping company, of say small pearl-fishing ships." The last was fondly meant, but even Pound's affections could be double-edged.

The imagery is trenchant, as would be expected, but its differences suggest that whatever imposition the form of *The Cantos* contemplated—and the form makes demands upon its reader beyond the translation of ideogram to moral action—the visual aspect was passive and contemplative. The visual image was the consequent form in English of the ideogram, and so not meaning represented but meaning embodied. This was an attempt, not to cut off the access of experience to the visual realm, but to secure for experience the innocence of visual authority (elsewhere *The Cantos* is all annotation and no denotation). *The Cantos* had to exact such disinterest if its metamorphoses were not to seem merely corrupt or partial; this it was never fully able to establish, as the ambition became contaminated by considerations only partly thematic.

There is a similar if minor movement in *The Cantos'* success at fending off all ironies that are not ironies of circumstance—that is, ironies that serve the movements of one history through another. This resistance, in a poet indulgent in his humors, is more flagrant when we compare the general ironic tenor of *The Cantos* (where the past is held up to the present, to the present's disadvantage) with the wit released from the bondage of argument. Humor in *The Cantos* is almost always anecdotal, protecting the poet from any suspicion that he is fouling or flouting his concerns; but

Quinn's story about the buggered sailor, which closes Canto XII, and the old admiral's tale of Lord Byron in Canto XVI are among the few instances where the humor is not exigent or hardened by effect. The pleasure we derive from these passages in *The Cantos* is partly that they are not quite of *The Cantos:* they are rank with the personal, and their power is in their separation from the poem's high-minded charge. Here, however, by standing off from the immediate welter, they establish a realm beyond that of mere argument, and so further the idea of a history whose seriousness is the mode of argument.

For comic relief to work at all, there must be something to be relieved from: relief intensifies the tragedy, because we are further separated from the world of innocence by being reminded of it. It was not that Pound was incapable of his humors (the letters are spattered with inky wit), but that humor could have only a partial and limiting effect in a poem that relied largely on the guilts of historical condition. The japes and jibes that are the easy currency of the letters ("Liberty's makes me feel as if I'd got into somebody's dressing room by mistake" [1913], "Had the ineffable pleasure of watching Fry's sylph-like and lardlike length bobbing around in the muddy water off the pier" [1916], "[Eliot] can't simply chuck her in the Thames., even if he were so disposed, which he aint" [1922]) must therefore be restricted or discriminated. This is why *The Cantos* is not *The Canterbury Tales.* Similarly, the dialect that was virtually a mirror of Pound's mockery, and that is shown to such amusing and then gradually arthritic effect in the letters, is in *The Cantos* almost always the portion of anecdote; otherwise the impersonality of ideogram would have threatened to become the personality of idiolect, and character would exist just where character needed to be absented.

We can see the effect of *The Cantos'* absorption of style in the area most open to misinterpretation, Pound's prejudices and his particular anti-Semitism. Pound's bigotry was despicable and repellent, and is the obstacle to a controlled reading of the poetry. The nature and name of his prejudices, however, cannot be dismissed as merely the poisoning of the literary by the anti-literary, cannot merely be subject to the prejudgments of others. To analyze them is not to excuse them, but to render their metamorphoses a mistake of the meaning.

Anti-Semitism, it must first be remembered, was nearly rigid in Pound's class and period. The saintly Dr. Williams could write his publisher, "There is the possibility that some smart Kike might make a fifty fifty deal with one of my protagonists" (1937). Eliot is altogether more circumspect in the published letters ("Burnham is a Jew merchant" [1917]), but we have the evidence of the poems and of such transient remarks as the one in his "suppressed" book, *After Strange Gods*: "Reasons of race and religion combine to make any large number of free-thinking Jews undesirable" (the context must not be taken as ameliorating).

Pound's letters do not escape the intolerance of the period; this may be expedient, if there remain romantic illusions about the company of poets, as an example of how even in the company of poets prejudice may be sustained. None of this can exculpate the virulence of the hatred or the progression of virulence. "The jew publisher," "[the magazine] had to sell out to the jews," "to withstand Guggenbergs and Picklesteins": these in letters to Quinn, who himself could write of trying to get financial backing from a "cultivated jew banker" and could rail against a "Jewish Number" of the *Little Review*. By the late thirties, in letters to Lewis, the language was worse: "BAD enough to have european aryans murdering each other fer the sake of . . . a few buggarin' kikes," "why the hell dont it occur to you that the lousy jews who run yr/ fahrt of an empire steal 7 bob to the quid from a mans royalties" (the conjunction of the anus and anti-Semitism is telling).

The forbearance of Pound's publisher James Laughlin is thoroughly on display in their letters. Over the course of forty years Laughlin was his diligent front man in America, a Maxwell's demon of intelligence and good sense. There is much to be said for a man who could be preached at by Ezra Pound for four decades without losing his composure. On one occasion, however, he stood up to Pound with great dignity and courage, in 1939 refusing to have any more to do with Pound's anti-Semitism, or to publish anything in *The Cantos* that could be construed as an attack on Jews. Laughlin in shame recanted his own youthful anti-Semitic remarks. Pound was flabbergasted.

Though the insistent mania of Pound's letters in the late thirties suggests a mind close to fanatic collapse, his remarks (made uglier by comments about Asians and blacks) are not words caught in the unstopped ear, not words others had poured in the porches of his ears. They form the pneumatic and base responses of a man who, beyond its collusive and unfeeling pleasure (the pleasure of intemperance, the pleasure of hatred), indulged in bigotry and then used (or was used by) the unstable identities it conferred on his art. A language of prejudice should not be mistaken for the pure fact of the prejudice, if we register the discontents and fictions with which language is charged; Pound's anti-Semitism is never confused by his friendships with Jews, his troubled remarks against intolerance, and his violent contempt for Christians. Yet the terms of his prejudice would not have been decent even if there *had* been a conspiracy of Jewish bankers.

When we come to *The Cantos*, we find that wherever the bigotry is indulged, the objects of hatred assume a weird transfigurative power. In any literary work the demonized become a nexus of force: without aversion, neither *The Merchant of Venice* nor *Oliver Twist* could proceed; and it is by anathema, almost entirely unexamined in either case, that Shylock and Fagin draw forth the imaginative sympathy neither Antonio nor Bill Sykes ever secures.

The model of transfigured power is Satan, without whom *Paradise Lost* could scarcely exist as a major poem. Most readers never overcome the sympathies the epic form focuses upon him. (Some of the tensions in the *Iliad* derive entirely from sympathies the heroism of Hector evokes.) Satan is a figure of action, however, and any reader of less than pure religious instinct must derive pleasure from the deception of Adam and Eve. The Jews in Pound's cosmology are never permitted active graces, and the purity of his distaste does not allow even the comic sympathies we feel for the minor fallen angels (they backed the wrong horse and were punished for it). Nevertheless, the Jews, linked to the incantations about money that form the disturbed and disabling chorus to *The Cantos*, are subject to a transformation nearly accidental—that is, not calculated by nor compliant to the poet's intention. Rothschild and the Jews become *The Cantos'* poor equivalent of Satan and the fallen angels, and it is Pound's responsibility for never having embodied them as arguments. They are assertions and not arguments, and so fail to inhabit the mythos of evil of which they are meant to be absolute embodiments. Pound's association of Jews and money was so fixed that the one was likely to call forth the other without intervening connection: note, in Canto XXXI, how closely "He believed all the Indians of / America to be descended from the jews" is followed by "an interest of exactly the same amount / (four million dollars)."

The fallen relations are further tangled (perhaps the hatred is tangled) by the possibility that Pound was mistaken for a Jew. His pushiness (the comic-book gesture of Jewishness), his odd gypsy manner, his wiry shock of hair, his Old Testament first name: these might be reason for the strength of his unreason. But Pound dismissed such mistaken identity as the accident of art. To Quinn in 1918: "Don't remember ever being taken for a Jew in real life; but ever since a member of the tribe of Ephrahim painted my portrait in Paris, putting in most of his own face, my photos have raised the enquiry: 'Il est Semite?'" He has forgotten the incident in the synagogue in 1908, commemorated in Canto XXII. It took a Jew to catch his Jewishness. (Robert Casillo has preceded me. In *The Genealogy of Demons*, he thoroughly and subtly investigates the mirrored feature of Pound's prejudice. We disagree about what happened in the synagogue: I sense Pound's pleasure in being mistaken for what he reviled. He put something over on the Jews.) Fixation is often a disturbed fascination, and in that fascination the moral order of the poem is corrupted.

If a poet is to be gripped by mania, he had better seem an innocent if he is not to seem a crank. No artist can succeed when he cedes to his material the transforming power that is his to control: in such cases the artist no longer grips the material; the material has gripped him. Pound's ambitions were defeated not by temptation (though all hatred may be defeat by temptation), but by purulent fables set forth as truth. What is opinion in the letters is belief in *The Cantos*: the literary form of the mania destroyed its protection from criticism. Pound failed in his own terms, the terms of an artist's independence from cant.

I have construed style in its broad aspect, to include what lingers just out of range of what we normally call technique. Pound was not religious, though many of his hatreds were, and his letters are unexpectedly affected by the fog of supernatural belief drifting through Georgian London. He was a hard-minded and gristly rationalist but, whenever he considered poetry, a rationalist with a mystic tinge. Yeats, he told Dorothy Shakespear (as she recorded in her notebook), was "one of the Twenty of the world who have added to the World's poetical matter." She asked Pound (this in 1909) whether he had seen things in a "crystal." "I see things without a crystal," he answered. He told her of the "Great Inspiration" he awaited, that "he wished above all things to be in readiness, open-minded and waiting, on the Great Day when it should come. For he evidently believes it will come to him." The words are hers, but there is no mistaking the background mysticism. Pound was in touch with that minor London milieu of theosophy and the occult, through Dorothy, Yeats, and Walter Rummel; and though eventually he could be harsh about Yeats's enthusiasms (to Quinn in 1918: "Yeats . . . will be quite sensible till some question of ghosts or occultism comes up"; and again in 1919: "Bit queer in his head about 'moon'; whole new metaphysics about 'moon,' very very very bug-house"), in 1912 he was willing to provide his birth hour so that Yeats could work up his horoscope and to entertain cracked notions about centaurs and about the dead Margaret Cravens. Even in 1922, he contributed an occult calendar to the *Little Review*.

Pound was not religious, but such supernatural urges infected any compensating replacement for the mysterious certainties and certain mysteries of organized religion—that is, a religion organized around a myth. This compensation was the reversion of the classical world to historical status. *The Cantos* begins with the Nekyia, the passage of Odysseus to the underworld, where by blood sacrifice he called up the shades of the dead. (Given the possible effect of *The Waste Land* on Pound's renewed ambition, it should be remembered that blood was spilled to call forth the shade of Tiresias. The first Canto predated *The Waste Land* but assumed its place only in Pound's later reordering.) The "So that:" with which the first Canto abruptly breaks off marks not just the poet's deference ("Venerandam") to Homer as the first cause, the prime mover, of Western poetry, but his recognition that blood sacrifice (the sacrifice obsession makes upon such altars) allows the presence of all the shades that haunt the poem. *The Cantos* is a book of the dead.

The Cantos had to measure its coherence against the secret strands, the secretive myths, of a history over which Pound was no master. The private, sustaining ambition, however, allowed Pound to cast the poem as a ritual raising of the dead; and it would mistake the privacy of his ambitions if we did not notice that his secret protocols repeatedly illuminate the world of pre-war and wartime London. The writer is always a medium, whether the forces be mystical or memorial; and *The Cantos* is haunted by the world that had vanished by the time Pound regained his interest in the long poem in 1922. The poem repeatedly resurrects the world of Hulme and Gaudier-Brzeska that he was then powerless to re-enter; and the recurring mortification of the poem is not just how the past endures into the present, but how the past—now forever cut off—endures *for* the present.

London after the war did not offer Pound the old challenge or the old gratification: the dispensations were gone, and he moved to Paris in 1921 and to Rapallo in 1924. He was never to recover the vortex; as the decade lapsed his letters show the signs of a man out of touch with his milieu. Times and avant-gardes had changed, and Pound was not capable of recognizing that in 1930 the new poetry in English was being written by Auden (Pound could only grudgingly admit that Auden was "among young England's best dozen" [1934]). Only a year later Pound began to use the Fascist calendar, marking a stage in the decline of his letters and *The Cantos* from which neither entirely recovered. He had become a consul of the second-rate.

If the life had moved from its *Paradiso* to its *Purgatorio* (to be followed, in Pisa and after, by its *Inferno* and the deep frigid silence of Pound's final years—the cold ninth circle of Hell was the circle for traitors), the collapse of experience only intensified the need to recover what was necessary from the past. Pound's experience, however severed or incomplete, becomes the metonomy of our shattered recognitions of the past. One of the many technical advances by which Pound managed the pastness of the past was the filtering of one culture through another: Homer caught the accent of Anglo-Saxon in his passage. This might have seemed adventitious, a literary art too artful; but Pound's subtle ear granted to Homer a sureness and swiftness not reached in English since Pope. The opening of *The Cantos* is one of the great monuments of English free verse. (The version published in Ur-Canto III [*Poetry*, August 1917] is less sure. "On that swart ship" was "on the swarthy ship," and "Bore sheep aboard her" was "Sheep bore we aboard her.") The scansion shows the regularity of its irregularities:

And then | went down | to the ship,

Set keel | to break | ers, forth | on the god | ly sea, and

We set | up mast | and sail | on that | swart ship,

Bore sheep | aboard | her, and | our bod | ies also

Heavy | with weep | ing, so winds | from sternward

Bore us | out on | ward with bel | lying canvas,

Circe's | this craft, | the trim- | coifed goddess.

Then sat | we amid | ships, wind jam | ming the tiller,

Thus with | stretched sail, | we went | over sea | till day's end.

The initial inversions and feminine endings, the anapests favored in medial or late positions, the rough spondees: of his characteristic rhythms these lines lack only his ionic feet. "Beat, beat, whirr, thud, in the soft turf" (IV). "Ear, ear for the sea-surge" (VII). From these elements Pound composed a verse not free but formal in its responses, free only in its formalities (here the inversions and endings launch the lines forward and outward). The indistinct elements compose a distinctive rhythmic voice, which is surely the point of meter. It is no wonder he disparaged the garden uses of vers libre.

Meter, as an imposition of form in time, is its own argument with the past and for Pound a symbolic action of change and difference, the most radical and effective of *The Cantos'* many metamorphoses of the past. Each transformation is itself an emphatic mask; and only by reconstructing, in this partial and inadequate way, what the mask of style covers can we grasp the heroic efforts and heroic failures of the enterprise. What was taken directly into the organization of *The Cantos* offered least to the poetry; the poetry required not the suspension of genius but the supplement of genius. If *The Cantos* fails in almost every generalization, what it secures in the particular it often betrays in general. The particulars could not exist, however, without the general failures, and indeed depend upon the failure of their medium for their luminous intensity. That is the fatal and tragic condition of a poem destined to be a magnificent ruin, but no less magnificent or ruined for that.

After poets are food for worms, they are food for biographers. The letters of a poet like Pound are the contingent reminders of a life that has increasingly little to offer the poetry. They remain the historical present, the present as it was in the past, while the poems become the past that is always present, the news that stays news. (This is not so with all poets—Byron's letters and journals are freshening reminders of a life that was active and original, while except for *Don Juan* his poems are historical documents.) As the publication of Pound's letters proceeds in haphazard fashion, each volume carries a voice out of the dead (it is an advantage that we are generally given both sides of the conversation). Each voice speaks in turn, and voice by voice the letters offer an antiphonal chorus to *The Cantos*. These are the voices that his voices masked.

chapter 8

Eliot among the Metaphysicals

Eliot was still a banker when Trinity College, Cambridge, invited him to give the Clark Lectures in 1925. By the time he began to deliver the lectures the following January he had taken a cut in salary to become an editor, with a five-year contract, at Faber and Gwyer. The lectures therefore fall at a crucial moment of marital exhaustion, occupational insecurity only recently alleviated (though at a cost), religious doubt, nervous breakdown, and gum disease. The private life's wear and tear had uncertain but compromising effect on the searches for confirming authority and for the sources of intellectual disintegration that form the substrate of these lectures.

Eliot the sometime poet and sometime chameleon had reason to remake himself as a historian of ideas: his powers were variously thwarted in verse, and he had recently abandoned *Sweeney Agonistes*. The lectures, thoroughly revised, were meant to serve as the initial volume of an exhaustive treatise to be called "The Disintegration of the Intellect," a criticism of the English Renaissance composed in three parts: *The School of Donne, Elizabethan Drama*, and *The Sons of Ben*. The project gradually collapsed, and the eight lectures remained unrevised and almost unpublished (the third lecture appeared in French). As so often in Eliot, there was a failure not of ambition, but in the structure of ambition. In 1933, during the American lecture tour that produced *The Use of Poetry and the Use of Criticism* (the Norton Lectures at Harvard) and *After Strange Gods* (the Page-Barbour Lectures at Virginia), Eliot spent two days in a sickbed quickly revising and condensing the Clark Lectures in order to remake the sow's purse into three Turnbull Lectures at Johns Hopkins. These were also unpublished, and it is from ancient typescripts that the two sets of lectures have now been rescued.

The Clark Lectures are more distant from our moment than Arnold's *Essays in Criticism* was from Eliot's. The theory of metaphysical poetry they present is therefore a curious fossil, and of considerably less importance than the literary judgments and misreadings in which it is embedded. Despite their defects in attention and organization, the Clark Lectures quarry the hardened sediments of the most influential critic of our century, and the one most sensitive to the poet's quarrels with his medium. Our understanding of Eliot is advanced furthest in his errors and asides, in part because he is finally a poet of error and aside.

The context of those errors, however, is a theory. In order to reform the idea of metaphysical poetry, Eliot had to argue for its presence four centuries before and two centuries after Donne. To secure relations between Dante, Donne, and Laforgue, his exemplary poets, the metaphysical had to be divorced from the purely philosophical, from poetry that mastered a system or poetry where philosophical thought was "so to speak *fused* into poetry at a very high temperature." Santayana's philosophical poets—Lucretius, Dante, and Goethe—were philosophical in a way that Donne was not: each wrote work that was intimate with a system and attempted a poetic costume of that system.

Eliot wished to use *metaphysical* in a sense peculiar to a kind of thinking in verse, and his terms were precisely the terms of his appreciation and indebtedness. *The Varieties of Metaphysical Poetry* is therefore a complex defense of the aspects of Eliot's verse that had been criticized as most modern, occult, and difficult. If Eliot could establish a genealogy of effect, the "metaphysical" in his verse could not seem merely an idiosyncrasy or a translation of certain gestures in Laforgue.

What interested Eliot was how philosophy, and the thinking of which philosophy is a part, became the conduit for an inspiration specifically poetic. He knew that simplification of a complex term was dangerous—"when one's subject matter is literature," he wrote, "clarity beyond a certain point becomes falsification." Clarity would also leave little room for the adjustments necessary to align the "metaphysical" with the practice of three very different periods. His definition was finely judged, a model of scientific tact: metaphysical poetry "elevates sense for a moment to regions ordinarily attainable only by abstract thought, or on the other hand clothes the abstract, for a moment, with all the painful delight of flesh." Metaphysical poetry was "the emotional equivalent of thought."

This was a definition as useful as a reversible raincoat. It allowed Eliot to claim for the metaphysical not just those moments when a philosophy is embodied in physical terms, but moments when emotion itself becomes, through its intensity, a kind of philosophy. He could therefore include (as idea moving toward emotion) the lines where Dante, in the midst of his almost inapprehensible divine vision, recalls Neptune watching in wonder as the Argo passed over him, or where Donne, in "A Valediction: Forbidding Mourning," figures the souls in concrete terms, "like gold to airy thinness beat." Here, Eliot comments, Donne is not diagramming a philosophical notion or a theory about the soul; he is creating the idea from the figure. The metaphysical does not demand the formal movement of philosophy; it is open equally to a "voluptuary of thought" like Donne and a "voluptuary of religious emotion" like Crashaw—they represent the inverse movements of thought into the realm of emotion and emotion into that of thought.

Samuel Johnson had confined the metaphysical in poetry to the conceit. Eliot considered this a libel on metaphysics, and required a meaning of the metaphysical detached from the overlays of critical practice and philosophical debate. To rescue the term from the limitations to which prior use had consigned it (Aristotle's *Metaphysica* was, famously, once merely the volume shelved after the *Physica*), Eliot had to show that it was not a fashion for contrivance in a particular period. If the metaphysical were the "sensuous equivalent" of thought, the conceit would be just the particular form toward which the metaphysical tended in seventeenth-century verse.

Eliot offered an acute insight—his mind grinding toward its prejudices—into the recurrent sources of the metaphysical. Behind each poet lay a shelf of books (a thought appropriate to a great borrower of books and the substance of books); and behind the periods with which Eliot was concerned (Florence in the thirteenth century, London in the seventeenth, Paris in the nineteenth) lay not just philosophy, as would be expected, but intellectual forms of mysticism. In the exemplary poets the inclinations of their reading in theology and philosophy ("No man of Donne's ability and attainments ever seems to have read more positive rubbish") found no creative expression in those fields.

The differences across these periods provided the revising ratios that proved, as one strain of Eliot's analysis always proved, the fallen state of the present. The thirteenth century had "an exact statement of intellectual order," the seventeenth "an exact statement of intellectual disorder," and the nineteenth "a vague statement of intellectual disorder." This was not to fashion the past at the expense of the present, but to attempt to understand the conditions under which the past flourished, conditions no longer available to the present.

> *I wish to insist that this poetry is not the quaint fashion of a primitive age, pre-Raphaelite, given to visions and Benozzo Gozzoli processions up to heaven, but the product of men who felt and thought both clearly and beyond the ordinary frontiers of mind. These were men of highly trained intellects, who also had their feet very firmly on the ground—a rather muddy ground of politics, amours and gang fighting.*

Between the age of Dante and the age of Donne, psychology had triumphed over ontology.

It was not by training with Bunsen burners that Eliot made his scientific metaphors (literary criticism's longing toward the scientific can be heard in I. A. Richards as well); but the confused passage on the catalyst in "Tradition and the Individual Talent" was only a rehearsal for the jazzy references in these lectures to catabolism, coal tar, and the dose of bismuth taken before an X-ray. However hotly up-to-date Eliot's metaphors, he required an analysis of sensibility for which science and scientific figure were inadequate:

> *With Donne the disintegration of thought produces the conceit, but the conceit springs from original thought; with Crashaw the disintegration of thought has, with the assistance of Italian models, become almost an aesthetic; Donne thought, whether he fabricated conceits or no; Crashaw thought in and for the conceit. And the conceit could be carried no further.*

This is a subtle passage, but the "disintegration" is no more useful to criticism (in fact distinctly less useful) than the "dissociation of sensibility." It may be a politic way for a period to advertise its inferiority, or its humility.

Eliot goes too far in thinking that the opening of Donne's "The Relique" (and the opening of the grave) "indicates that something was beginning to go wrong with civilisation about that time."

> *When my grave is broke up again*
> *Some second guest to entertain*
> *(For graves have learned that woman-head*
> *To be to more than one a bed)* . . .

Eliot was a critic whose emotional need tended to infect his thinking—one can almost trace the collapse of his marriage in his bearing toward religion. But to give the criticism over to the life is to simplify the one without salvaging the other. The life can more easily be understood as a creative misreading of the criticism: as a critic, Eliot (whether spurred toward, or spurred by, his terrors) was greater in reaction than in synthesis.

The opening of the grave is a convenient metaphor for the defects of Eliot's close reading. Graves had to pitch their lovers from bed in crowded churchyards: Eliot was disturbed by (though he admired) Donne's association of the infidelity of the grave with the infidelity of women. If we believe in Judgment Day, as Donne did, we expect eventually to be pitched from our graves willy-nilly; the infidelity of our last resting place is mordantly responsive to the fidelity of the lovers. Infidelity, like death, is what their love denies.

Donne's insolence, his audacious defiance of death, carries into the next stanza, where his lover becomes Magdalen and he becomes "a something else," a way (as in communion) of having your Christ and eating Him too. And of suggesting without quite saying that Magdalen and Christ were lovers. Even if this last sentence goes too far (my point is Donne's brassiness, not his blasphemy), there is nothing "ominous" in this conceit of the unfaithful grave, though by 1933, when this nervousness entered the Turnbull Lectures, Eliot had grown decidedly uneasy about inhabiting a grave with Vivienne, perhaps feeling they were already sharing one. The more religious he became, the more he would have to face the thought of lovers reuniting on Judgment Day.

Eliot's fine eye for absurdity is exercised on the opening of "The Exstasie," a quatrain not quite as marrowless as he would have it ("Here are four lines wasted to let us know that the lovers sat on a bank"). The beautiful exaction of his prose is full of dry comedy:

> *To compare a bank to a pillow (it is surely superfluous to add "on a bed" since a pillow may be presumed to have much the same shape wherever it be disposed) does neither dignify nor elucidate; but the simile comes into sharp collision with a metaphor—the bank is pregnant. Having already learned that the bank was shaped like a pillow, we do not require to be told that it was pregnant, unless an earthquake was preparing, which was not the case. I pass over the question of the beauty of obstetrical metaphors in general. . . . The pregnant bank swells, which is just what it should not do, for the whole scene that follows is represented as static; otherwise it would not be an "ecstasy" at all.*

Much of this is relevant, and all of it witty in its wary primness; but Eliot mistakes a low embankment under a hedge or along a pond or garden (as in Cambridge), against which violets might grow and on which a lover might rest his head, for a steep hillside or riverbank ("if the bank swelled only sufficiently to support the head of the violet, it was hardly of great enough size to deserve the name of bank"). The pillow-bank-bed is probably a commonplace of the period ("Hermia: 'For I upon this bank will rest my head.' Lysander: 'One turf shall serve as pillow for us both.'" [*Midsummer*

Night's Dream]), but Eliot did not bother to consult the *OED* (part 2 of which, from *Ant* to *Batten*, had appeared in 1885). It may be a shabby opening to a rich poem, yet "on a bed" prepares the idea of a bed for flowers—a flowerbed; and the pregnant bank, while ridiculous, reminds us of what comes after lovers lie on beds.

I am not trying to rescue Donne from Eliot, but to suggest that Eliot is not always trustworthy when marking a tone or prescribing from particulars. When the author of the Martin Marprelate tracts slanders a bishop who "has a face like old wainscot, and would lie as fast as a dog would trot," it's a little unfair of Eliot to say that "it is meaningless" to make such a comparison. The joke is not just that wainscot "lies fast" against a wall, but that *lie* (taken differentially, as lying down) contrasts with *trot* when we take *lie* in its third aspect, as the bishop lies through his teeth as fast as a dog can trot. This impacting is itself a kind of lying down together (of lying down with the dog and picking up fleas), of quibbling about a quibbling man. The slyness of the simile is the manner of his misspeaking. (This figure must also have been a commonplace. In the film *One-Eyed Jacks*, Karl Malden says to Marlon Brando, "I think you're lyin' . . . faster than a dog can trot.") The matter of misspeaking is made no better if, as the editor here informs us, the Marprelate passage actually read "seasoned wainscot." In trying to limit the figures to rhetoric rather than reason, Eliot has lost some of the rhetorical complexity by which figures move beyond reason while on behalf of reason (or here, perhaps, a little mocking reason)—it is a limitation observed in his poetry, if not by his poetry.

Eliot composed some of these lectures far from his library, and he was notoriously careless in setting matters right after he had set them wrong (misquotation was the guarantor of his interest). The editor's fastidious notes are a hilarious catalogue of Eliot's misquotations: "sharp-tongued" for "sharp-fanged," "melancholy" for "mournful," "Violets" for "Snowdrops," and, quite miraculously, "alimented" for "elemented." Eliot mistakes Appleton House for Marlborough House, invents a curious volume called the *Pensée* of Descartes, misremembers a passage in the *Iliad*, and believes that in the *Odyssey* Elpenor fell overboard and drowned. A few lines after drowning Elpenor his subconscious guiltily encourages him to write of "floating ideas." In Eliot's version of *The Hunting of the Snark*, the Butcher and the Beaver march "from necessity," not "merely from nervousness," and the confused rhythm of this and one or two other passages suggests that Eliot's ear was even more trusting than his eye.

Criticism is not always in the particular (the criticism's in the putty), and Eliot's gaze is often focused a little aslant its target. His best criticism proceeds in the crabwise way Coleridge, laboring to define fancy and imagination, to set up the conditions for our comprehension of terms, ended by defining not the terms but the conditions.

Already in the Turnbull Lectures the lure of religion and social critique, toward which Eliot's criticism was unhappily drawn, began to interfere with his literary judgment, which showed conflicting loyalties. If the "ultimate purpose, the ultimate value, of the poet's work is religious," only a remarkable intellect under remarkable control (or quietly deranged) can assert, in the same paragraph, that the "artist . . . is the perpetual upsetter of conventional values, the restorer of the real." For Eliot, the logic is plain: religion was the real.

Eliot had a love of personal extinction not exceeded by that in James, but he had a more cunning humor. The higher civilization he thought available through a marriage between "acute sensation and acute thought" immediately suggested the possibility of a society in which the one always refused the other, "a society in which everyone was either a Marcel Proust or an Einstein. . . . it is merely the existence of a highly perfected race of insects." The fear here, the metaphysical fear, goes beyond humor; it is the discomfort of Kafka's "The Metamorphosis." The same disquiet haunts some of Eliot's most striking asides: that "contemplation is probably the most ecstatic emotional state possible" (no criticism of static ecstasies here), that "real irony is an expression of suffering," that "influences . . . occur very frequently through misunderstanding," that "the poet in a man does tend to spoil everything else."

Such brilliantly tortured criticism (the asides echo from one of the middle circles of the *Inferno*) explains the private costs of a singular poetic imagination—Eliot was hardly one to repent in haste after sinning at leisure. When he borrowed—having burrowed into—the substance of other writers, they stood as the philosophical ground to his contemplative and modernist figure (his emotional ecstasies were all inferential): his poetry was the impersonation, the sensuous apparatus, of the thoughts on the dusty page. In this he was a metaphysical poet quite unlike his metaphysical forebears—a poet all too knowing of the processes of disintegration and willing to make, from disintegrating material, an integrating statement of intellectual disorder. His readings of other poets, in his poems as in his lectures, were most fruitfully misreadings, his influences misunderstandings, his ironies suffering. He kept his metaphysics warm—the poet was the disintegrating form of the personal and the personal the spoiled remnant of the poetry.

The editor of these lectures has provided a model commentary, tracing the obscure and tracking down the curious, translating foreign passages, and dispensing much necessary information on Eliot's philosophical interest and the evidence of his library. The notes make clear how well Eliot's classes at Harvard served him. They also make clear that Eliot loved certain quotations as much as Arnold did and dragged them in wherever possible—his often praised ability to quote was subject to cruel repetition. Half a dozen typos have escaped the editor's correcting eye (and perhaps a typescript with "unplumbed depths" shouldn't be a "veritable watershed"), but these are small flaws amid such splendidly informed attention. The belated publication of these lectures underscores how desperately we need a collected edition of Eliot's fugitive prose.

The undercurrent in Eliot's lectures is that a poetry without belief, religious or philosophical (and preferably mystical), will be circumscribed or crippled: belief is transcendence. This is bad news for atheists.

chapter 9

Classics and Commercials

Christopher Logue

The past is always with us, but it is with us in translation. If each generation must remake the past in its own image, our translators are hardly at fault for whatever violence they visit on their texts. We are increasingly bound by English; and as our horizons narrow we are apt to treat translation as yet another "creative" act, rather than an act of homage, fealty, or submission—and yet, as poets know, at times the greatest homage is a form of betrayal.

For the past quarter-century, the British poet Christopher Logue has been working fitfully on a translation of the *Iliad*. He would be no one's adequate idea of a translator of one of the two great poems from the preclassical—the prehistoric—Western world (his own poems are garden-variety avant-garde). He has no Greek and is indebted to a shelf of Greek-reading scholars and poets, from George Chapman down. The results have often been brilliant—and always cantankerous, a little dotty, full of heroic grumbling and swearing. Passages are the best Homer we have had since Pope—a music-hall Homer, violent and vicious. Logue has regained in English some of the eerie world, so different from ours in idea and so similar in emotion, that was Homer's dream of his distant Mycenean ancestors.

Logue has learned at the feet of Ezra Pound, our wayward master of translation, though Pound's method has often been disastrous in other poets (consider the attempt by Louis and Celia

Zukofsky to translate Catullus *by sound alone*). The method requires a deep (and incalculable, since it can't be scheming) sympathy with the original—Pound tried to bring into English the mood and the meaning at once, deceiving and even deranging the original where it would not suit the use in an English poem ("We must try its effect as an English poem," Samuel Johnson said of a new translation of Aeschylus). It is a method that lives in error and inventive corruption. I am among those who feel that *Cathay*, and *Homage to Sextus Propertius*, and Pound's "Seafarer" are the height of his achievement. Logue has at times equaled that achievement in his Homer.

> *Think of those fields of light that sometimes sheet*
> *Low tide sands, and of the panes of such a tide*
> *When, carrying the sky, they start to flow*
> *Everywhere, and then across themselves:*
> *Likewise the Greek bronze streaming out at speed,*
> *Glinting among the orchards and the groves,*
> *And then across the plain—dust, grass, no grass,*
> *Its long low swells and falls—all warwear pearl,*
> *Blue Heaven above, Mt Ida's snow behind, Troy inbetween. . . .*
>
> *And what pleasure it was to be there! To be one of that host!*
> *Greek, and as naked as God, naked as bride and groom,*
> *Exulting for battle!*

The echo of Henry V's speech before Agincourt is exact to the intention, and Logue drags in the literature and even the technology of all the centuries that lie between us and Homer—helicopters and A-bombs and Tennyson clutter the imagery of the Trojan plain. Logue has regained on the terms of English literature some of the original's moral and emotional force.

Some, but not all. *The Husbands* is an "account," as he calls it, of the third and fourth books of the *Iliad*, and in it the defects of his method are as plain as the virtues. He has been too enticed by the idea of a radical Homer in English to be faithful to the original, and in the deviations some of his triumphs and many of his disasters occur. The faults of *The Husbands* are not fatal to its best passages; but those faults, which severely damaged the movement and passions of *Kings* (1991), his account of the *Iliad*'s first two books, are almost always a failure to trust Homer.

The onslaught above is actually from the second book of the *Iliad* and does not capture the seething of Homer's images, images surprisingly domestic—the soldiers swarming, for example, like insects above a sheepfold. To suit his translation Logue has foreshortened and disordered his events (and, more culpably, invented them), reduced the epic similes to asides (the *Iliad* is a narrative that to a large extent proceeds through the body of its similes), and corrupted details small and large, often to no advantage. He insists on telling us exactly how gigantic the ancient warriors were: "He is as tall as Hector (8'9")." He even imports weird and un-Homeric names like Quibuph and T'lesspiax. To update Homer does not require that Zeus and Athene be spoiled brats ("I definitely did not." / "Did-did-did-did—and no returns") or Menelaos an embittered schoolboy ("I hate that man. I am going to kill that man"). These are not just unfaithful to the original; they are contemptuous of the characters. Admittedly, Logue's characterizations can have humor—his young Paris (perhaps not so young after ten years cooped up in Troy) is an affected decadent. Homer's own scenes among the gods may be the forerunners of soap opera; but when Logue makes Athene say to Zeus, "Signor?" and Zeus answer, "Choo-Choo . . . how nice," we are lost in a trashy supermarket paperback. We miss the Homer who shows the artful ways that gods influence men (Athene doesn't *become* Pandaros—she appears in the guise of a friend and persuades him to try to murder Menelaos, breaking the truce between the Greeks and Trojans). We miss the Homer who describes the silence of the advancing Greeks and the cacophony of the Trojans speaking an incomprehensible welter of languages.

Logue has removed some of the worst excesses of the version published in Britain last year. *The Husbands* is still a messy work, given to a comic-book Alice-in-Wonderland tone we do not expect in Homer ("Off with his cock! Off with his cock!" shout the troops). But how many splendid lines and phrases there are! A poet who can write, "Your altars smoke on every empty coast, / To catch

your voice grave saints in oilskins lean across the waves" or "Now
see the beauty to be fought for with long spears" could give us—
has already given us in fragments—an incomparable English ver-
sion of this distant, uncomfortable, alien poem.

Alice Fulton

Alice Fulton is a nervy, skittish, bandbox of a poet, thrilled by
image and image and image—the reader's afraid to dart out into
the traffic of all those images whizzing by. Sometimes everything is
thrown into her poems except the kitchen sink; then that gets
thrown in, too. You long for one still, quiet moment. She's so eager
to get on with things, she'll run the title into the first line. "The
Priming Is a Negligee" begins:

> *between the oils and canvas. Stroke the white*
> *sheath well into the weave. The canvas*
> *needs more veil. The painting*
> > *should float on skins of lead*
> *white coating—or its oils will wither*
> *the linen they touch, its colors gnaw*
> *at cloth until the image hangs on air.*
> > *The canvas needs more veil.*

This is language charged with idea, even if the logic goes awry
(gnawing is not at all the same as withering, and a negligee isn't
much protection against either). Fulton's poems have linguistic fa-
cility and appetite, but she can't write even of small matters except
in this fanciful, Edith Sitwell way: of a man sanding, "I guess he
meant to open the finish, / strip the paint stalled on some grain /
and groom the primal gold."

Simulation, fraud, imitation, protective coloration: *Sensual
Math*, her fourth book, is a book of *otherness*, to use the term fash-
ionable in academia. The high spirits of her earlier poems have
found subjects increasingly ambitious, though often ill-suited to
the calculated cuteness of her style. In "My Last TV Campaign,"

an ad man is lured from retirement by a mysterious organization that wants advocacy ads for—if I can make it out—embracing the enemy, the other ("An ad that pushed viewers to incorporate-embrace / rather than debase-slash-erase the other / gal-slash-guy"). Fulton has a feeling for the American huckster—in her relentless amphetamine style she's sometimes a huckster herself (though the ad slogans she dreams up are worse than the names Marianne Moore suggested for the Edsel). The point of this campaign is never clear (except that it's clearly preposterous), and after two dozen pages Fulton has ventured little about advertising beyond a few dressy clichés. She quotes from real campaigns; and the slogans have more bite, more splendid vulgarity and wit, than anything in her verse. It's hard to put your phrases up against Madison Avenue's.

Fulton's poetry ought to have the tragedy of myth, but the fussiness keeps tragedy out. The associative logic, giddy images, and idiosyncratic indentations and punctuation are highly reminiscent of Jorie Graham's poetry. (To disrupt the plain gestures of a poem, Fulton sometimes uses a kind of spastic colon, a double equals sign [==], just as Jorie Graham uses her notorious lacunae or single-line stanzas.) Not surprisingly, Fulton is drawn to Ovid's *Metamorphoses*; and the showpiece of her book is a "re-imagining" of the myth of Daphne and Apollo. The forty pages of forced-march invention (Ovid needed only a hundred lines or so) show her at her most appallingly frivolous and wearyingly meaningful—Apollo is a Vegas lounge lizard with a taste for camouflage outfits and Daphne a compound of Emily Dickinson and Amelia Earhart and Marianne Moore and Annie Oakley. Her Apollo threatens,

> *"You can lose a bay leaf*
> *from a laurel tree—lose-a lose-a your lunch, dear—*
> *but you'll never lose me, uh-uh-uh—*
> *no siree," defends*
> *"Doggone it, Bachelor-Girl, I'm Phoebus not a fibber,*
> *so be a Natural-Girl,*
> *not a hairy Ladies-Libber," sweet-talks*

> *"Inky-Dink Nymphie, don't say toodle-loo—*
>> *I'm Apollo, not some moron out to oo-*
>>> *oo-oogle you," wheedles*
> *"Yo! Miss Daphne, doncha say amscray—*
>> *How 'bout it baby,*
>>> *wanna hear 'My Way?'"*

The facetiousness never quite rises to humor or descends to po-
etry—you don't get closer to the idea of gods and men, or men and
rapists, with such mincing campiness, all dimples and self-con-
gratulation. We're a long way from Ovid's apologetic lovelorn sap.
The bad parts of this improvisation are as awful as anything I've
read by a young poet of substance. But though too often a poet of
trifles, Fulton is not always to be trifled with. When she describes
"the spine's / expansive gossip and / the prophet in the cell," all
that self-conscious daring, all that frenzy of image, has become a
little poetry. Her showy performances destroy whatever animal
sentiment the poems mean to establish—there's an odd heartless-
ness at the center of her fancy. It's dangerous for this poet to say of
Daphne and Apollo, "deep down they were profoundly / superfi-
cial."

chapter 10

In the Lectureship of Verse

Seamus Heaney

The Redress of Poetry began as the lectures delivered by Seamus Heaney during his term as Professor of Poetry at Oxford. The election of an Irish poet to that most English of posts was itself an act awash in politics; and Heaney took as his subject the adequacy of poetry in a world, in responding to a world, of violence and political crisis. The *redress* he proposed was not just reparation for wrongs sustained, but a restoration of spirit in the rubble of history.

This might seem a wish foolishly utopian, were Heaney not keen to establish that poetry can only dangerously aim at or design political change. Though it may on occasion intervene in the world, poetry offers what Auden called an "affirming flame," an alternate world where words have transcendent potential and fulfilling force.

Heaney, who won the Nobel Prize in literature last year and has often been a compelling analyst of the role of a private art in a public world, has nervously accepted the fur-lined mantle of T. S. Eliot as the poet dragged onstage to pronounce on poetry and culture. These notes on the language of poetry and its purpose in politics (the government of the spirit within as well as of statesmen without) are most forceful when furthest from the intention of the lectures. Some of the poets crucial to Heaney (Marlowe, Oscar

Wilde, Dylan Thomas, among others) were displaced from their natural dialect, while others tried to redress the dialect they spoke (John Clare and the eighteenth-century Irishman Brian Merriman) or reinvent one no longer spoken (Hugh MacDiarmid).

As an Irishman who writes in English, Heaney is particularly sensitive to the politics and transgressions of language. His comments only rarely skirt his own practice; but, where he troubles his own revisions (on using *worked* in a poem rather than the *wrought* of his local dialect: "Once you think twice about a local usage you have been displaced from it") or writes on poets with whom he suffered some early wrestle of influence, he offers a private understanding of the art. Heaney has the most flexible and beautiful lyric voice of our age, and his prose often answers his poetry in a run of subtle and subtly resonant phrasing (as well as in the witty brilliance of his imagery—he describes "the dead-pan cloudiness of a word processor"). Heaney's language is often the particular pleasure of these lectures, and it is therefore disturbing to find it so permeable and unresistant to the brutal vocabulary of contemporary criticism—to *multivalent, devalorizing, empowered, marginalized, phallocentric, patriarchal,* and *the other.* Such language urges, in its blind but coercive way, all the easy political solutions his argument otherwise opposes.

The essays in *The Redress of Poetry* have more cumulative force than individual character—seldom striking in themselves, they are convincing in the residue of their attentions, in their belief that poetic invention "represents not a submission to the conditions of [the] world but a creative victory over them." If Heaney has not developed the original prose voice of Auden or Eliot, he has maintained for English poetry a responsive, gratified, and radical ear.

Helen Vendler

"It is still not understood," thunders the formidable Helen Vendler in the introduction to *The Breaking of Style,* "that in lyric writing, style in its largest sense is best understood as a material body." The schoolmarm opening to such a sentence, the unnecessary exaggeration of the two superlatives, the leaden repetition of "understood," and finally that outrageous (but outrageously fashionable) metaphor of the body: this is rhetoric gone wild with self-esteem.

It is odd that a writer on style can be so insensitive to style herself. Style is no more a "material body" than it is a bowl of soup (we speak of a writer's "body of work," but we don't mean one with myopia, bad breath, and an unpleasant husband). Vendler needs the metaphor to claim that by changing style the poet "perpetuates an act of violence, so to speak, on the self." This is to make every change in style a scar or a suicide; but many changes in poetic style might be called natural or organic, the residue of mad growth or slow invention, the sin of wisdom or the virtue of calculation.

Vendler is one of the most acute of contemporary critics; and her close reading of stylistic changes in the work of Gerard Manley Hopkins, Seamus Heaney, and Jorie Graham attends to aspects of style not always given formal notice—Hopkins's adoption of sprung rhythm may be familiar, but not Heaney's concentration on parts of speech or Jorie Graham's changes in line length. Vendler wants to establish that "the first duty of any poet is to reconfigure felt experience in an analogical rhythm—prosodic, syntactic, or structural"; and when she escapes the duties of her metaphor (a duty that leads her into language like "Hopkins' new zigzag stylistic body . . . is more nervous and fluctuating than his younger stylistic body"), her readings (of, for example, Heaney's "in betweenness") have all the force and ingenuity of which this capable critic is capable. She is unfortunately all too vulnerable to shabby theorizing and wishful thinking.

These chapters on style began as the Richard Ellmann Memorial Lectures at Emory University and have been published simultaneously with *The Given and the Made*, Vendler's T. S. Eliot Memorial Lectures at the University of Kent. These books have been published by the same distinguished press, so it is odd that while one has an index the other does not and that a list of Graham's seven "dual self-portraits" in one becomes a list of six—a slightly variant six!—in the other. The latter lectures, on the *donnée* or "given" in a poet's life that is transfigured into art, pair two older postwar poets, Robert Lowell and John Berryman, with two much younger contemporaries, Rita Dove and Jorie Graham.

The pairing—intriguing, unbalanced, entirely to the advantage of the older poets—reveals the weakness of Vendler's critical vision. She is superb on Lowell's "public and private forms of poetic history" and particularly on his "disloyalty," both to family and to art; and her consideration of Berryman is fond but overstretched (if she is unconvincing in arguing that the enclosed form of Berryman's *Dream Songs* restages Freud's analytical hour, her suggestion that "Successive sessions of psychiatric therapy may be seen as another form of the 'sessions of . . . silent thought' which generated Shakespeare's sonnets" is sidesplitting). Like all these lectures, *The Given and the Made* is limited by its occasion—a lecture requires a specific length more than a specific subject, and becomes a Procrustean bed for the partial ideas or rambling observations that in an essay might receive precise development.

Vendler has a soft spot for younger poets, though her taste has been wildly uneven. Her close consideration of Rita Dove cannot conceal the utter dullness of the poetry, while her critical loyalty to Jorie Graham claims a major reputation for a poet more interesting to read about than to read, whose philosophical musings do not yet have the depth or resonance of Wallace Stevens's, and whose trilingual childhood, Vendler's biographical "given," has little effect on her poems. Vendler argues that being raised in three languages produced Graham's sense of the "virtual" world—as with much biographical criticism, a case of *post hoc, ergo propter hoc*. You could argue, just as irrelevantly, that being the daughter of a sculptor produced Graham's "sculptural" long and short lines. Apart from one early poem, foreign language and Graham's identity in other languages feature little in her work—the detachment of the sign from the thing is familiar to anyone who studies language young. Vendler will go to some length to protect the ingenuity of her readings or the reputation of a favorite: when Dove persistently misdates Haitian massacres by two decades, the critic writes, "Here and elsewhere the correct date . . . is mistranscribed."

Vendler has attempted a higher biographical criticism that risks being biographically reductive: her analysis of the ways the life is transposed or transformed into art is without insight into the means: we remain ignorant of why Berryman and Lowell could return as art the ruins of manic depression or family history.

The stylistic emphasis of the one book and the biographical concerns of the other avoid judgment on language—its currents of meaning, ambiguity, and betrayal, its life as memory. Vendler is too susceptible to hall-of-mirrors notions that poems are mimetic responses to themselves—she is always looking for and applauding a "structural and rhythmic enactment" (mimetic accuracy is "the virtue, the fundamental ethics, of art"). The critic who writes of Berryman's "layer of psychic squalor beneath high artistic convention" or the "inescapable social accusation of blackness" suffered by Dove is worth the attention of close argument, but rarely makes an appearance here.

Anthony Hecht

Anthony Hecht is our country's darkest, most brutal and moral, most magnificent living poet, an heir to Elizabethan manners. He richly deserves the Nobel Prize (though, in the way of fallen things, Ginsberg or Ashbery is much more likely to receive it). His Andrew W. Mellon Lectures in the Fine Arts, now published as *On the Laws of the Poetic Art*, are a defense of certain traditional understandings of poetry—that poetry is an art most eloquent when impersonal and complex, full of tension and contradiction, ripe in mythological or literary relation.

The lectures are informal and discursive affairs, and in their slapdash desk-learning recall a certain Victorian mode—a précis of a particularly jumbled half-paragraph might run: "Book of Job a sublime poem—imagery drawn from architecture—architecture the oldest of the arts—earth described as building in Old Testament—God a builder-architect, embraced by Masons—Haydn a Mason—Baron Gottfried van Swieten, too." There are curious facts galore, but facts never marshalled into argument. Hecht's method is to support some entirely uncontentious notion with a list of examples and quotations, some absurdly long. The Laws of the Poetic Art seem finally to be that poetry is sometimes visual, sometimes musical; that sometimes the wilderness is paradise; that sometimes poetry is public, or private, or composed of contraries. This is not a distinguished addition to a series that included Kenneth Clark's *The Nude* and E. H. Gombrich's *Art and Illusion.*

When Hecht argues that, contrary to much modernist thinking, poetry does not have to reside in "things," or suggests that "the framed limits of a painting" may be a rough equivalent to Aristotle's dramatic "plot," or writes of "this restless ambition to render the visible world in words," you have a sense of how charged with idea these lectures might have been. But the manner is so often professorial, and the prose occasionally so flyblown ("he had not evinced the normal attempts at verbal articulation"), it's like watching your great-aunt dress up as Dr. Johnson. Poetry will not be rescued from the philistines in this way (and there's a lot of tub-thumping about philistines). Hecht's poems remain a far more eloquent defense of the art.

chapter 11

The Bounty of Derek Walcott

Derek Walcott has lived in the quarrel of two languages, the patois of his Caribbean birth and the drenched, nightingale tones of British literature, one a harbor of memory and the other a heritage of guilt and betrayal as well as gratitude. Among poets writing in English in our late half-century, Walcott has been the most tortured by divisions of the tongue; and his stateless, passport-clenched existence (international poets live in airports) has only increased the fatal lure of home. His last book, the windy and flawed *Omeros* (1990), attempted to shrink the *Iliad* and *Odyssey* into the tiny sins and squabbles of some Caribbean fishermen and bewildered colonials. The present enacted the myths of the past, as if all our odysseys might be the *Odyssey;* but the present could not replace the past by remaining in debt to it.

The Bounty is a retrospective volume, full of elegy and apologia, turning from the death of the poet's mother to a long sequence coiled in the comforts but wary of the confines of his home island St. Lucia. The brazen confidence of Walcott's verse refuses the map-drawn boundaries of politics:

> *Between the vision of the Tourist Board and the true*
> *Paradise lies the desert where Isaiah's elations*
> *force a rose from the sand. The thirty-third canto*
>
> *cores the dawn clouds with concentric radiance,*
> *the breadfruit opens its palms in praise of the bounty,*
> *bois-pain, tree of bread, slave food, the bliss of John Clare,*

torn, wandering Tom, stoat-stroker in his county
of reeds and stalk-crickets, fiddling the dank air,
lacing his boots with vines, steering glazed beetles

with the tenderest prods, knight of the cockchafer,
wrapped in the mists of shires, their snail-horned steeples
palms opening to the cupped pool.

Walcott is a master of such easy, careless abundance, the stunned eloquence of his lines descending from the heavens to the homely beetle. Here the biblical prophet rises from Caribbean sands, the sky is Dante's *Paradiso*, and the doomed *Bounty* brings its breadfruit trees (a bounty themselves) from the South Pacific to feed the slaves. For Walcott life is lived in its literature, the wanderings of mad John Clare also the wanderings of Tom o' Bedlam, the real poet acting the rule of fiction. The sly ironies that give the Tourist Board a "vision," as if even our commerce were prophetic, permit this mirage of the real in the false realm of literature. "I myself am a fiction," Walcott says in one poem. When are we not heir to our fictions?

Walcott is a great charmer, his language full of pleasing vanity, preening before the mirror of the literary past. He can pack a poem with allusion as if stuffing a Christmas goose, but you can tell how much he longs to seduce himself—he's so busy with seduction he sometimes forgets the poem has somewhere to get to.

The epic scale of *Omeros* exposed Walcott's concentrated talents to his considerable flaws. Line by line the poem flaunted the exhaustive verbal gift not matched in his generation by anyone but Lowell (Walcott's imagery as rich if not always as original). The poem had dozens of dazzling occasions, but the characters were insectlike versions of their Homeric selves; the masterplot of the *Iliad* broke down in the middle (as the narrator began to gallivant from city to city like a poet on a reading tour); when the protagonist Achille had a sunstroke dream of Africa, it was a sentimental rehash of *Roots*. The poet's climactic "duet" with Homer was introduced when Homer asked, about a young woman, "Did you, you know, do it often?"

Despite his fluent and deceptive language, despite a career restless in its forms, Walcott has written few poems memorable as poems. There is intoxicating writing, with striking images by the cartload (if they come from the warehouse at times, most poets work out of a shed), but rarely a poem that bullies its way into memory the way poems by Lowell or Bishop or Larkin or Auden or Hecht often do. What you remember in Walcott is the texture, never the text.

The long sequence that forms the greater part of *The Bounty* is badly organized and diffuse, composed less in verse than unmetered rhyming prose (though a gorgeous oratorical prose). Walcott revisits his old haunts—St. Lucia, New England, Europe—with mortality in mind; and the way he nurses his wounds, his refusal of his native tongue (he's a Philoctetes of old poison, and his wound is his tongue), makes the ancient difficulties darker and more depriving than ever. Walcott worries the artist's position, the distance art demands from his life. Nervously attentive to his literary airs, deeply immersed in the language of empire, he fails to see that his poems are drowning in the empire's dreams. His romantic wish to merge with the paradise he's been driven from wallows happily in romantic blather ("O leaves, multiply the days of my absence and subtract them / from the humiliation of punishment, the ambush of disgrace"), but he understands his paradise is haunted by Europe. His vision of Europe, of European literature, is of merchandise and the hot appetites of capital:

> *Europe fulfilled its silhouette in the nineteenth century*
> *with steaming train-stations, gas-lamps, encyclopedias,*
> *the expanding waists of empires, an appetite for inventory*
> *in the novel as a market roaring with ideas.*
> *Bound volumes echoed city-blocks of paragraphs*
> *with ornate parenthetical doorways, crowds on one margin*
> *waiting to cross to the other page; as pigeons gurgle epigraphs*
> *for the next chapter, in which old cobbles begin*
> *the labyrinth of a twisted plot.*

In both worlds, the lines are heavy with habitat, never one image when half a dozen will do. This surfeit of the visual cannot repay the losses the poet has suffered, the life estranged in the medium of its language. The poems run on in near panic, their once crisp images an impressionist blur.

> *In late-afternoon light the tops of the breadfruit leaves*
> *are lemon and the lower leaves a waxen viridian*
> *with the shaped shadows greenish black over the eaves*
> *of the shops and the rust-crusted fences that are Indian*
> *red, sepia, and often orange; but by then the light has*
> *ripened and grass and the sides of the houses and even a*
> *rooster crossing a yard blazes like a satrap.*

Walcott has to try hard to write badly, but *The Bounty* often lacks the language of resonant detail that takes the attentions of the visual beyond mere decoration. His rhetoric is as powerful as a trumpet, but every line has the same emphasis—you scarcely know where the crescendi are, because they're all crescendi.

The Nobel laureate's early poems were jagged, nervy celebrations of the seen (a young man's one-man talent show). Though I admire the idiosyncratic autobiography of *Another Life* (1973), his strongest poems (often influenced by Lowell) were in books of his middle period, *Sea Grapes* (1976), *The Star-Apple Kingdom* (1979), *The Fortunate Traveller* (1981), and *The Arkansas Testament* (1987). *The Bounty*, in its airless and sublime self-indulgence, its dissolution into mere writing, resembles the tedious run-on grandiloquence of *Midsummer* (1984), another book of days. It is in his briefer lyrics, and not the rambling sequences or ambitious epics, that Walcott's vision discovers the anatomy of his loss.

chapter 12

Verse Chronicle: Martyrs to Language

John Ashbery

I have criticized John Ashbery so often for what he is, I would like to praise him for what he is not. American poets have always been uncomfortable with a poetry whose designs remain in language. We are a content-minded country, where language is a McCormick reaper, an old manual typewriter, a Frank Lloyd Wright house. Ashbery writes as if language were a medium. With its swooping declensions into the colloquial, its quick-change-artist's unmasking, his poetry reminds us that the soiled, complacent manner of our poetry—its do-it-yourself Romantic style—is slavery of our own invention. Ashbery is a tone, not an argument; and he has sprayed graffiti on every monument with puckish delight, all the while without writing a memorable poem except on the rarest occasion.

An Ashbery poem begins in the following way:

A loose and dispiriting
wind took over from the grinding of traffic.
Clouds from the distillery
blotted out the sky. Ocarina sales plummeted.

Believe you me it was a situation
Aladdin's lamp might have ameliorated. And where was I?

Among architecture, magazines, recycled fish,
waiting for the wear and tear
to show up on my chart. Good luck,

bonne chance. *Remember me to the zithers*
and their friends, the ondes martenot.

Here is the confidence of tone and vagueness of reference, the absurd and irrelevant statement ("Ocarina sales plummeted"), the slangy phrase (what other poet would dare say, "Believe you me"?), the Scheherazade allusion, the rhetorical question (immediately answered), the surreal list (those recycled fish owe Dada its due). His poems are always daring in this wintry, winsome way—one of the delights of Ashbery's poetry is that anything might happen, and one of the despairs that so often anything does.

Reading such stanzas, you feel they might have been arranged in another way without loss, that a typesetter might have jumbled two or three poems together without anyone noticing—without even Ashbery noticing! Ashbery is our Nabokovian genius (at times he seems invented by Nabokov): he's the great lepidopterist of language and life in our dark century. He delights in English as if it were his second language, or not his language at all; and like Nabokov's fictions Ashbery's poems talk best when they talk about themselves. No poet argues better about poetry; perhaps it's best that he does so offhandedly. As he says in one poem, "He had forgotten the art / of knowing how far to go too far."

There's a weird compulsive mania beneath Ashbery's work (the poems in *Can You Hear, Bird* are arranged alphabetically by title). Among repetitive poets, you think of Clare, not Hardy, of Felicia Hemans, not Emily Dickinson. In the past four years Ashbery has published six hundred and fifty new pages of verse—it's not just too much, it's too much by a fabulous, Arabian Nights amount. Those readers of the future, our inevitable critics, may be grateful for every scrap; but they haven't been born yet, and we are stuck with the readers we are.

The finest poem in this new book reads like deranged Beckett.

> *A hears by chance a familiar name, and the name involves a riddle of the past.*
>
> *B, in love with A, receives an unsigned letter in which the writer states that she is the mistress of A and begs B not to take him away from her.*
>
> *B, compelled by circumstances to be a companion of A in an isolated place. . . .*

And on through A-4, A-5, A-8, Angela, Philip, W, Petronius B. Furlong, and dozens of other characters related by happenstance. It's a comic soap opera, preposterous and long-winded; but it provides what Ashbery so rarely offers now, the illusion of narrative, of motion through character, of a past.

Ashbery uses one part of his imagination with genius—the random, absurdist, associative part—and the other parts not at all. I'm sure that critics like Helen Vendler are right, that Ashbery makes sense more often than is said; but when his poems make sense they are rarely likable: they seem pinched and competent. It's in the making of nonsense—or the not making of sense—that he becomes a larger individual, a Stevens without the galumphing philosophy (though there's plenty of galumphing in Ashbery).

Compared to Ashbery, most poets look diminished in their language, trapped by their conception, not just of what verse does, but of what it *can* do. His limitations are more peculiar than those of any poet writing, perhaps among the most peculiar of any poet who has written in English. Who would have loved Ashbery's work? Christopher Smart, and Lewis Carroll, and Erasmus Darwin. This isn't to say that Ashbery too isn't trapped by the machinery of his verse, merely that his poems are often the triumph of their illusions.

Adrienne Rich

Anyone who likes jeremiads will want to own Adrienne Rich's new book. *Dark Fields of the Republic* has more of the sketchy, angry

poems she has been writing for the past decade—they're like jot-
tings torn from a notebook, like dark scribbles of Goya's. Who are
her enemies? Society, Capital, Law, Men—they're never named,
but you hear them conspiring behind the lines:

> *There's a place between two stands of trees where the grass grows*
> *uphill*
> *and the old revolutionary road breaks off into shadows*
> *near a meeting-house abandoned by the persecuted*
> *who disappeared into those shadows.*

Who or what is being persecuted is not explained, but Rich doesn't
have time for explanations (when she's not preaching to the con-
verted, she's just preaching). Rich makes a cunning point, that ours
is a poetry leaning toward pastoral even when steeped in blood;
but she wants to have it both ways, wants to ride her high horse but
keep her romantic landscape, too.

With every book Rich has sunk deeper into a malaise of hatred,
of wronged innocence, of violated trust. Her poems have become
censoriously sincere, unbearably high-minded, self-important,
Babbittlike, and yet driven helplessly to dissection of pain. The
causes of pain are disembodied and abstract—her enemies are
looming presences, unnameable gods of the machine, her poems
like raw wounds:

> *Narrow waters rocking in spasms. The torch hand-held and the*
> *poem of entrance.*
> *Topless towers turned red and green.*
> *Dripping faucet icicled radiator.*
> *Eyes turned inward. Births arced into dumpsters.*
> *Eyes blazing under knitted caps,*
> *hands gripped on taxi-wheels, steering.*
> *Fir bough propped in a cardboard doorway, bitter tinsel.*
> *The House of the Jewish Book, the Chinese Dumpling House.*
> *Swaddled limbs dreaming on stacked shelves of sleep   opening*
> *like knives.*

"Here / it is in my shorthand," she says in another poem. At times,
even now, she can't help being a poet; but the hair-shirt purity of

such lines is that of a martyr to language. Only a poet beyond argument resorts to the tawdry insinuation of lines like "Swaddled limbs . . . opening like knives." It's not that her poems make assumptions (all poems make assumptions); it's that they start so long after the assumptions are finished. They never have the startling rough vision of any old political line of Lowell's.

When the best poem in the book is cast as one of Karl Jaspers's letters after the war, you know that something has gone terribly wrong. The lines may be invented (I can't find them in the Hannah Arendt correspondence); but Rich can no longer suffer such pained self-knowledge or necessary regret, such a pathos of attention, in her own voice. A poet as good as Rich shouldn't be capable of writing lines like "worms have toothed at your truths" or "She could swim or sink / like a beautiful crystal." These new poems revel in so narrow an emotional realm, reading them is like staring into a dark closet until the monsters appear. What they reveal is almost more surprising than emotion. Imagine Adrienne Rich not knowing that "the dyer's hand" comes from Shakespeare.

Rich now lives in an icy tundra of abstraction. Her "Narratives" and her "Inscriptions" suggest how much she wants from the present for the future: she has become the myth of herself. In her poems there are only victims, only the unidentified "you," the shadowy "I." In the absence of argument, the poetry of witness becomes just another poetry polluted with self-advertisement.

August Kleinzahler

When you read August Kleinzahler's work, you think of William Carlos Williams. You think that everything half bad in Kleinzahler was half good in Williams; you think that whatever Kleinzahler does well, Williams did better. How deft, how economical, how unassuming the line in Williams; but you can't try to be just as unpretentious as Williams without being pretentious. The economical in Williams becomes a famine in Kleinzahler.

Kleinzahler is a cool, knowing student of urban grunge. He knows the bar scenes of Bukowski, the sidewalk shoptalk of O'Hara ("and asparagus already / under two dollars a pound"), the beaten and broken characters of Selby and Rechy and Auster—he knows them all from books, and his poems read like an encyclopedia of secondhand responses. He's got all the bad of his models and little of the good: the poems are full of false bonhomie, cities by Piranesi (and landscapes by Laura Ashley), intellectual anti-intellect (Catullus becomes "Heyho, loverboy / is that a radioactive isotope you've got / burning through your shirtfront / or are you just glad to see me?"). Like tough guys everywhere, he's got a heart of Ivory soap, and it doesn't take much to turn him frothy and sentimental:

> *There is an abundant peace to be found here*
>
> *in the blue, then gray and mauve eyes*
> *of the voluptuous women cutting bread into an embossed tureen.*

That's "Follain's Paris," and the rest of Kleinzahler's poems about Paris read like a brochure for the Chambre de Commerce.

For a poet like this, someone else's tragedy becomes a celebration of the knowing eye. He wants an audience that appreciates blackface and minstrelsy:

> —Are you an *Ex-is-ten-tial-ist,*
> Mr. Mister?
>
> —Oh, no, no,
> I would prefer to think
>
> of myself, ahem,
> as a *Collision-Ecstasist.*
>
> —You undress on impact,
> sir?
>
> —Oh, hohohoho,
> not no more.

The poems are so full of dumb, joky moments that you may miss the quiet clamor of beauty, a beauty Kleinzahler obviously distrusts but doesn't know how to argue against. In the strange fable of a Weasel and a Ponce, or the narrative of a sailing trip, you see the mark of a very different poetry; but, wedded to his minor and repetitive designs, to finding the trivial and leaving it trivial, Kleinzahler makes it hard for any other poetry to get hold of him. His best poems are direct forces, lacking that "poetic" attitude that makes poetry more depressing than daily life (that makes daily life more depressing than daily life). He has a taste for beauty, but then it's off to writing ludicrous "sapphics" ("Festinating rhythm's bothered her axis"), or a Gulf War poem of broken phrases ("Assault plasma star launch"), or a dream (*"Gland burgers excrement /* If it's a dream / Give the projector a flip, willya"). Poetry has to be more than infinite variety and finite shallowness. It has to be more than Renoir rewritten as film noir.

Billy Collins

Billy Collins has a sideshow owner's instinct for hoopla and a taste for one-ring-circus ideas; but his poems are gentle, mild, and awfully dull. It's like finding that the weightlifter is an accountant and the bearded lady a housewife. He has an unthinking passion for nature that makes you long for a few polluters—his is a nature of continuous and helpless loveliness. In his peaceable kingdom, the mourning doves look like Robert Penn Warren and the titmice like Marianne Moore.

Collins is an idea man—ideas are his shtick. Auden was an idea man, and so is Les Murray; but Collins wants to be a comedian, too. He'll start a poem, "How agreeable it is not to be touring Italy this summer," and he'll tell you everything he won't be seeing (it's hard to stop Collins from telling you everything); then he'll tell you what he *will* be seeing back home at the coffee shop. It's all very agreeable; but you don't believe him for an instant, because *you* want to be standing by that sarcophagus in Italy. His poems start with the hypothetical and end with a view.

An idea man is hungry for subject, and the titles of Collins's poems show how starved a poet can become: "Death Beds," "The Biography of a Cloud," "Thesaurus" ("It could be the name of a prehistoric beast"), "On Turning Ten," "Keats's Handwriting," "Budapest," "Man in Space," "The Invention of the Saxophone,"

"The End of the World." It's no great shock a lot of the poems are poems about poetry.

Oddly enough, just when you've grown irritated with this nattering, sweet, educated voice, there are one or two surprises. "Workshop" is a poem I would have thought impossible to write— it's composed of the things students say in writing workshops; but Collins has found a way to make these comments the poem itself, a poem that devours itself like a hall of mirrors:

> *The other thing that throws me off,*
> *and maybe this is just me,*
> *is the way the scene keeps shifting around.*
> *First, we're in this big aerodrome*
> *and the speaker is inspecting a row of dirigibles,*
> *which makes me think this could be a dream.*
> *Then he takes us into his garden,*
> *the part with the dahlias and the coiling hose,*
> *though that's nice, the coiling hose,*
> *but then I'm not sure where we're supposed to be.*

It's a haunting little Magritte, the better for being perfectly insubstantial: nothing said is the least interesting, except as it creates— as it is—the poem you see.

There are other signs of the poet Collins might be, if he weren't afflicted with terminal whimsy. At his best he sounds like Elizabeth Bishop: "In the dining room there is a brown fish / hanging on the wall who swims along / in his frame while we are eating dinner." That poem ends deliciously possessed by the fish's "one, small, spellbound eye," but Collins tries too hard for his lightness of being. Then it isn't lightness anymore. He's a glutton for every hokey moment of transcendence, for "the vast, windless spaces between the stars," for "the immensity of the clouds," for a woman "offering a handful of birdsong and a small cup of light." Some poets get sentiment the way others get religion: "But now when I fall upon the sidewalks of life, / I skin my knees. I bleed."

Collins is a good representative of the mild-mannered middle voice of American poetry. It's the voice of sensitive middle-class middle-aged American men (or younger poets who write as if they *were* middle-aged)—the honorable time-servers. Like parodies of moderation, they take nothing too far—they make failures of extremity like Ashbery look like virtues.

Rita Dove

Mother Love works like mad to jazz up the story of Demeter and Persephone, but Rita Dove's fragile, prosy talent cannot turn life into myth. She has a naive and antagonistic relation to her chosen form—"I like how the sonnet comforts even while its prim borders (but what a pretty fence!) are stultifying; one is constantly bumping up against Order." Her sonnets are therefore laggard, ill-kempt, weak-spirited things, sonnets that condescend to have fourteen lines. The lines tend to run like this:

> *In the sixth grade I was chased home by*
> *the Gatlin kids, three skinny sisters*
> *in rolled-down bobby socks. Hissing*
> Brainiac! *and* Mrs. Stringbean!, *they trod my heel.*
> *I knew my body was no big deal*
> *but never thought to retort: who's*
> *calling* who *skinny?*

If I tell the reader this is better than the average, he'll think me cruel. There are responsibilities in the sonnet this poet doesn't accept and freedoms she doesn't understand: that's why her substance and her movement are so restricted. She would like to pretend that writing sonnets is a kind of slavery ("all three—mother-goddess, daughter-consort and poet—are struggling to sing in their chains").

Sometimes the poems are about Dove and her daughter, sometimes Dove and her mother, sometimes about other people entirely—knowing the myth doesn't help much. Though I see the point (every Persephone becomes a Demeter), it's hard not to find all this odd psychologically. A number of poems play out a mysterious vengeance against children (one mother wants to appear before young boys in her daughter's skin, another roasts a baby on a spit—with mothers like this, who *wouldn't* want to spend half the year in Hell?). The poetry would be more interesting if it accused the violence at its heart.

Instead, two of the sequences (one of them "Persephone in Hell") rehearse a postgraduate year in Paris and an ill-considered love affair. Perhaps the Grand Tour qualifies as Hell these days; but the myth makes Dove's experience vacant and privileged, the love life of another spoiled American abroad. It takes courage to cast yourself as Persephone, courage and an unlimited capacity for self-pity: "He only wanted me for happiness: / to walk in air / and not think so much, / to watch the smile / begun in his eyes / end on the lips / his eyes caressed." Bathos is not exclusively the property of greeting-card writers.

The former poet laureate ends *Mother Love* with a crown of sonnets (or "sonnets") on visiting temples in Sicily—they're witty, alert to landscape, and almost always too pat; but they show a poetic intelligence absent from the rest of this self-indulgent and painfully misguided book.

Stanley Kunitz

When Thomas Hardy died at eighty-seven, among his papers was the manuscript of his final poems, *Winter Words*. Its unfinished introduction read in part, "So far as I am aware, I happen to be the only English poet who has brought out a new volume of his verse on his . . . birthday." The touching blank remained when the volume was posthumously published.

Stanley Kunitz, the old and honorable warhorse of American poetry, has exceeded Hardy by publishing new poems on his ninetieth birthday. Kunitz was long into his sixties before his work became distinctive, and then much of the distinction was his friend Robert Lowell's. *The Testing Tree* (1971) took over Lowell's characteristic movement and burly, shifting language (reading Lowell is sometimes like watching the land slip during an earthquake).

> *That year of the cloud, when my marriage failed,*
> *I slept in a chair, by the flagstone hearth,*
> *fighting my sleep,*
> *and one night saw a Hessian soldier*

stand at attention there in full
regalia, till his head broke into flames.
My only other callers were the FBI
sent to investigate me as a Russian spy
by patriotic neighbors on the river road.

Oh, you think, that's from *Life Studies*—no, *For the Union Dead.* The influence salvaged Kunitz from an earlier poetry with too many phrases like "rose-gilded chamber" and too many lines like "On the anvil of love my flesh has been hammered out." Such poems survive only in the museum of period diction; and Kunitz has excluded from this volume of new and selected poems everything he published before *The Testing Tree*, an act of courageous rejection and scarring renewal.

Kunitz's poems are lessons in the sickness of history. Drawn to visions of hell, he courts the victims of history's great bland mill of neutrality. The four exemplary anecdotes in "Signs and Portents" relate the sad condition of the last giant tortoise of Saint Helena; the pollution-scarred caryatids on the Acropolis; the decaying mummy of Ramses II; and the caves of Lascaux, their paintings slowly eroded by people's breath. An Ozymandias in every direction.

The nine new poems in *Passing Through* are intelligent rubbed-over recollections and allegories, a little round-eyed and professorial—the work of a professor trying to forget he's a professor. They have his homely, courteous, shambling manner, as well as his mawkish insistence that "art is that chalice into which we pour the wine of transcendence." The worst of Hardy's last poems were far worse, but the best were much better. Kunitz has often gone as far as intelligence can in humble organization, without the lines ever seeming unbearably right or revealing. Even his good lines never quite escape the prison of impersonation. I wish he had written more Kafkaesque fantasies like "The Custom Collector's Report," or fits of tragicomic morality like "The Gladiators," or Landorian epigrams like "The System."

The anthologies of the next century will have great swatches of Auden and Lowell, half a dozen gorgeous miniatures by Bishop (changing from anthology to anthology but always and depressingly including "The Fish"), Roethke's "The Waking" (and Thomas's "Do Not Go Gentle into That Good Night" and Empson's "Missing Dates"—the future will think the age wrote only villanelles, but will still fall helplessly in love with Bishop's "One Art"), four Dream Songs and "The Death of the Ball Turret Gunner." If Kunitz will not be among them, neither will many poets more deserving; there will be readers who discover him by accident, the way we now discover and are pleased by Churchill or Sandys or Barnes.

Kunitz's work is isolated and lonely, with an almost biblical presence, where mysteries half-revealed call down the centuries. The patriarch in poetry is no longer admired, and Kunitz is too mild and flinching to be much of a desert father, though he has seen the vacant spaces and acknowledged them. Occasionally, in his verse, the desert places have spoken back.

Elizabeth Spires

Most of the poems in Elizabeth Spires's new book are stiff with contemporary sentiment, but toward the end a voice of surprising grace and moral resilience appears—she manages to write lightly about the most mortal of subjects. The opening half of the book is a sequence about the birth and childhood of her daughter, and you have to like baby photos a lot to get through it. Maternal pride shades too easily into something coquettish and hectoring and flooded in tears.

Children bring out the worst in poets, giving them leave for all the sententiousness ("*I have had a child. Now I must live with death*") and self-flattery ("Through corridors of birth and death we were wheeled") daily life won't allow—all irony disappears with the severing of the umbilical cord. Spires is much given to little unconvincing fables—at times you feel you've stumbled, not into Grimm, but into Andrew Lang's gauzy wings and fairy dust. All Spires's bad habits are reflexive—she has to search for her good ones. *Worldling* is her fourth book; though she has always been an ambitious poet, the poems have been thinner than the ambition.

Half a dozen poems in the second half of the book are simply and impossibly lovely, about mortality but also mortal. They face the loss of youth and beauty with the calm resolution of Elizabeth Bishop. Spires did a fond and thorough interview with Bishop twenty years ago (decades apart, they were both students at Vassar), and one or two of her earlier pieces are the most uncanny, exact reproductions of Bishop's manner I can imagine. But they did not prepare for the warm mastery of this:

> *Dusk. The light on the water contracts to a tear*
> *   where only a minute before*
> *it lay like a long spill, and out of the shadows*
> *   the great blue heron appears*
> *to stand on the periphery of what is and what is not.*
> . . . .
>
> *But the hour approaches when you must fly—fly off!—*
> *   fly through the needle's eye*
> *to save yourself while I must see the winter through,*
>
> *carrying this moment as lovers do—meeting, parting*
> *   how many times over one life, two?—*
> *as the night closes in, and cold cuts to the marrow,*
> *   and, distantly, the lights*
> *begin to come on in the great houses of Baltimore.*

This has a mute observing splendor, absorbing the landscape without making it partial or romantic (we are a minor industry of nineteenth-century landscape painters). It is Bishop, but it is Spires too. Bishop, after all, was for years haunted by Marianne Moore; but when we look back now we see what Bishop made her own, not what she borrowed. Bishop wouldn't have written in quite this way, and the passing on of the good in other writers (sometimes the good concealed, sometimes the good remade) is what we call tradition.

In "Good Friday. Driving Westward," "The Rock," "Mansion Beach," "Two Watchers," "The Great Sea," and "Roman Lachrymatory Bottles," Elizabeth Spires has come into her poetic maturity—touched by the metaphysical, the threat of age and fear of the transitory, but also taking them in a fine cautious embrace. I want to recommend these poems to anyone who cares about contemporary verse. Spires has captured a moral universe at the moment it realizes that innocence is no longer a form of knowledge, the moment it embraces the fallen condition that is the world.

chapter 13

Verse Chronicle: Gravel on the Tongue

W. S. Merwin

W. S. Merwin's new book is so dreary, I had to recite *Henry V*'s battle speeches just to get through it. Merwin gave up the burdens of punctuation so long ago it's hard to remember he began as a perfectly conventional poet of the fifties, one of those sons of Auden who lost their way. But who would have thought that the later master of barefoot surrealism, who could make a phrase about stars or bones or stones (those Dutch still-lifes of the late sixties) shimmer with numinous life, who could tease a nerve out of the dull flesh of prose, would end as a village explainer, as Stein called Pound? *The Vixen* doesn't want to be read; it wants to prose its readers to death:

> *and now I have come to ask you to say what will*
> *   free me from the body of a fox please tell me*
> *when someone has wakened to what is really there*
> *   is that person free of the chain of consequences*
> *and this time the answer was That person sees it as it is*
> *   then the old man said Thank you for waking me*
> *you have set me free of the body of the fox.*

Mnemosyne is the evil goddess of these poems: the onslaught of syntax renders the life of a lost world. Merwin lived for years in a village in southwest France, and these poems are laments for the death of old culture (there is something primitive about that region of Albigensian heresies, so close to where the Basques speak Western Europe's one remaining pre-Indo-European language). This is *ubi sunt* poetry filtered through the Romantics, and the last words of the poems are a little thesaurus of belated gesture: *forgotten, gone, autumn, waiting, past us, rusted over, vanishing, looking back, the only time, finished stars, late summer, already gone, going, remembered, afterward, disappeared, remember.*

Where once Merwin used line breaks to give mystery to his phrases, now the sentence is pursued with unmediated vengeance, as if form itself were the crime. This style foregoes all the rhythm of attention punctuation confers—of pointing in its other sense. Punctuation shocks, withholds, hesitates, retards, reviews, resurrects. The advantage of a prose landscape without landmarks—the breathlessness, the giddy rush of speech and image—seems small recompense for the losses.

One might argue that Merwin's sentences are at times the imitation of an action: "the wind-scorched leaves . . . whipped in the hissing rush / over restless litter and cracked ground until the boughs / groan crash finally snap striking back flailing." They're a textbook example of why imitation is a dead form of syntax. The technical problem of denoting the end of a thought drove medieval copyists to invent that series of extraneous and interpolated scratches we know as modern punctuation, our miniature collection of dots, slashes, and curls. (Merwin succumbs to capitals, as in the inset passage above, for the direct representation of speech—otherwise it's every sentence for itself.)

Though he describes the tangles of ivy, the flash of streams, these are dreams of experience, what experience would be if it were prettier and bought retail, like wallpaper. The past underlies the present in ghostly palimpsest, but this retrospect without governance almost requires a sentimental cast: otherwise why look so firmly back? Occasionally there's a whiff of the personal, a bright turn of nature ("the twisted flags / of dried irises knuckled into the hollows"). A few historical monologues, and the memory of a local holocaust, show how edgy this style might become. It's easier to forgive a lack of punctuation in our ancestors.

Merwin has already written about this land in *The Lost Upland*, his stylish autobiographical fiction. He is one of our best memoirists—his prose is redolent, modest, attentive—and he is still a translator of great gifts. It isn't simply that his poems are a species of prose—his *prose* is a species of prose, and it's lovely. In his poems the writing is now so wordy and lifeless, so lacking in the virtues of prose knowledge—I've never thought before that punctuation is a moral choice. This run-on, the-sentence-is-everything-that-is-the-case style (like Molly Bloom on Prozac) is an aesthetic decision, not mere laziness. It just looks like laziness.

Sharon Olds

Sharon Olds has Large, Important Emotions and some fairly odd ways of expressing them. *The Wellspring*, her fifth book, is a family epic, the life of Sharon Olds from unfertilized egg to wife and mother, from before the cradle to before the grave. Olds has raw, wounded energy; an almost animal directness; a savage way with metaphor—it's hard to know exactly when her lines lapse into the comic-book vulgarity that is her only medium of emotional exchange.

Olds is so raptured by family (her book *The Father* was one long autopsy), it almost excuses her rather creepy voyeurism—relentlessly high-minded, as most lowly things are. She invades her parents' bedroom with the cheerful officiousness of a social worker:

> *Today, I thought of that blood, rippling out,*
> *and the blood that seeps up, out of the side*
> *of a trout when a pressed-down blade breaks through,*
> *silvery salty sweet fish*
> *of my mother's maidenhead. It was in the dark,*
> *the harsh shantung blinds drawn down, the*
> *ruffled curtains unloosed at the waist.*
> *She was naked with a man for the first time,*

the intricate embroidery silks of her
pudenda moist upright alert
terrified, thrilled, each hair
reaching out and curling back, she was
there in the bed like her own parents,
there at the center of the world. Now
she was the loaf laid into the pan
raw and being fed now into the bright oven.

This must be the poetry Freud had in mind, a poetry completely devoured by the family romance. But it would be a mistake not to admire the confident violation of our well-meant privacies and well-earned proprieties. That gutted trout, for instance, is a bad joke about a bad joke; but the withheld metaphor is as calculated as an analyst's fee. Olds exceeds your worst dreams of "honesty," and it seems to cost her nothing—her poetic voice is numbing as Novocain, deadening to anything it might say. (Plath and Sexton were mere innocents compared to her.) She's like a girl dancing too long in a peep show—her naked skin has become her clothing. But a loaf in a pan!

For bad taste and preening Isadora Duncan passion, for a ballet of steely insecurities and a twinge of moral ugliness, Olds can scarcely be bettered. If she writes of an abandoned farmhouse, it's abandoned because the army has taken the Japanese-American owners away. We are all on the right side now—it's easy to be, fifty years after the war. What would be hard would be resisting the temptation to secure your moral authority by condescending to the dead, to your parents ("ignorant people"), to people in the grip of war's irrational fears. She's the Tammany Hall of venal sincerity.

She'll write of her son, "I think of your penis, its / candor and virtue"; or of her mother, "Half of me / was deep in her body, dyed egg / with my name on it, in cursive script"; or of a dead gerbil, "trans- / mogrified backwards from a living body / into a bolt of rodent bread" (*transmogrified* isn't the word she wants, but neither is *bolt*—a bolt of bread!); or, imagining herself inside her father's testicles, "My brothers / and sisters are there, swimming by the cinerous / millions" (*cinerous* may be the word she wants, but it's hard to imagine why). She's never gotten over the idea that her children were once inside her—she writes as if she wanted them there still.

There's a great need for erotic poetry in English; our poetry is all emotion without sex (sexual intercourse may not have begun for Larkin until 1963—he was *joking*—but for most poets it hasn't started yet). Olds is our poet laureate of oral sex, and as erotic as a greasy sock. She reports on her private acts with innocent *joie de vivre*, but they're mechanical as a scratchy old porn movie—there's something sad in the sleaze. She has taken voyeurism a good deal farther than most poets, but it's herself she loves watching.

It makes matters worse and not better that Olds is a poet of no mean talent. No one without some of her gifts can be a good poet, but a poet with all of them can still be a bad one. Just when you're caught by a turn of phrase, thinking she's not so dreadful after all, she'll write something that leaves you dumbstruck: "In the middle of the night, when we get up / after making love, we look at each other in / complete friendship." It's not like being told about sex by your eighth-grade health teacher—it's like watching your health teacher demonstrate it.

Virginia Hamilton Adair

Virginia Hamilton Adair is eighty-three, and the poems in *Ants on the Melon* have emerged from a long self-exile. She seems like an Ovid come home from the Black Sea after everyone has forgotten him, speaking a language slightly fussy, preserving in amber its archaisms and conventions. Adair published poems in *Saturday Review*, the *Atlantic Monthly*, and the *New Republic* in the thirties and forties, so she wasn't working in a vacuum—she had a long and mostly content family life on the edge of academia, and suffered one great tragedy in the suicide of her husband, a historian. She is now blind.

Adair was born a little after Elizabeth Bishop and a little before Amy Clampitt; a reader cannot help remembering, from the circumstances of this belated first volume, that Clampitt didn't publish her own first book until she was sixty-three. Parts of Adair are remarkably close to Clampitt: the love of nature and narrow landscapes, of the Wordsworths, of life in London (and travel in general). They are not at all similar as poets—Clampitt was worddrunk, a baroque free-verse poet of great flair and daring (and much repetition); Adair is smaller and mustier, given to whimsy, stultified and arthritic diction, and often placid rhyming. At her worst, she sounds like a parody of a parody of Yeats:

My life's great tower fallen, from base to rafter,
Across this deranged bed with its blot of blood,
Appalling lover, where are the flowers of our laughter,
The bright river of your thought in flood?

She'll write of surfers "oaring with their arms / toward the horizon whence comes their hope" or, of a drowned girl:

No push of pulse, no battle in the blood
finally disturbed the saline melody
when last the swell through dissonance of surf
bore her, loose-fingered and with heavy hair,
to resolution on the empty shore.

At times you're back at some debutante's 1929 ball, hours after the Crash. Resurrected here are the tones and structures of the period when Adair began to write—not those of early Auden or Stevens or Frost or Eliot, the great exceptions, but of the mass of poets now forgotten, who thought themselves original and wrote like everyone else.

Too much of Adair's work is fustian amateur poetry of that bygone age. But some of her graces come from that age—enough time has passed for those old conventions to seem fresh again. There's an inconsequent clumsiness in most of her poems, but much verve, too. She sets a melon rind on an anthill, and sees it blacken

with antmen out of hand
wild for their melon toddies

just like our world next year
no place to step or stand
except on bodies.

The "toddies" are giddy (her sprightliness is almost Bishop's), but they prepare that sudden descent into Swiftian ferocity in the last line. You think you've understood the limitations of this poet, and it takes you aback. She has a good ear for speech (a conductor says, "If you hungry, we wire / ahead to a widow lady, fixes / a fine box supper for you-all"), but almost never employs it (an ear for speech is not the same as an ear for diction—we're often deaf to our own diction). What Adair has presented in lines and stanzas, and once or twice in almost a whole poem, is a gift whose demands were callously ignored.

The biographical afterword, by her kind and solicitous friend Robert Mezey, suggests just what one *ought* to think—that, by not publishing, Adair escaped the need to uphold a reputation or respond to reviewers, to preserve favor or court expectation. I would say that it kept her from the jolt of challenge, that it insulated and stifled her. What would one give for a few more poems in the voice of her Eve?

Not sure how I got there,
But a perfect location: smogless,
Free food & 4 unpolluted rivers.

The man I took to at once—
Our bare bodies made us forget
Our parents (if we ever had any).

Adam was given a desk job, naming
Species; I typed the name tags,
Kept the files, fixed coffee, dusted,

Found the best plants for food, picked
Perma-press leaves for rainshawls
& little aprons to keep off gnats.

. . . .

The snake was sure I'd ratted on him
& bit me. Adam stomped him. Now his kids
Can't play with our kids any more.

We were evicted from Eden Gardens.
Those goons with the flamethrower!
You better believe we went quietly.

Despite the near-religious wonder elsewhere (there are some dire poems about Zen), the moony ghost-struck plangency and a diction nearly ludicrous, Adair has more jazzy surprise—though always, always in fragments!—than poets half or a quarter her age. Piecemeal there's a rare spirit at work.

Mark Doty

Mark Doty's *My Alexandria* won awards from the National Book Critics Circle and the *Los Angeles Times*, was a finalist for the National Book Award, and most recently won the T. S. Eliot Prize in Britain. I'm perhaps the only reader who disliked it, who thought it a bland and dispiriting example of contemporary free-verse Life and Times. Being gay and writing poems is an important occupation just now, but wasn't it an important occupation for Whitman, and Housman, and Auden? Being gay didn't stop Auden from writing good poems; I don't know why it should stop Mark Doty.

Atlantis is a confident performance—confident in the way that comes in middle age to poets who have won a few awards (that's when overconfidence comes, too). The poet begins to trust the contrariness of his impulses, begins to speak against himself. Doty has a life, and the life is written to the terms of his art:

My salt marsh
—mine, I call it, because
these day-hammered fields

of dazzled horizontals
undulate, summers,
inside me and out—

how can I say what it is?
Sea lavender shivers
over the tidewater steel.

A million minnows ally
with their million shadows
(lucky we'll never need

to know whose is whose).

This has his self-absorbed, whimsical, and irrelevant grace, taking pleasure in the passages of nature. The voice, in rhetorical questions and parentheses, keeps breaking in on itself. "I could go on like this," he says a few lines later, and the trouble is, he does. He doesn't know when to stop talking, and the poems natter on, little shivering shallows of talk. His poems tend to be about pointless walks through town or visits with friends, walks and visits so sweetly dopey you feel mean for pointing it out—at best they're little descriptions of nature in a sub-Marianne Moore mode, without her refreshing and cruel eye. His poems have instead that kitchen-pantry-by-Ralph-Lauren look.

AIDS hovers at the edge of these poems like an unbidden guest. Doty doesn't stand on a soapbox—he lost his lover to the disease and in many poems seems bewildered and stunned. His friends are victims, but he doesn't convey their lives especially well; their stories are sad, professionally sad, but they're also dull. We've become accustomed to the narrative of AIDS, to the arguments and denials, the rapid diagnosis and slow grief, to the whole architecture and religion of the disease. All the privacy has leaked out (when a subject has been too long public it becomes professional). The pressures are all toward genial confession; and when confession is genial, it isn't confession any more—it's public relations.

This is what I imagine will happen,
the spirit's release. *Michael,*
when we support our friends,
one of us on either side, our arms

under the man or woman's arms,

> *what is it we're holding? Vessel,*
> *shadow, hurrying light?*

The poet and his friends suffer devastating loss. Your heart goes out to them; but he still isn't able to turn loss into poetry, he's only able to make it "poetic." And this often involves a revelatory flash of light. After *day-hammered, dazzled, haloed, brilliance, gleam, flashing, brightness,* after *flame* and *brilliant* and *flickering* and *coronas* and *licks of fire,* after *haloed, luminosity, brilliant, glitter, sunstruck, luminosity, radiant, iridescent, rainbowed, iridesce,* after *shimmer* and *flashing* and *rainbowed* and *brilliant* and *gleaming,* you're only a dozen pages into the book, with Roget's barely thumbed through.

The light show, the clutter of rhetorical questions (over a hundred of them, often huddled together as though they might get lonely), attempt their dramas in a poetry essentially passive: in the face of death, Doty has a deadpan flatness and loss of affect (other poems are scored by Rodgers and written by Hammerstein, as if at any moment Doty might get down on his knees and sing "Oklahoma!"). In a momentary gleam of description ("veiled like the marsh / gone under its tidal sheet // of mildly rippling aluminum") or an act of sexual cruelty, you see the harshness of desire the contemporary rhetoric is holding back; mostly you get lines like "you can see every bloom's // the multiple expression / of a single shining idea, / which is the face hammered into joy." Then it's on to a talking lighthouse.

Louise Glück

Poetry is a species of fiction, but also a species of autobiography. The reader is dispossessed of the facts, and the dispossession makes poetry more permeable to myth and parable. Louise Glück has taken sustenance from myth in a poetry sometimes starved of all else: her hollow-voiced language is as full of self-conscious angst as a Bergman movie. *Meadowlands* is about the death of a marriage, played out against the *Iliad* and the *Odyssey*.

In Glück's poems myth must be considered broadly, as the devastation of historical narrative by religious longing—Christian, pagan, what matters is the refraction of the sins of the present through the sins of the past. She is an underhanded and suggestive poet, and when she titles a poem "Cana" you cannot expect to find a Jesus there. Cana was the site of a wedding where a miracle occurred, a minor and perhaps silly miracle by a god. The poem talks vaguely of forsythia, an estranged lover (or husband, as other poems make plain), of "emblems of light / which are more powerful, being / implicitly some earthly / thing transformed." This collapses the notions of a god made man, a wedding at which the sign of that godhood is manifest, the fall toward martyrdom that the first miracle signifies, and the transformation toward which all religion (and all love) yearns: one thing turned into another is the silence beneath the sacraments. It's a lot to suggest that your husband assumes the guise of Christ, but Glück is subtle in her means and bitter in her suggestions.

The dozen poems at the heart of *Meadowlands* are brute dialogues of marital squabbling and pure meanness, more vengeful than anything Glück has written:

I said you could snuggle. That doesn't mean
your cold feet all over my dick.

Someone should teach you how to act in bed.
What I think is you should
keep your extremities to yourself.

And again:

You should take one of those chemicals,
maybe you'd write more.
Maybe you have some kind of void syndrome.

You know why you cook? Because
you like control. A person who cooks is a person who likes
to create debt.

These lines are the husband talking, but the wife is no better. They're quarrelsome, childless, deeply unsympathetic adults (though they don't act like adults)—you can imagine what the sitcom will be like, but it would have to be written by Albee and star Taylor and

Burton. Little said by this couple is said without intent to wound (they're like Greek warriors, armed to the teeth). In a dozen lines you learn more about them than you ever want to know; they're appalling, but they're also sad and ridiculous.

Glück seems to realize how airless and closeted these scenes are, and much of the rest of the book returns the marriage through Odysseus and Penelope, the straying husband and patient wife. Glück also assumes the voices of Circe and Telemachus, as if she were, or wanted to be, at once wife, mistress, and the abandoned child of her own childless marriage. Even at her most passionate Glück is a thin and bloodless poet (each character allows a different form of self-pity). She doesn't seem to mind that casting her husband as Odysseus and herself as Penelope might be grandiose. Freud meant that we enacted the myth, not that we became the myth.

Glück's style, a deadened management of the senses, steals the emotional resonance from these marital remains. Her harshly beautiful lines are the living impulse of claustrophobia—they lack image, figure, anything to move them beyond their own small means. When she tries to analyze despair, she sounds like an issue of *Psychology Today* ("I realized I *was* / actually a person; I had / my own voice, my own perceptions"). The poems work hard to evade responsibility for this moral landscape. They seem, in their trashy tabloid way, more like "Oprah" than opera—Odysseus and Penelope are just one more couple who need counseling.

Seamus Heaney

As a title, *The Spirit Level* is a typically Heaneyesque bit of whimsy: a carpenter's worn tool, wood and brass and a bubble in liquid (the dust jacket makes it so), it is also a supernatural idea, the very plane or level of the spirit, even a moderation of spirit (Heaney is our Lucretius of spirit). Heaney, his Ireland still half medieval, half modern, loves the moment when the religious wells up within the secular—it is the political disaster of Irish life. In Heaney there are always two worlds, and his idea of carpentry would be a device to make the canted spirit level again.

Heaney has become an institution now, and dangerous in the way institutions are: his Nobel Prize marks him wrongly as a spent force. As a poet ages he has to fight against his own inclinations, even his own past—not just what has made him what he is, but the made past of his writing.

Heaney's poems start almost anywhere, like the unguarded and mild banter of conversation. We've seen these poems before, in other versions: elegies for friends (the "held-at-arm's-length dead"), turns on classical themes, poems about the land (ploughing up a field often means ploughing up a poem about poetry), transformations of everyday objects. Heaney can be as routine and predictable as Hardy, but as shocking and bewildering as Hardy, too. The routines are part of the deception (sometimes even the deceptions are part of the deception). A poem about a whitewash brush, so mild and homely Heaney seems the Andrew Wyeth of domestic interior, builds slowly toward an unbearable murder. The whitewash is a metaphor ("Of course," you want to mutter—but it's not *just* a metaphor): in Irish politics, what would have been pastoral is too often elegy.

Even his classical themes (his long sequence "Mycenae Lookout" is a camp version of the *Agamemnon*) speak from the Greek past to the Irish present:

The little violets' heads bowed on their stems,
The pre-dawn gossamers, all dew and scrim
And star-lace, it was more through them

I felt the beating of the huge time-wound
We lived inside. My soul wept in my hand
When I would touch them, my whole being rained

Down on myself, I saw cities of grass,
Valleys of longing, tombs, a wind-swept brightness,
And far-off, in a hilly, ominous place,

Small crowds of people watching as a man
Jumped a fresh earth-wall and another ran
Amorously, it seemed, to strike him down.

The "time-wound" is a bit of Heaney's guff, but how strange and unlikely the ending! The quiet manner of these poems is often part of their secret working.

Heaney can raise a lyric uproar when necessary—his "downpour, sluice-rush, spillage and backwash" delight in the warble and wastage of language. He still nestles adjective after adjective one against the other ("slabbery, clabbery, wintry, puddled ground," "grey-blue, dull-shining, scentless, touchable"), as if tapping bricks into mortar—though he isn't a laboring man, he has a feel for doing a job of work.

You get a little tired of the country sentiment (the last poems are all wet weather and moss), of the good and uncanny nature of things; but Heaney always reminds you there is evil in things, too. He has a remarkable way of opening up the sides and floor of a poem:

> *It was more*
> *Hans Memling's light of heaven off green grass,*
> *Light over fields and hedges, the shed-mouth*
> *Sunstruck and expectant, the bedding-straw*
> *Piled to one side, like a Nativity*
> *Foreground and background waiting for the figures.*

This looks easier to do than it is to do. The painter's moment is the moment during, or just after; Heaney wants the moment just before. Heaney is rarely a visual poet; it's his other senses that are preternaturally active. Many of these poems live on a sound, or a taste, or a texture, and his language is all gravel on the tongue: we haven't had as personal and craggy a poet since Auden (I'm talking about the verse, not their good looks). If at times the writing seems reflexive, that's not a bad thing for a poet in middle age to be: his verse has become as natural as breathing.

chapter 14

The Unbearable Lightness
of Elizabeth Bishop

The beauty of Elizabeth Bishop's poetry lies in the keenness of its reserve, and the duplicity such reserve demands from language. No poet this century, other than Auden, has written so many likable poems or suffered more from the consoling attentions of critics. Her readers cannot be blamed for having mistaken her: it is the condition of a poet of limited means to be mistaken, and usually in her virtues rather than her vices.

Her vices were of course often taken for virtues. Bishop was once pigeonholed as a poet of visual scale, of specious ornamentation and frivolous detail. She was a Florida coastline stocked with rare birds, tediously pretty, littered with beautiful shells: "with these the monotonous, endless, sagging coast-line / is delicately ornamented." Robert Lowell wrote that "when we read her, we enter the classical serenity of a new country"—the visual seductiveness of her poems has the passivity of landscape.

In poetry the instinct of communication is often exceeded by the poetic means. The means can bear a burden in excess of their commitment, and in a poet like Bishop the innocence of those means may become part of the troubled drama of understanding, may agree to be the carrier of less innocent messages. Poetry is not a code, because it is more ambivalent than code—its most immaculate expression may not seem genuine unless betrayed by the archeology beneath it.

"Land lies in water," begins "The Map," the first poem in her first book, marking at the outset a devotion to appearances, even when appearances are deceiving. Every schoolboy knows that water lies on land (there are undersea mountains taller than the Himalayas), but Bishop has a more primitive conception of the physical world. Her ideas often rely on pretending to have the untamed eye (if not the heart—her heart was always a civilized broken one) of the innocent.

A reader may delight in the faux naive (readers love playacting) but appreciate it only when it returns the wrongs of common sense. There, all lands are islands—and islands float in the isolation of their waters. The cajoling quality of Bishop's rhetoric—her seduction of the reader's judgment with her intimate "we" ("We can stroke these lovely bays"), the dry irony of her questions ("Are they assigned, or can the countries pick their colors?"), the fine hesitation of her perceiving instinct ("Shadows, or are they shallows . . .") —conceals the purpose to which the rhetoric is put, here to blur the distinction between the map and the world it represents.

The map is not the world, but as rhetoric it becomes a world, just as our printed representations don't merely refer to a world but are a world in themselves. In that world the guileless observation may be the most guilty of suggestion.

> The names of seashore towns run out to sea,
> the names of cities cross the neighboring mountains
> —the printer here experiencing the same excitement
> as when emotion too far exceeds its cause.

History has complications if no subtlety; but the complications have been resolved on the map, the visual equivalent to the blind work of civilization, where the names of ports are carried to sea on ships and the names of inland cities traded across mountains. Such commerce of course required the making of maps; but commerce was already ancient before someone looked down on the world like a god and drew a picture of it.

Emotion that exceeds its cause is usually labeled sentiment, but here the printer has experienced the excitement of the discoverer. It's easier to be a god than to act like a god, and the power of naming has encouraged the printer to write the names in water and impose them on scarps. That is a kind of civilization, too, and an example of the fate that countries suffer from the inattentions of history rather than the attentions of mapmakers. From above we see none of the hatreds that run over borders, none of the wars that have put borders in place. (From a plane we would see no borders at all.) That detachment allows the mapmakers to devote their art (and this is a poem intimate with the detachments of art) to choosing a palette for history's winners and losers. The colors of history are bold strokes, as the poem reminds us: "More delicate than the historians' are the map-makers' colors." The understandings of the poem proceed by what they ignore: art has here imposed on history.

Many early readers of Bishop must have felt that their emotions too were outrunning the cause, a common reaction to minor poets or private favorites—Housman, Hardy, and Larkin have also excited the wary eagerness of readers unsure whether their fondness did not exceed their judgment. The properties of her poetry are slight and conditional, and the subtlety of her arguments is felt neither as a compelled candor nor as a compelling passion. As a poet of the tentative, she bears the frailties of a resistance not in the language so much as beneath it: the intimacies her poems trouble to create are sometimes desperate in their resolve, and even her unbearable prettiness—so tempting and so ingenuous—often cloaks the unpleasantly real. The virtue of her language, like the virtue of her emotion, is in its privacy and reservation; what it reserves is not just the announcement of its causes but the retrieval of its motives.

Bishop therefore did not have—perhaps could not have had— any significant influence on the direction of American poetry in the postwar period; her sensibility was more precarious and less cautiously disposed than the period demanded. She did not grapple with the religious or formal or personal responsibilities that tormented Robert Lowell, against whose poetry hers sometimes acted as a subtle counterirritant—the softer inflections of his middle period were among the few signs that a poetry might be written to allay her influence. Their regard was mutual and their echoings of each other sometimes concordant; but everything Lowell touched turned to poetry, and it was impossible for Bishop not to measure herself against such fluent self-transformation— her disappointments and impediments never seemed of artistic value, at least to her.

Bishop was treated as a peculiar case, a deviant and unhelpful example like Marianne Moore, to whose poetry—similar in its observant miniatures—hers was often compared, at times to her disfavor. She had accepted Moore's friendship and patronage, which came bound with the misapprehensions of critics. Moore's early poems had radical force, in their carapace of poetic manner (her early poetry has still not been completely absorbed, but then later in life Moore apparently had little liking for the uncomfortable burs of that poetry). Bishop was a poet more conventional, whose timidity and mordant self-deprecation never seemed virtuous to her ("One has wasted one's talent through timidity," she once wrote in a letter). You might see in her sequence of prose poems, "Rainy Season; Sub-Tropics," the barely concealed triptych of a personality and its defeats: of all the tropical fauna, why else choose a poisonous toad that longs to be touched; a wandering crab ignorant of its terrible fragility and far from home; and a huge lumbering snail, asking for pity, that can never see its own gorgeous shell? Each has been crippled by its limitations.

Bishop's major gift, what might be called the stimulus to the higher and less provisional reaches of her art, was a nakedness of the observing eye, the curse of seeing the world as if it had never been seen before—she seemed to come upon objects with a small delighted gasp ("Why couldn't we have . . . looked and looked our infant sight away"). To put it another way, she saw the real through the artifice of sight—of the sights possible, the analyses undertaken, in the complex of metaphor and simile: *armed vision*, in Coleridge's phrase. Marianne Moore had a similar gift; yet despite her imaginative priority the gift was original in its effect on the younger poet—the characteristic turns in Bishop's early drafts might have come after reading Moore's poems, but they are already part of a sensibility more warmly functioning, more intimate, and quite different in its occupations, if as yet more tentative (compared to Bishop, Moore is a finicky clipper of news articles, her gift more scientific, more primly precise, and therefore much cooler).

The course of Bishop's poetry is largely a history of the use of this gift, its development (and taming) and temptation. Poetry functions supremely well in the visual frequencies, since language trades not just in observation but in the metaphorical transformations that lie deep as etymology or shallow as simile. At its simplest, Bishop's gift was formed not just in the saturated depths of individual comparisons but in the variation of emphasis and strategy, and the passivity of their forced beauty:

> *Here and there*
> *his brown skin hung in strips*
> *like ancient wallpaper,*
> *and its pattern of darker brown*
> *was like wallpaper:*
> *shapes like full-blown roses*
> *stained and lost through age.*
> ("The Fish")

> *White, crumbling ribs of marl protrude and glare*
> *and the boats are dry, the pilings dry as matches.*
> *Absorbing, rather than being absorbed,*
> *the water in the bight doesn't wet anything,*
> *the color of the gas flame turned as low as possible.*
> ("The Bight")

> *The world seldom changes,*
> *but the wet foot dangles*
> *until a bird arranges*
> *two notes at right angles.*
> ("Sunday, 4 A.M.")

> *Now flour is adulterated*
> *with cornmeal, the loaves of bread*
> *lie like yellow-fever victims*

laid out in a crowded ward.
("Going to the Bakery")

Other poets have had striking descriptive gifts, but rarely has a poetry been organized to take better advantage of this gift in particular. The lyric arrangement of her poems often became subordinate to the images, which sometimes (in "The Bight," "Seascape," and "Florida," most obviously) overwhelmed argument. In such poems one detail succeeds another but, within the margins of subject, the details often have little to do with each other. The poems, not surprisingly, offer the critic a progressive freedom of interpretation as well as a regressive constriction—the argument is not apparent at all or is apparent only in the interstices.

The danger of this gift (every literary gift harboring disadvantages to offset its advantage) lies precisely in its quarantine of beauty. The more the object is raised above the surface by the hard strike of description, the less available it is to the poem's plainer function. Bishop worried about using "this accumulation of exotic or picturesque or charming detail" and thought she might "turn into solid cuteness in my poetry if I don't watch out—or if I do watch out."

An artist reveals by her anxieties many of the terms of her enterprise, even if the enterprise finds ways of exceeding or compromising those terms. Bishop's nervousness about the picturesque lies beneath the various ways she absorbs picturesque detail or forces the centrifugal energies of image to serve the inner torsions of idea. The intrigues are visible even at their slightest and most ingratiating, when the stakes are modest or the tone requires merely the ingratiations of fancy. (Bishop was a poet who found new depth in fancy, but the frailty of her fancy calls forth the protectiveness of her readers.) "Ports are necessities, like postage stamps, or soap," she writes in "Arrival at Santos,"

but they seldom seem to care what impression they make,
or, like this, only attempt, since it does not matter,
the unassertive colors of soap, or postage stamps—
wasting away like the former, slipping the way the latter

do when we mail the letters we wrote on the boat,

either because the glue here is very inferior
or because of the heat. We leave Santos at once;
we are driving to the interior.

As so often, anything as troubling as emotion is overlaid by an insouciance (one of Bishop's many insulating virtues) as pliable as veneer. The careless play of images admits, partially in the form, partially in the way form holds off introspection or dread, the disorder of emotion beneath the surface.

The postage stamps and soap, at hand for extraneous comparison and ornamentation, are converted to terms of debility and complaint. That "wasting away" quietly suggests the fate of all tourists who remain too long abroad, but the remark about the quality of the glue or the intensity of the heat is beguiled by the ending—the tourists, so intent on their "immodest demands for a different world," will not turn back. In blind desire, they want to drive forward, further into inconvenience and difficulty.

Even in her travels Bishop was likely to remain a placid and housebound observer. A critic might make more of the circumstances of a woman who, until late in life, rarely had to work (like Robert Lowell's, her life resembled the lives of poets of another century). Compared to most poets, she took few trips. She stayed in Brazil, having suffered an allergic reaction to a cashew, because she fell in love and there she could piece out an existence from a modest inheritance. She said, speaking to an interviewer about her childhood, "I was always a sort of a guest, and I think I've always felt like that," and yet she had homes, and made homes (and lost them) wherever she went. A woman of her disposition would have felt homeless anywhere—but she was a traveler and not a tourist, and could find the consolation of beauty wherever she was invited.

Bishop often tests the consolations of beauty, the very beauty enforced by her description—this control prevents her poems from a movement toward disintegration. That her powers of organization were equal to her powers of observation is apparent as early as "Wading at Wellfleet," where the argument balances on the fulcrum of one image: the ocean compared to an Assyrian chariot, its rolling breakers the murderous wheels (the speaker must be wading on the Atlantic side of the Cape).

The point of the comparison is not that the terms negotiate with each other but that the negotiation breaks down. The sea is preparing to go to war:

This morning's glitterings reveal
the sea is "all a case of knives."

Lying so close, they catch the sun,
the spokes directed at the shin.
The chariot front is blue and great.

The war rests wholly with the waves:
they try revolving, but the wheels
give way; they will not bear the weight.

The image, too, has not borne the weight of comparison; but the poem's argument rises just where its movement has collapsed, and the ending takes unawares the mildness of tone (a tone misleading in its allurements). The sea has only been plotting ("A thousand warriors in the sea / could not consider such a war / as that the sea itself contrives // but hasn't put in action yet"), but we are aware of the violence of which the sea is capable (the hurricane of 1938 devastated the Massachusetts coast).

The burden of the failure is not that the image has failed to complete its transformation, but that the waves have been inadequate to their desire; in the futility of desire the sea is condemned, for the moment, to its glitter. The function of the image *as* an image is thus parallel to its function in the argument: the yearning of the ocean to be the murderous chariot is little separate from the yearning of image, or the poetry or art of which it is an example, to have an effect beyond the moral condition of the poem, to be equivalent, in its way, to the "arts" of war—in the immorality of technique, the poem is driven to destroy its own prettiness. The poem, which might be dismissed for the narrowness of its aesthetic focus, has a deeper and more troubling argument in the aesthetic realm. Bishop's visual conceits are so charming—so warmly enchanted, however slightly or slyly detailed—that they tend to corrupt her melancholy. As the eye attends to the mere wash of prettiness, even of stubborn glamor, we ignore or repress the moodier Bishop, whose vision is subject to its revealed need, and so sacrificial.

The interior tensions of metaphor and simile are often severely underestimated, even (perhaps especially) by the artist liberal in using them. Bishop might write casually, in the draft of an unfinished prose piece: "I noticed the white vertebrae of larger fish, heaped up or scattered. I found myself staring down at them, like an aeroplane up ten thousand feet, say, over the ruined columns of a Greek temple." Even the ornamental simile may have devastating pressure if conceived by an imagination continually under pressure and desperate to achieve (or helpless to avoid) remarkable acts of transfiguration. The simile works upon its broken identities; and the whiteness of Grecian ruins, as well as their fragility when seen from the air, provides further tenors of and supports to the comparison. But surely the authority of the comparison lies in the observer's realization that in each case something grand and beautiful has been dismantled, has been rendered subject to mortality and decay. A sense of collapsed religion, vanished majesty, haunts the simplicity of the fishbones (a simile functions effectively only when one of its terms haunts the other); and what might have been merely visual ends by becoming nearly moral, less a concealing decoration than a revealing attitude: otherwise the observer would not find herself "staring down at them."

The intense gaze of such description is rarely available to Bishop's formal prose, though frequently if chaotically present in her letters. Prose did not call forth the same sustaining or organizing powers of her imagination (her papers include a number of abandoned book reviews), because prose required a narrative largely inimical to the latent conduct of such images: prose needs an argument in the surface of the telling, not beneath it. For that reason her stories seem slight and fussy (and often overworked at the symbolic level), while her memoirs—so easily confused with her fictions—supply very little material beneath their cheery good manners: she was almost obliged to say, however self-mockingly, "It's almost impossible not to tell the truth in poetry, I think, but in prose it keeps eluding one in the funniest way."

The artist has no obligation, however, to work equally well in different modes, though Bishop's failures in prose cast an oblique light on the successes of her imagination in a mode less defensive to the form and execution of her gifts. The exercise of an artist's gifts is more or less efficient, depending on accidents of talent or timing; but the resonant uses to which the gifts are put depend on the resonating character of the subject. Bishop seems almost immune to the specific world of war and politics that loaned the substance and shaped the formal response of almost every other poet of her generation—her aloofness is mustered as a refusal, a conscientious objection to a world inimical to her poetry. And yet the plasticity of her gifts was such that within that modesty she could shape a response blasphemous in its repose.

Her moral universe was agnostic. The grimy little paradise of the "Filling Station" benefits from an unseen feminine agency— the small orderings beneath its oil-soaked exterior give rise to a series of doubts that can be answered only by a vague assurance that "Somebody" performs these tasks: "Somebody embroidered the doily. / Somebody waters the plant, / or oils it, maybe. Somebody / arranges the rows of cans / so that they softly say: / ESSO— so—so—so / to high-strung automobiles." And, finally, "Somebody loves us all." This ought to be comforting—it *would* be comforting, but the "Somebody" remains invisible, inapprehensible, and unknowable. And if this agent remains so vague and anonymous, perhaps it does not exist at all—the repeated "Somebody" conceals the terrifying idea of "Nobody at all" and seems increasingly uneasy and forlorn.

If the filling station is raised to metaphysics by these doubts, the universe is by an equal degree reduced. The unseen maternal presence is doing what it can, but the small world of the station is hopelessly squalid. This might be depressing if the poet were not so obviously in love with squalor—Bishop's poems delight in the untidiness of life, the losses endured (a philosophy not stoic but sanguine—only the messy, viscous, unctuous oil *could* whisper comfort to "high-strung automobiles"). The poems accept how little control we have, however much we desire; a poetry may itself be the tidiness that permits artistic misrule (in the restrained compass of the poem, Bishop's charm could never wear thin, or tolerate doubt equal to its size). It would be wrong to mistake the economy of her means (and the repetitions of thematic design) as a simple lack of resources, just as it would be wrong to find in the missing maternal presence at the filling station merely the helpless fact of Bishop's biography; but the economy and the absences suggest—as a lesson for American poetry—where to position the inner life, if the poet has an inner life.

"The Riverman" speaks of nature untouched by the political, and so available to sympathy. It was not unusual for Bishop's nature to serve as an ars poetica ("The Bight" is a disquieting reflection of the poet's imagination, that workshop of "old correspondences," that quiet harbor where the sediments of the past are dredged up). The riverman wishes to become a witch doctor, and believes or pretends to believe that nature will reveal its secrets to him in a private language he understands "like a dog, / although I can't speak it yet."

The appeal of a private language, to a poet who has also apprenticed herself to water spirits (her poems invoke water the way Larkin's invoke the land), should be apparent; but what is crucial to the correspondence is not that nature serve as the metaphor for imagination—nature often *was* her imagination—but that the explanation derive from the civilization nature would exclude: "the moon was burning bright / as the gasoline-lamp mantle / with the flame turned up too high," the rooms of the river spirit "shine like silver / with the light from overhead, / a steady stream of light / like at the cinema," and the river worms have "tiny electric eyes / turning on and off and on." The poet can consider nature only in the language of progress, which fosters the tragedy of misunderstanding embedded in the pathos of her work.

The impulse works quite differently when nature is not the absorbing metaphor but the surrounding circumstance. "The Burglar of Babylon" is also about a man who would disappear into nature, here the burglar and murderer run to ground on the hills above Rio. The hills have gradually been overrun with the shacks of the poor; but from the unfeeling distance of the rich who watch the drama from their apartments, through binoculars, the spread of the poor is a "stain," or "like lichen." The poor have mastered nature in their own fashion—the hills have become the names of poverty: "There's one hill called the Chicken, / And one called Catacomb; // There's the hill of Kerosene, / And the hill of the Skeleton. . . ."

"I've got to disappear," says the burglar Micuçú (with an irony unrecognized). His doomed spirit as the soldiers hunt him down lets the reader ignore his crimes—he becomes another victim, as desperate as the poor who have come to Rio and cannot go home (the victim is sacrificial as well as symbolic). The ballad provides the remoteness of fiction, a fiction that permits these conflicts in order not to incur the pieties a closer observer might invoke. This may seem like the cruelty of aloofness rather than a merely troubled respect, which requires the irony of respect; but Bishop knew the tension of disintegrating observations held in delicate relation.

A more difficult example of political ambiguity occurs in "Pink Dog," whose rhymed triplets seem jazzy and unfeeling, while the surrounding politics are murderous:

> *Didn't you know? It's been in all the papers,*
> *to solve this problem, how they deal with beggars?*
> *They take and throw them in the tidal rivers.*
>
> *Yes, idiots, paralytics, parasites*
> *go bobbing in the ebbing sewage, nights*
> *out in the suburbs, where there are no lights.*

Nothing in the poem dissociates the poet from the uncharitable voice, a voice that thoughtlessly dismisses the unsightly beggars to advise the pink dog on how to avoid a similar fate. What should the dog do? Dress up in carnival costume, in which it won't look out of place. But the idiots and paralytic beggars drowned by death squads won't go away—they possess the poem long after they cease to inhabit the city that has tacitly consented to their murder. The poem depends on their eerie presence to lay bare the masquerade of emotion that underlies the poem—Bishop often gains access to a darkening vision through the whimsy or slightness of her manner (few poets have ever been so severe in their irrelevance); perhaps it is appropriate that here one masquerade counsels another, revealing itself through another. The ignoring voice cannot bear the murders, but its silence does not silence them—they poison the contrived gaiety and expose its frantic inconsequence.

Bishop found ways of disturbing the dainty and inconsequential surfaces of her work without destroying them—that is, of being true to the manner without ignoring its constricting limitations. This is not special pleading: the etiquette of Bishop's work often contains the pleasures of her work, but it does not entirely determine the meaning that exists partly on behalf of such surfaces and partly in ironic or inimical relation to them. Is there any prose, for example, that more adequately portrays the absurdity and tragedy of the ruin of Ezra Pound than Bishop's nursery rhyme, "Visits to St. Elizabeths"?

Certain ironies are available to a poet willing to use, and use harshly, the availing forms, however despised. Bishop's slowly accruing stanzas, based on "The House That Jack Built," elaborate Pound's condition in a way not far distant from a madman's continual reckoning of his estate; though here the details alter slightly from stanza to stanza, as if that world were hallucinated. If these are "visits," however, each stanza represents the greater detail noticed and recorded on each new occasion, with the slow additions to the visitor's understanding and the complications and adjustments in that understanding. The adjectives describing the man, Ezra Pound, are subject to the most radical change: he is stanza by stanza *tragic; talkative; honored; old, brave; cranky; cruel; busy; tedious.* In the penultimate stanza what lies beneath these varying guises is exposed: "the poet, the man / that lies in the house of Bedlam." But the perception does not end there—the last stanza goes deeper, to "the wretched man / that lies in the house of Bedlam." Here the condition of the man and his circumstance are set at one, and the condition begins to atone for the circumstance. *Wretched* has a double force—as a moral judgment and as an admission of sympathy.

The apposition of "the poet, the man," however, has its own cunning: the phrase balances (or weighs) the two states into which all moral biography falls, but it also separates them. The equality is also equivocation, and upon that division most criticism of Pound has faltered. Bishop's little twist of syntax has left Pound the author of his own circumstance; that judgment is wretched in its sympathy.

It was not Pound but Eliot who was the author of much of Bishop's imagination, and his influence was more deeply absorbed and is therefore more difficult to trace than an influence on style like Moore or an alter ego and negative example like Lowell. The tracings must be more hesitant and less stable, but absorptions offer a more accurate calculus of a poet's strength than the influences stalled in style. Eliot was a poet who halted the development of two generations of poets seduced by his example or provoked into reaction against it: Bishop's modest but assuming use of a poet who proved so resistant might be called a fine example of reticence, an example of how her protective timidity permitted her to wrestle with poets more pertinent to her imagination than those who affected the play of her language.

Perhaps I have overstated a case that cannot go beyond mere inference. In "Love Lies Sleeping," the observed world conceals a unifying myth, a vision available only to the hungover speaker and the drunken or dead (or dead-drunk) man at the end:

> *for always to one, or several, morning comes,*
> *whose head has fallen over the edge of his bed,*
>   *whose face is turned*
>   *so that the image of*
>
> *the city grows down into his open eyes*
> *inverted and distorted. No. I mean*
>   *distorted and revealed,*
>   *if he sees it at all.*

The minutely traversed city ("made delicate by over-workman-ship" in one of Bishop's languid, scarring puns, which reaches back to touch the poet at her desk) is lurid in its beauty and dangerous and perhaps even toxic in its occupations (the city seems to have grown "from fused beads of iron and copper crystals, / the little chemical 'garden' in a jar"). Even though specific details—a water-wagon "throwing its hissy, snowy fan," the water drying "light-dry, dark-wet, the pattern / of the cool watermelon"—soften the harsh-ness of the waking city, this softness does not disguise the nature of the inhabitants.

The poem addresses the "queer cupids" whose evening meals will be prepared by the people "dragging in the streets their unique loves"—the cupids "will dine well / on his heart, on his, and his." But there are other victims who will not wake, or will wake to the distorted, revealed vision of the city: the victim at the end is appar-ently one whose heart has been eaten. There is a profound loneli-ness in Bishop's poem, profound because this figure reminds us of another martyr to knowledge. If he is a victim of those devouring cupids, his fate is Promethean—for the Greeks the liver was the seat of the affections, and for the eagle to eat Prometheus' liver is functionally no different, to the anthropologist, from the queer cupids preparing a meal "on his heart, on his, and his."

I don't want to push the myth too far, at least not past the point where it is suggestive; but the insinuation of myth (and not its jus-tification *as* myth) gives the poem its subterranean intensity. And in this use of myth Eliot's influence has been felt. Those "queer cupids" may not be related to Eliot's "golden Cupidon," but the still glance of the dead or drunken man, his open staring eyes, ought to remind us of Phlebas under water (Bishop's city seems to "waver" in "skies of water-glass"). And what is the supine man on the bed at daybreak (his upside-down vision distantly recalling the posture of St. Peter in martyrdom) but a right-side-up morning version of the most famous modernist image, Eliot's patient anaes-thetized on an operating table, the image of inverted evening?

The echoes of Eliot's stage props confirm Bishop's appropria-tion of his use of myth—she has taken on Eliot as Eliot had taken on Dante. Eliot is not the ghost in the machine of the poetry but the gatekeeper to the bleaker zones of emotion (emotion and influence might be called the obverse and reverse of one battered shield), which her brittle and whimsical surfaces disguise when they cannot protect.

"Sleeping on the Ceiling," for example, a pendant to "Love Lies Sleeping," again evokes the inverted etherized patient—here the sleeper who has floated to the ceiling, an upside-down Paris, its crystal chandelier a fountain in the Place de la Concorde. But there is no peace in that helium lightness, and ("Let us go then," wrote Eliot) we must make a visit—"We must go under the wallpaper / to meet the insect-gladiator, / to battle with a net and trident. . . ." This is a dark and compromised sleep. The insect gladiator may not seem threatening, but the threat depends on the scale of our meeting. The pleasures of the unconscious have been set against the terrors of real battle "under the wallpaper," in the id's closeted domain—we have gone from the civilized splendors of Paris to the bloody circuses of Rome (cockroaches are fond of the organic glue on the underside of old wallpaper—they also love to breed in the enclosed spaces under sagging wallpaper). Loneliness and doubt are the forms of this dream work, and the danger of the battle with the insect is no less than the danger of Prufrock's waking to drown. In this way Eliot supports Bishop as Dante supported him.

I have invoked the shadow of Eliot as another way of arguing that Bishop is neither a poet of pure glassine surfaces nor a poet without deeply abiding and maturely conserving transactions with her influences (one might impose the template of Eliot's "Journey of the Magi" over Bishop's "A Cold Spring"). The tendency to see Bishop as a special case isolates her in the literature from which she drew a luxuriating vigor, even if she chose to use it offhandedly—or bury it so deeply in the poem it is fossilized there.

Most of her critics are warmly employed scratching up the fossils of biography. The life of an artist will always have the appeal of an unpleasant (even slightly seedy) secret, merely because it stands behind the art as a compound ghost, sometimes alluded to, sometimes bearing upon, sometimes revealed—or seemingly revealed.

But critics can rarely make more than an inferential appeal to biography. No fact was ever less a fact than one tortured into poetry. We know that poets distort, cobble, trim, and refract. If we find a "fact" that seems to align with a poem, it is no proof that any other poem is aligned with fact. The life is only a fallible guide to reading the poem, and the poem an open lie for reading the life.

Since poets have a contempt for the small details (Bishop insisted on keeping the February 1918 date of the *National Geographic* in the poem "In the Waiting Room" even after the fact checkers at the *New Yorker* assured her the actual date was March 1918), we should not expect them to have respect for larger ones. Where the life imposes itself on the art is in the shadings and obsessions, the compulsions—perhaps even in the manner of the distortions.

Bishop was an orphan, or nearly an orphan (her father died when she was eight months old and a few years later her mother was permanently lodged in an asylum). Scenes of abandonment have an obvious resonance in her work—perhaps too obvious. Such "rhymes" are appealing to biographical critics because they so neatly observe the psychological proprieties. But what ought to be interesting is not the aligning of the life with the art, but the misaligning. A poem like "Sestina" may draw its emotional ruptures from the poet's memories, but the scenes of grandmother and granddaughter have been transfigured, almost into fairy tale. Even the title seems to remove the acts from the private room of the personal (and, from a certain point of view, more deeply lodge them there).

In the peaceable kingdom of the poem, with its six domesticated end words, the word *tears* is the unexpected fluid element (*house, grandmother, child, stove,* and *almanac* are hard properties of the setting). The grandmother "sits in the kitchen with the child / beside the Little Marvel Stove, / reading the jokes from the almanac, / laughing and talking to hide her tears." We know of the sorrow without knowing the source, and what we know is that it must be suppressed. The tears are "equinoctial"; but, even if the grandmother suffers them only twice a year, they cannot be stopped.

They appear everywhere—on the teakettle, in the teacup, as a man's buttons in the child's drawing, in the little moons of the almanac (whether projected or insinuated makes no difference). The surface is matter-of-fact and almost lighthearted, and here Bishop imitates the grandmother's attempt to keep her sorrow from the child—to keep the child's own knowledge of sorrow at a distance. The poem never mentions a death, never implies the child is an orphan. And yet there are ominous indications all around. Four things are said in the poem. What the grandmother says (*"It's time for tea now"*) maintains the bland illusion of domestic harmony; but the Marvel Stove says, *It was to be,* and the almanac says, *I know what I know.* Fate and secrecy are invoked just before the child draws a picture of a house and a man with "buttons like tears."

Perhaps there is nothing wrong. Here biography is almost too explicit. Little moons fall like tears from the almanac into the flower bed the child has drawn. The almanac says, ominously, *Time to plant tears.* If the tears are seeds, we don't want to know what will grow from them. It is not the business of the poem to disclose what these tears suggest about the inner life of an adult who recalls such a childhood. The life shadows a certain reading of the lines, but even without the shadow the poem (where in the end "the child draws another inscrutable house") reveals too much about houses and bitterness and memory. The poem, in other words, attempts to secure its own boundaries, to remain in the realm Bishop calls "self-forgetful." ("What one seems to want in art, in experiencing it, is the same thing that is necessary for its creation, a self-forgetful, perfectly useless concentration.") But in a sestina the return of the end words serves the return of the repressed.

Whether or not the poet has an intention here, the poem has difficulty fending off the pressure of biography. Of course a poet has intentions and the intentions have effects; but the intention is not always, perhaps not ever, the same as the effect. Here biography provides, or seems to provide, an enriching and complicating circumstance, without being necessary to our understanding (but dictating terms likely to disable or simplify that understanding).

A similar case is "Crusoe in England," where the rescued Crusoe looks back upon his island. At least one critic has drawn the parallel between Crusoe mourning the death of Friday in England and Bishop mourning in New York the death of her Brazilian companion, Lota de Macedo Soares. The poem luxuriates in such attentions, and other details seem to confess the inner life of an exile (Bishop spent more than twenty years in Brazil): "I often gave way to self-pity. / 'Do I deserve this? I suppose I must. / I wouldn't be here otherwise.'"

The reader must be wary of accepting Crusoe's life as a mirror life of Bishop. Whether Bishop's biography is applied in its bearing and particularity to the fiction or whether the fiction is instead a medium for expressing a private vastation is a very different thing. Treating the poetry as the transcendence of fact is more difficult than exposing it as the mere imposition of fact. We must read such work in self-division if we are neither to trespass on artistic proprieties nor hobble ourselves in ignorance.

Critics sometimes forget that psychology is not the only thing that determines the course of the poem, that much a poet writes is found in the heat of engagement, and much that he rewrites is colored more by accidents of talent than by the masks and fetters of psychology. It is fashionable to think of the writer as helpless before psychology, yet many writers deploy their imaginations in frustrating the demands of the inner life. Not *every* deviation from biography is pathological, or driven by repressive instinct; nor is every mask a protection. An artist has keener orders of fidelity and loyalty than an autobiographer, and the poem has demands more radical than tales of the past. This is not to say that psychology is irrelevant to the arraignments of the imagination, merely that the assumption of relevance is often a presumption of helplessness, the author's impotence before his own psychology. (If not all deviations can be referred to psychology, none can be securely referred.) The critical evidence must ignore, because ignorant of, the private sense of authority with which a writer writes.

That is the artist's duplicity and his only hope of escaping the mere priorities and prior arrangements of the life. The artist's fidelity requires a withdrawal from the life if there is to be any solace in the art, and the fact of that withdrawal lies in the success of an art that is not minutely mined by the life. The poet may be alive to the inner meaning but keen to preserve its lack of standing as meaning. Half-hidden, it retains the same influence emotions exert in life—the force of a poem comes not from actual disclosures, but from our sensitivity to their latent presence. There a poet whose pleasure lies in her transparency, in the seeming perfection of a minor art, has a troubling coerciveness, even if her flinching retreat from its sources leaves her art permanently mangled or crippled. Her vices, like those of Emily Dickinson, are intimate to her best work and inseparable from it. Bishop is one of the best examples in our poetry of how the eccentric course of meaning documents both the major and minor terms of an art nearly perfect in its clarity and constricted by its fastidiousness. The terms of her limitations are likely to be, to readers not wholly conditioned by the grotesque expanses of poets not nearly her equal in the psychological realm, the modest terms of our respect.

chapter 15

Lowell in the Shadows

Our longing for literature has the force of a prejudice, and to account for the mystery and method of that prejudice we need a distinguishing case. Since Robert Lowell's death in 1977, his reputation has suffered slow-motion collapse. Even the most distinguished poets are eclipsed by death (we are as worn out by the mediocrity of the bad as by the brutal magnificence of the good). It is a shallow thing, reputation, and its standing before death bears little relation to its standing afterward. This would amuse a family with the long history of the Lowells: such a family can wait for the justice of history, if history is just.

Lowell was the form and the shadow of postwar poetry. *Lord Weary's Castle* shaped the mannerisms of the fifties, and the sixties were a long footnote (we are still writing that footnote) to *Life Studies*. This simplifies the sources and ignores the exceptions, but for forty years after *Lord Weary* Lowell was the poet who troubled the sleep of other poets. The great modernists who preceded him have also been dead twenty years or more, and we live in the diminished landscape after such genius. Those who believe we are in a major phase of American poetry have closed their ears to the past. We must retire the past to prepare a revival, however; and perhaps we should be grateful that for all its suppressed power Lowell's poetry has been rendered mortal by disfavor, by familiarity, by the small contempts of biography.

Lowell's life like his art was a series of set pieces, in part because he worked so much of his life into the nakedness of art. He was born to a prominent Boston family, beneath the silhouette of the state house, on the verge of American entry into the First World War. The models for the brownstone pillars of his grandfather Winslow's front doorway stood at the Temple of the Kings at Memphis. The wealth once concentrated in that generation of Winslows left his parents set up on the thin stilts of trust funds and a navy salary—he later wrote that his mother had "a genius for squeezing luxury out of rocks."

The scenes from such a life fall helplessly into anecdote; but the anecdotes have the symbolic force of Melville, where tragedy and the Bible have mocking undertones: Lowell the Harvard dropout and would-be poet, pitching a tent on Allen Tate's front lawn, having misunderstood Southern irony for invitation; Lowell, blind drunk, ramming the family Packard into a wall and ruining the face of his fiancée, Jean Stafford; Lowell, a Catholic C.O. during the Second World War, imprisoned—for refusing to kill—next to the czar of Murder, Inc.; Lowell, like a young Senator McCarthy, nosing out communists at an art colony; Lowell in the grip of mania, holding Allen Tate out a window while reciting Tate's "Ode to the Confederate Dead" in a bear's growl; Lowell on mad ward after mad ward, the manic attacks coming every two years, then every year, then twice a year. The incidents are misleading in their notoriety, and the duty of biography is to face down the notoriety and find the small still context of the original sins.

Lowell was a religious poet, early and late; and we miss the transforming character of his work if we fail to understand his politics, his politic evasions, his evasive confessions, in terms of the failed sanctities of a religious life. The early summer retreats to an isolated stretch of Nantucket for regimens of reading, the later retreats to monasteries and art colonies (his months in prison allowing a monastic asceticism, too), the conversion to Catholicism and the later apostasy, and the various failed recourses to psychiatry fix successive stages of a life that gradually exhausted the defenses of the will. (If we do not quite expect the grace of communion at the hands of psychiatrists, the rituals of the couch are little different from the rituals of the Cross—and there was a point when the shock-treatment table was almost the altar of American intellectual life.)

Properly speaking, however, a poet doesn't have a life. He may go through the motions of St. Mark's and Harvard and Kenyon, of marrying three women and having daughter and son, of betraying his spouses or his friends, of dying in a taxi cab; but his actual life is all the while in language. The biography of the art is never the biography of the body, however much the ravages of the body leave their scars on the art; and we do the man and the poetry a disservice by trying to make the marks on one equivalent to the marks on the other. The calculus that would measure the value of one in terms of the other has never been discovered.

Lowell, as it happened, composed prose fragments of a life during a period of mental breakdown in the late fifties (the only portion he published was "91 Revere Street" in *Life Studies*). These fragments, some of which appeared posthumously in *The Collected Prose of Robert Lowell*, have remarkable emotional texture and symbolic example, even if the characters all too often talk not as if they were kin to Robert Lowell, but as if they *were* Robert Lowell ("Great-aunt Sarah lifted a hand dramatically to the mute keys of the dummy piano. 'Barbarism lies behind me,' she declaimed grandly. 'Mannerism is ahead.'")

A poet is never a reliable witness to his life, for all the nonpoetic reasons (perjury being our daily bread) and for one intimately and mordantly poetic: that the life is too rich not to become a source of the art and too limited not to be transformed by the processes of art. It becomes art not in its faith but by its falsity. These are old matters to aestheticians and philosophers, and Plato would properly have driven us out of his Republic. We would have gone to live happily among the Cretan liars. In "91 Revere Street" Lowell mentioned his boyhood love for some lead soldiers from Dijon. A young poet, thinking to ingratiate himself, sent Lowell some lead soldiers found in Dijon—but Lowell had made up the detail, "on the Flaubertian principle of always being particular."

This cautionary anecdote is repeated in *Lost Puritan: A Life of Robert Lowell*, Paul Mariani's fact-heavy new biography, meant to replace Ian Hamilton's of a dozen years ago. Despite the caution, which lies quietly among his notes, Mariani uses Lowell's fragments as if Lowell had been under oath. And yet Lowell's fictive use of himself surrounds every story—the fragments about his boyhood show the ordinary unhappiness of a coddled childhood, none of the potential violence or obsessive will to power that began to disfigure his adolescence. Mariani's portrait of the young Lowell is therefore attenuated by the limits of the man in his own mirror and, most witnesses being dead, the lack of other evidence. Even Lowell's tales from the mental hospital—written in bemused, equable style—reveal little of the associative genius or brilliant intuitiveness to which his friends and early students attest. We would not know from Lowell why he commanded such loyalty, or why he was memorable before he was significant. Most men are mysteries to themselves; they are fascinating when they are mysteries to others.

Every biographer suffers the fable of his biography, and usually a fable of hero worship or parricide, the one sometimes becoming the other. Here the biographer has so restricted himself to the closed border of the particular, the fable of factuality, it is not surprising that so many of his facts are immigrant fictions. By not admitting that the fictions *are* fictions, he must pretend that they are something else—gospel truth, for instance.

Sometimes it is not clear, except to a scourer of notes, when such fictions are dressed as facts:

> *"That awful summer!", Jean would remember, when "every poet in America came to stay with us. It was the first summer after the war, when people once again had gasoline and could go where they liked. . . . And then all day I'd cook and wash the dishes and chop the ice and weed the garden and type my husband's poems and quarrel with him."*

But this is not memoir; this is a story composed decades later called "An Influx of Poets." Mariani is fond of the evidence of this story, and when using it earlier seems to understand the problem of evidence:

> *Forty years later, in her short story/memoir "An Influx of Poets," Jean would describe a thinly disguised version of Cal: "Half a year*

after we were married, [Cal], immersed in the rhythms of Gerard Manley Hopkins the poet. . . ."

This is not quite good enough. A "short story/memoir" promises the fact within fiction and conveniently ignores its inconvenient status as fiction; just as the biographer's sleight of hand in replacing the fictional "Theron" in that quotation with Lowell's unfictional nickname "Cal" allows him to claim the disguise as no more than the man. Jean Stafford had trouble with facts even when they were not fictions—but we are not obliged to treat a story as a concealed affidavit, and neither is Lowell's biographer. If it were an affidavit, we would have to wonder why the Lowells' house in Maine was purchased not with a bequest from a fictional aunt, but with royalties from Stafford's first novel; and why the biographer fails to pursue the claim that "Theron Maybank" is anti-Semitic. "An Influx of Poets" is not really a story at all, but all that her editor Robert Giroux was able to patch together from her failed novel, "The Parliament of Women." (Mariani has trouble with his sources. A vilification of Gertrude Buckman attributed to this story in fact comes from a letter by Stafford.)

Lowell's poems are everywhere taken as precision instruments of recall: "Lowell would remember a 'sand-red sow / grubbing acorns by a cinder pile.'" Even if we allow the intimacies between the life and the art, this is from a poem written more than a decade later about the day Lowell was driven to prison. Are we to trust as untampered memory a symbol as convenient as a pig grubbing up its living beside the ashes? *Lowell would remember.* It may be within the permissible limits of speculation to write, regarding the fictional use of violent fact:

while she was dreaming of a former lover, Cal had awakened her to make love and, still half asleep, she'd repeated her lover's name. In a perfect frenzy, Cal tried to strangle her. . . . In an unpublished draft of "A Country Love Story," Jean would play the scene again, having the wife, alienated by her husband's absorption in his work, fantasize instead about an imaginary lover.

It seems beyond those limits to write in the next paragraph about Lowell's long poem, "The Mills of the Kavanaughs," in which a woman recalls the violence of her husband (called Harry, not Robert Lowell), that in the published versions Lowell "could not bring himself to speak even then of his attempt to take her against her will." What the life has endured the poem may not require.

Lowell could be violent, in and out of mania, and the roster of his assaults includes boyhood friends, his father, Jean Stafford (he broke her nose months after ruining her face), his friend Frank Parker, Allen Tate, Delmore Schwartz, a wealthy lover (whom he took by the neck and threw to the floor during an argument about Shakespeare), and any number of policemen and psychiatric attendants. There is at least one possible strangling and attempted rape (alluded to above), and numerous threats (the month before he drove the Packard into a wall, he threatened to do so). These do not require the speculations of fiction or the tainted evidence of poetry. But since biography is commonly an assault on the life, why should it not be an assault on the imagination as well?

Some of this might be forgivable in an interpretive biography, a dark Freudian masterpiece like Berryman on Stephen Crane—Freudians are usually able to tell the dream from the declaiming. Mariani's is an archival biography, a biography of petty fact, of itinerary, guest list, street address, of performances attended, books read, records heard. He knows the life like a travel agent—"Afterwards, the Lowells . . . sailed from Brindisi to Turkey to encounter Constantinople, Bursa, Smyrna, and Ephesus, before sailing on to Greece (Priene, Delphi, Athens, Corinth, Sounion). . . . Then on to Venice, Vienna, Paris, Versailles." If you want to know to which floor Lowell was dragged in a mental hospital, Mariani will remember; and he will insist on telling you. By antlike drudgery he has produced a thorough chronology of a life, thereby modestly correcting trivial mistakes by his predecessor and bringing from dusty files forgotten paragraphs of that life, like Lowell's long, warm correspondence with Santayana.

The petty faults of such an enterprise are almost beneath notice—the scattering of typographical errors or solecisms (*New york*,

Cincinatti, miniscule, Boden for *Bowden* Broadwater, *Gunther* for *Günter* Grass, *St. John* for *St.-John* Perse, *Stonybrook* for *Stony Brook, St. Elizabeth's* for *St. Elizabeths* [a mistake Hamilton also makes throughout]), the wayward syntax, the occasional ludicrous sentence ("even as the war came to a horrifying but swift conclusion with the dropping of two atomic bombs on Japan, Jarrell pored through Cal's poems line by line." *Even?*), the overcharged or trite phrasing ("they could feel rebellion crackling in every fiber of their son's body," "he could have cut the chill . . . with a knife"), the inadequate index, the irritating hearty familiarity ("Cal" and "Lizzie" for Lowell and Hardwick). None of this would matter if Lowell were the living presence of these hoarded facts, these errors; but these are facts starved of interpretation. They pile up, little dust heaps of forgotten events, with scarcely a pause for analysis or motive or insight or intuition. The poems are quoted for the factual cob beneath the kernel (though usually we get just the kernel); yet fewer than half a dozen are examined, and these the old warhorses or sawhorses, to the dissection of which Mariani brings little of interest, and less of passion.

One might shelve such a vast hulk of biography if there weren't intermittent signs of where the shimmer of facts might lead. Mariani dryly contrasts the fond recollections of Lowell's old teachers, Eberhart and Ransom, with their harsher judgments written at the scene. When he says that in Holland Lowell would find "a new way of seeing, closer to the mode of the Dutch realists," or that Lowell "was not yet fully aware of translation's links for him to schizophrenia and manic depression," we face a differential intelligence and integrating comprehension. These are the beginnings of an unwritten book.

Hamilton was roundly criticized for his concentration on lurid and violent episodes. Those episodes recede into the dailiness of Mariani's biography; and within the recitation of days when nothing much happened we remember that outside the months of madness were years of literary production at a harrowing and original level, that outside the lightning streaks of breakdown was the steady rain of sanity (or something unlike sanity, the sanity of minor genius), that the tropical love affairs were banded by temperate zones of marital affection. Lowell was humbled by his illness, contrite on his return to the living. On the other hand, Hamilton has a sharper intuition of how men act and why things happen. He tells how *Land of Unlikeness* came to be published, gives a thorough account of the scandal over the award of the Bollingen Prize to Ezra Pound, and explains the whole bungle behind Lowell's failure to win election as Oxford Professor of Poetry: to these Mariani is largely indifferent (he forgets even to mention the outcome of the election). Passage by passage, Hamilton is vivid and specific, and his anecdotes remain memorable gossip, if still gossip. He has a leisurely eighteenth-century way with narrative, and his very long quotations let numerous characters speak for themselves. Mariani treats the same quotations with a butcher knife.

I have concentrated on the unsatisfactory aspects of this biography because there the form of the prejudice is most apparent: where literature becomes not the end but an interference or impediment, a concealing scrim placed between the reader and the life. But what if matters were reversed, and we accepted that literature had its own psychology, its own biography, and these were lived in different valences from the flesh? It is useful to know the terms on which Lowell and Stafford lived in Black Rock, but that does not make "Colloquy in Black Rock" a transcript of their lives. We may know more about the poem by knowing the circumstances surrounding its composition; but what we know is the contingent force, not the impenetrable action. It is more likely that the life is the lived issue of the poems. These are ancient arguments.

There is a further problem. Mariani expresses in his acknowledgments his great debt to his predecessor, but a reader casually comparing the two books finds greater debts left unacknowledged. Consider a typical incident in Hamilton:

> Peter Taylor had organized a Writers' Forum (really a kind of Kenyon reunion, with old classmates Robie Macauley and John Thompson there, as well as Taylor and Jarrell).

And the same incident in Mariani:

Taylor had organized a Writers' Forum there, in effect a Kenyon reunion which included Robie Macauley, John Thompson, Warren, Cal, and himself.

Or Vienna in Hamilton:

The Seminar in American Studies was held in an eighteenth-century rococo castle called Schloss Leopoldskron—it would have been hard to find a less mundane location for this multilingual gathering of some one hundred poets, artists and musicians from all over Europe.

And Vienna in Mariani:

the Salzburg Seminar in American Civilization, located in an eighteenth-century rococo castle called the Schloss Leopoldskron. . . . It was a vibrant, multi-lingual gathering of some one hundred poets, artists, and musicians from all over Europe.

Or a dinner party in Hamilton:

he attended a dinner party given by Caresse Crosby . . . for the French poet St.-John Perse and was there introduced to a wealthy Georgetown neighbor, Mrs. Carley Dawson.

And a dinner party in Mariani:

Cal attended a dinner party given by Caresse Crosby for the French poet, St. John [sic] Perse, and was introduced that evening to a wealthy Georgetown neighbor, Mrs. Carley Dawson.

Or genealogy in Hamilton:

there were the Pilgrims, the frontiersmen, the Indian killers, the colonial governors, the Revolutionary War hero General Stark, and even a reputed witch.

And genealogy in Mariani:

puritans, frontiersmen, Indian killers, colonial governors, a Revolutionary War general, even a reputed witch.

Or a list in Hamilton:

These poems included final versions of "Beyond the Alps," "Words for Hart Crane," "Inauguration Day: January 1953" and "To Delmore Schwartz" (this last a poem he'd begun in 1946). The new poems were "Skunk Hour," "Man and Wife" . . . , "Memories of West Street and Lepke," "To Speak of the Woe That Is in Marriage" [sic] . . . , "My Last Afternoon with Uncle Devereux Winslow," "Commander Lowell" and "Terminal Days at Beverly Farms."

And a list in Mariani:

Out of this period would come final versions of "Beyond the Alps," "Words for Hart Crane," "Inauguration Day: January 1953" and "To Delmore Schwartz," the last begun in 1946. The new poems would be "Skunk Hour," "Man and Wife," "Memories of West Street and Lepke," "To Speak of Woe That Is in Marriage," "My Last Afternoon with Uncle Devereux Winslow," "Commander Lowell," and "Terminal Days at Beverly Farms."

Or Jarrell in Hamilton:

his tennis, the girlfriend he had in town, his sometimes scathing view of Ransom, and also his conceit, his intransigence, his primness.

And Jarrell in Mariani:

the way he played tennis, the teacher girlfriend he had in town, . . . his criticism even of Ransom, his conceit, his intransigence, even his primness.

Or Eugene McCarthy in Hamilton:

Lowell almost did lose him votes by telling the owners of the sweater factories that the workers in the shoe factory seemed so much happier than their own employees.

And McCarthy in Mariani:

Cal did almost lose him votes when he told the owners of several New Hampshire sweater factories that workers in the shoe factories seemed much happier than their own employees.

Or a night in Ireland in Hamilton:

> *first the telephone failed, then the electricity. He tried to leave the house to make calls from the nearby village . . . but, in the dark, was unable to locate a latch on the one door. . . . It could not have been easy even to find his way back to his top-floor apartment; when the cleaning woman "released" him in the morning, he complained that Castletown "was a very bad place; it needs an elevator"; then, she says: "he went down with one lot of suitcases and then he came back up again and gave me three dollars."*

And a night in Ireland in Mariani:

> *First the telephone failed, then the electricity. When he tried to leave the darkened house to make a call from the village, he could not find his way out, and had to grope back up the stairs to his top-floor apartment. In the morning, it was the cleaning woman who released him. . . . he told her that Castletown "was a very bad place" and needed an elevator. Then he carried his own suitcases down, climbed back up, and handed her three dollars.*

None of the passages in Mariani acknowledges Hamilton as its source, and none seems to derive from some unacknowledged third source. The passages on McCarthy and Ireland come from interviews done by Hamilton. There are dozens of such parallel passages, and many others where the writing seems to have been done with one eye on Hamilton and the other on the computer screen. Hamilton's prose and Hamilton's quotations are the paraphrased and filleted matter of this book.

The violence men do to others is as nothing to the violence they do to themselves. Lowell used his estranged wife's letters in the poems of *The Dolphin*—a punishment that was no less a punishment of himself (though the insensitivity of Caligula is more despicable than the self-mortification of Caliban)—and the ruptures and upheavals of his life found transfigured form in the poetry. That poetry, however undervalued in our age of prose, is the raw and unkempt visage of our late century—the torsions in Lowell, political and personal, have torn further since his death (his books tended to pair into raw and cooked forms of the same formal and expressive tendencies: *Lord Weary's Castle* and *The Mills of the Kavanaughs; Life Studies* and *For the Union Dead; Notebook* and the simultaneously issued *History* and *For Lizzie and Harriet* and *The Dolphin*). This is a minor period for a major poet. Even so, the force and influence of this personality have overwhelmed his biographer. Lowell, after all, plagiarized his own life.

chapter 16

Verse Chronicle:
Old Guys

Charles Simic

Mitteleuropa surrealism isn't what it was when the Balkans, the Orthodox Church, and the Ottoman Empire brooded in the background. Surrealist poems, those uncompromising, gritty, erotic protests against logic or meaning, were once the dreams Kafka suffered, the dreams of an insurance clerk. In America, surrealists like Charles Simic write like this:

> *They had already attached the evening's tears to the windowpanes.*
> *The general was busy with the ant farm in his head.*
> *The holy saints in their tombs were burning, all except one who*
>   *was a prisoner of a dark-haired movie star.*

Fanciful, mild-mannered (you're in danger of stubbing your toe on the meaning), the poems in *Walking the Black Cat* often sound like translations, or merely like translators. (Many American surrealists seem to know the originals only in translation—why *shouldn't* they sound like translators?) Surrealism isn't the same in Simic's land of hamburger stands, snack food, and drive-in movies.

Simic's recent poems favor whimsical, offbeat subjects: bad TV reception, kitchen implements that talk back, a charm-school proprietor, a garden of barbed wire. Or they're about wives, playing cards, cats (a lot of cats), ghosts, any old thing, as long as it can be treated in easy-chair fashion. At worst the poems break down into a shudder of random statement and low-voltage detail: "The blue trees argue with the red wind. // The white mare has a peacock for a servant." Who would have thought even surrealism would come down to its clichés?

Simic wasn't always so civilized. His childhood was spent in Yugoslavia and his first language was Serbo-Croatian, so he knew about war (as a boy he stole helmets and ammunition from dead German soldiers). There was a quiet menace to his early books, *Dismantling the Silence* (1971) and *Return to a Place Lit by a Glass of Milk* (1974), the precision of nightmare made flesh. When he was young, he knew how to be savage (the arthritis set in long before he won his Pulitzer). Now he can barely be bothered to put two spirited words together. His poems exist in moral negation—there's no living emotion anymore, just literary hamming (for him, the emotion was once in the seeing). His wiseguy manner is a defense against feeling, which is fine if your readers are refrigerators.

Rocky was a regular guy, a loyal friend.
The trouble was he was only a cat.
Let's practice, he'd say, and he'd pounce
On his shadow on the wall.

When a poem begins like this, you hope it was written at gunpoint.

Sometimes Simic starts smirking, as if he thought he were Ashbery or James Tate. Few lines remind you of the poet he once was (when time and eternity "Cast no image / As they admire themselves in the mirror," you think—Oh! Vampires!). A poem titled "Slaughterhouse Flies" ("Evenings, they ran their bloody feet / Over the pages of my schoolbooks") is suggestive and creepy, and "Cameo Appearance" treats politics as Beckett might. But too often now Simic sounds like a poet working on a merit badge. Poetry isn't suited to aesthetic denial, unless you're an ascetic; and it isn't suited to emotional denial, either, unless you're one of the living dead.

A. R. Ammons

A. R. Ammons has always been a crotchety, damaged, unlikely poet, a modern Diogenes living in a bathtub and grousing about nature and metaphysics. If he starts a poem, "Rock frozen and fractured / spills, a shambles," you know he'll soon come to phrases like "tiers of time" and "metaphysical debris." He can't walk through a forest without being bushwhacked by mortality and ontology (you end up thinking he couldn't *possibly* walk through that many forests). Most people go to the forests to get away from the metaphysics.

Words like *thicket* and *parameter* are always suggestive together, as long as you don't try to explain *why* they're suggestive. The naked concrete noun and the naked abstract term are a marriage made in Plato's cave (and attended by Shrödinger's cat). Ammons records the transient, devious nature of mind at meditation; and his best poems tend to be large, unfolding road maps of passing fancy, AAA itineraries through all the small towns of the brain.

> *In a time of big cars, a small car raises eyebrows:*
> *this law, lowly derived, is as high as any other sky:*
> *contempt, amusement, curiosity: but if then the cars*
>
> *switched, big to small, the law would remain the same:*
> *another law, older than Kepler: (trilliums by the*
> *trillion whitened the slopes broken down by brooks,*
>
> *I noticed the other day as I rode in my car, small, as*
> *it happened): I don't know: I just have a few words*
> *to say: it's not my world, no: even though it is*
>
> *the only world and, so, mine or not, mine.*

This is an ungainly mixture of genius and junk—Ammons would be preening at the Apocalypse, but always noticing, noticing, noticing. He's a poet whose faults are hard to like and whose virtues hard to respect. His last book, titled *Garbage* (with a leaden dose of irony), was a splendidly out-at-elbows treatise on all our junk dreams. *Brink Road* is a bottom drawer of a book, some of the poems uncollected for more than two decades, most of them expressions of a mode long perfected: the poems jigger this way and that, argue out of both sides of their mouths—they're pell-mell, hobble-knobble, zigzag affairs, fretful and confounding by turns.

There's little to protect such poetry from prose, and often all that salvages it from prose are the white spaces—only the spaces of poetry make this poetry. Without them, we would be left with:

Poems are forms of protective coloration by which a person insecure in his true colors takes trial stances of coloration to imitate true colors or to baffle detection, either by simple baffling or by adopting disguise of common conventions or to direct attention from his differences by putting on the unconventional act.

Ammons's flaws are so disfiguring it's impossible not to notice them: a lot of his poems are tedious (you trudge through the metaphysics to get to the nature, but it wasn't worth the trudge); they're ponderous, muddled performances, terrible and trivial at once, like an elephant balanced on a pinhead. Just when you fall in love with a stripped-bare description of the natural world, or an improbable insight into the human, he'll start a poem, "Anxiety clears meat chunks out of the stew, carrots, takes / the skimmer to floats of greasy globules," or succumb to blather like "The flow-finding of the making impulse / rounds the curves of what-is / and shakes out scaffolding / suitable to the outline of the perception." He'll end a confused rumination on the limits of nature with a line so awful it ought to receive some sort of prize: "remarkable sucked fizzy drinks burning the mucous."

Ammons doesn't always take himself seriously—a big galoot of a poet, he's proud of being nearly unreadable (his poems "bowing to no one, nonpatronizing and ungrateful") but knows he likes to be read. You can tell it gets under his skin when a review says he falls "far short of Stevens"—but it's true, he does fall far short of Stevens. Often he falls far short of Ammons (when he refers to Stevens, he soon drags in the Flintstones, too). He's not the philosopher-in-a-banker's-suit Stevens or the woodsy moral-hunter Frost, though he's a bit of a Yankee (by adoption) and was once a bit of a business executive. And yet. And yet, he's a much deeper poet than he sometimes appears to be (a poet who can write, "The quickest / way / to change // the / world is / to // like it / the / way it // is," has no business being deep); and in glimpses, at odd angles, the mortal lessons take the prosy metaphysics into pressures you never thought they could survive. He thinks about the world in a way poets rarely do, but only his "tinctured core of brutality" redeems means so limited and yet so grandiose.

Robert Hass

Robert Hass is a man of letters in the California mode, devotee of Eastern philosophy but also Eastern Europe, translator of classical haiku as well as Czeslaw Milosz. His rangy, laid-back essays, collected in *Twentieth Century Pleasures* (1984), are the record of a reader, a reader in love (such a meticulous nurse of his own pulse he's almost a hypochondriac). There's a goofy, Summer of Love innocence to his poems (few serious poets would attempt an aria about snot), but also a sharp-eyed suspicion of authority, especially the romantic authority of poetry itself.

Sun under Wood is full of romantic gestures. Hass can scarcely pass a tree without falling into a swoon—he would love to have written "This Lime-Tree Bower My Prison."

> *This morning in the early sun,*
> *steam rising from the pond the color of smoky topaz,*
> *a pair of delicate, copper-red, needle-fine insects*
> *are mating in the unopened crown of a Shasta daisy.*

Such lines are ravishing, blooming into vision like Impressionist paintings; but every swoon comes with its little load of guilt and shame. Hass has grown increasingly skeptical of poetry's illusion, and many of these poems are about writing poems. He'll start a poem, "Maybe you need to write a poem about grace," or remark on a description of creek stones, "'It is good sometimes that poetry should disenchant us,' / I wrote, and something about 'the heart's huge vacancy,' / which seemed contemptible." A poem titled "Layover" is followed by the prose poem "Notes on 'Layover,'" details and incidents he might have included, but did not.

The fashionable term for such radical nihilism is deconstruction (not so fashionable, if even poets are familiar with it), but it's often hall-of-mirrors narcissism. Most readers assume a poem was written, that a writer did not compose in the heat of battle or passion the words that lie so easily on the page. Few readers want to be told, line by line, that the ink dried up, the writer was hungry, the visitor from Porlock was knocking on the front door again, because few readers want to be treated as slightly retarded.

Hass's dry self-examinations have a faintly puritanical edge, as if the reader's sublimation in pleasure were illicit. The midget commissar at the center of his verse can never admit that even the breaking of illusion is an illusion—the writer was writing then, too. Many of the poet laureate's new poems, when they aren't about his own poems, are ragbag suites or odes, flitting from subject to subject (a poet tired of "subjects" is often reduced to writing about writing), their concerns unified only by the writer's illusion of impulse—they are the progress of their own pathology. A poem that moves from his broken marriage through his brother's crack addiction, a trip to Korea, Derrida, and torture yearns to make things whole. The memorable lines have nothing to do with arthouse artifice.

> *In the town center*
> *of Kwangju, there was a late October market fair.*
> *Some guy was barbecuing halfs of baby chicks on a long, sooty con-*
> *traption*
> *of a grill, slathering them with soy sauce. Baby chicks.*

This has the studied common touch ("Some guy . . ."), but it's direct and discomforting. When he writes of his marriage or his alcoholic mother, the intensity of emotion overcomes his primness about illusion; yet such passages cannot atone for the aimless notebook narratives, the occasional giddy awfulness (little songs about his mother's nipples: "What could be more fair / than les nipples de ma mère?"), or a few lines of callow self-absorption ("There ought to be some single word / For the misery of divorce. / It dines upon you casually / duh-dduh-duh-duh-dduh-fierce/remorse/pierce").

Hass is at times a rare and original poet. He's willing to try things no one else would and willing to fail at them, too (and contemplate the failure, and bat it around with his paw). His sweet, aw-shucks reasonableness can get on your nerves—he doesn't have much time for catharsis or pity. If he's a blander version of Rexroth, he reminds you of a time when we *had* autodidacts and iconoclasts like Rexroth. Hass's better poems sustain themselves within their ambiguities, acknowledging the pain they work hard to avert.

> *She says to him, musing, "If you ever leave me,*
> *and marry a younger woman and have another baby,*
> *I'll put a knife in your heart." They are in bed,*
> *so she climbs onto his chest, and looks directly*
> *down into his eyes. "You understand? Your heart."*

In a poet uncomfortable with the sly suggestiveness of language, "musing" is all too suggestive of a muse whose looks could kill.

C. K. Williams

Sigmund Freud of voyeurs, analyst and analysand of complex states of watching, C. K. Williams has accepted the labor of observation with an almost religious devotion. We look to religion for words like *passion*, which has infected our image of love with a theology of suffering. In *The Vigil*, as in his recent books, Williams has turned the long verse line of Whitman, that brawny lover of men, of laborers and loungers, into the medium of modern urban anxiety, of naked souls in the naked city. It is not without religious instinct that such densely neurotic notation of the inner life has been called *confession*.

Williams is a small-town, Sinclair Lewis busybody about the lives of others—a store clerk murdered in a holdup, his dying caught on camera; an old acquaintance beaten to death in an alley; a retarded woman given a peanut to eat before a little audience of ladies; a neighbor who keeps a wretched menagerie in her apartment:

> *Her five horrid, deformed little dogs, who incessantly yap on the*
> *roof under my window;*
> *her cats, god knows how many, who must piss on her rugs—her*
> *landing's a sickening reek. . . .*

If you're not squeamish, Williams makes you *want* to be squeamish. Soon that poor old woman is not just mad, she's Medea. Williams's gift, if it is a gift, is to turn the most loathsome observations against himself; the ravaged presence of this woman is shadowed by memories of a lover he'd once been cruel to—as if, in some Borgesian reality, they might be the same woman. They're not, and he knows they're not; but at the center of his disgust is a kind of erotic longing. His own sins are the first to be written.

Unfortunately, Williams also has other designs upon the reader. He loves the extra gush of significance that places his poems deep in the annals of bathos: "the true history I inhabit, its sea of suffering, its wave to which I am froth, scum" or "Quickly, never mind death, never mind mute, oblivious, onrushing time: wake, hold me!" or "the leaves quake, and Oh, I throw myself this way, the trees say, then that way, I tremble, / I moan, and still you don't understand the absence I'll be in the void of unredeemable time."

Such lines confirm your worst fears—that the poet is a little too aroused by his own nakedness. Many of these poems are anatomy lessons (you feel Williams would like to buy a textbook and take out his own appendix). The poet watches himself, watches those around him (in a way that must be excruciating to them), watches the poems that will never relieve him of responsibility for what he observes. Here and there, in "Hawk" and "Insight" and "The Lover," Williams achieves a passionate despair that rivals Edwin Arlington Robinson's lesson in neurotic psychology, "Eros Turannos."

> *at first she thinks it's just coincidence; after all, she knows she's*
> *sometimes wrong,*
> *everyone is sometimes wrong, but with him now all there seem to*
> *be are sides, she's always wrong;*
> *even when she doesn't know she's arguing, when she doesn't care,*
> *he finds her wrong,*

in herself it seems she's wrong, she feels she should apologize, to
someone, anyone, to him;
him, him, him; what is it that he wants from her: remorse, con-
trition, should she just die?

The rising panic is precisely pitched on the rhyming of wrongs. At such moments the poet's loss of shame becomes a perfected form of guilt. Far too many poems, however, are like watching a dog eat its own vomit.

Williams must hope, vainly, that watching can change things, even when he knows that nothing can change (why else would he be so attracted to transformation, to poets like Ovid and Rilke?). If things could change, we would not have to die. Williams's poetry seeks absolution, and confession must always come before absolution. You leave his poems, as you leave most rituals, feeling more soiled than ever.

Joseph Brodsky

The death of Joseph Brodsky last January invited the usual pieties for an unusual public career. Brodsky had been adopted by this country with old-fashioned warmth, the way it adopted Nureyev and Baryshnikov and would have adopted Solzhenitysn, had he not retreated into his Vermont gulag of barbed wire. Brodsky, forcibly exiled from the Soviet Union in 1972 (therefore passing most of his adult life in America), was a rakish, engaging, impish character—the Byronic gestures were not unconscious—and it was hard to see beyond that character to the poetry. The poems were obscured not just by the difficulties of translation.

Brodsky was fortunate in his translators, at least until he took the major role himself (if a lawyer who hires himself has a fool for a client, a poet who translates himself has an idiot for a translator). Earlier translators gave his work English sense and style, at the cost of making him sound like Wilbur when the translator was Wilbur, Hecht when the translator was Hecht (many American poets would like to be translated into the English of Wilbur or Hecht). It was not clear, however, how much of this Russo-Wilbur or Russo-Hecht was Brodsky.

Most of the poems in *So Forth* were written in English or translated into English by the author; reading their wayward, tone-deaf lines makes you admire Nabokov and Conrad. Languages may be acquired late, but foreign words are first learned in equal weight or measure—it takes years to absorb the nuance necessary for literary composition. Nabokov and Conrad are test cases of English acquisition (as Beckett might be the parallel case for French); but Conrad didn't write poetry, while Nabokov's *Pale Fire* and his translation of *Eugene Onegin* prove how difficult English poetry is for a foreign ear (Nabokov was a genius in English prose, a minor workman at English poetry). Brodsky wrote English prose with rapacious appetite and fluency, but his poetry often sounds like verse by Humbert Humbert. You hear, as if through a lath-and-plaster wall, a noble, muffled intelligence. In his essay "To Please a Shadow," Brodsky claimed he wrote in English only to get closer to Auden, and some of his poems sound like Auden read through a pair of tin cans connected by string.

What are we to think when a poet as gifted as Brodsky, a Nobel laureate, writes, "one keeps carving notches only / so long as nobody apes one" or "the tear could be mine, chin-bound" or "the eye tracks the sinking soap, though it's the foam that's famous"? Or "the battle looks from afar like—'aaagh' carved in stone" and "seven / years later and pints of semen / under the bridge" and "a cross between muscular torso and horse's ibid" and "O if the transparent things in their blue garret / could hold their eye-dodging matter in second gear"? The words are generally right, but all their music is wrong (the words aren't always right—"you'll cock up your double-barrel," he says, cocking it up). When a foreign poet writes as if his fingers were in casts, you blame the translators—and Brodsky wasn't always his own translator. He worked with another translator to produce this:

Twilight in the new life. Cicadas that don't relent.
A classicist perspective that lacks a tank or,
barring that, dank fog patches to obfuscate its end;
a bare parquet floor that never sustained a tango.
In the new life, no one begs the moment, "Stay!"

Brought to a standstill, it quickly succumbs to dotage.
And your features, on top of that, are glazed enough anyway
for scratching their matte side with "Hi" and attaching the
*   postage.*

This sounds like Edith Sitwell on a good day or Ashbery on a bad one. As his own translator, Brodsky succumbed to:

Sweetheart, losing your looks, go to live in a village.
Mirrors there crave mildew, no maiden's visage.
A river, too, comes with ripples; and fields, in furrows,
clearly forgot for good about stocky fellows.

And in English he wrote,

"Right," says the Emperor. "Our enemy
*   is powerful, mean, and brash.*
But we'll administer him such an enema
*   his toilet won't need a flush.*

Rhyme was a method of organization disastrous to Brodsky's style, yet he used it like an addict. English is resistant enough to a foreign tongue, likely to pronounce all sorts of unlikely words as if they were rhymes; but Brodsky could torture his syntax for a rhyme perfectly awful, and even rhymes Cole Porter would have loved (*Noah / spermatozoa*) don't have lines to make them lovely.

When we read poems that go wrong in so many ways (almost always the ways of the ear), we're reminded how much we know about our language without knowing it. A native speaker would never write, I hope, "However you hide the ace, / the table gets hit with jacks of some odd suit and tailor" or "the world changes so fast, as if / indeed at a certain point it began to mainline / some muck obtained from a swarthy alien" (probably not a man from Mars).

Brodsky wasn't always this bad. "Nativity" opens:

No matter what went on around them; no matter
what message the snowstorm was straining to utter;
or how crowded they thought that wooden affair;
or that there was nothing for them anywhere. . . .

"Utter" and "affair" are off-key, but the simplicity of this is otherwise its salvation. Or consider this Audenesque quatrain:

Birds acquaint themselves with leaves.
Hired hands roll up their sleeves.
In a brick malodorous dorm
boys awake awash in sperm.

Brodsky's career in English was a career of might-have-beens. He plainly wanted to stake his claim in two languages (his essays may be his lasting achievement in English); but his pride could not accept his limitations, while mere ambition could not overcome the absence of what a native speaker absorbs through his pores. We read foreign poetry not for its music—for what is lost in translation—but for its angle of vision and strangeness of attack, for an architecture foreign to us, not imprisoned in the conventions of English verse (which for most poets mean the practices of their contemporaries). These autumnal poems of death and decay, turning often to elegy, show beneath the dead matter of translation that freshening of the foreign. But the poems themselves are now an elegy for great ambition.

Anthony Hecht

Anthony Hecht's new book, *Flight among the Tombs*, opens with a collaboration with Leonard Baskin, whose nearly two dozen engravings of Death are densely inked nightmares of skeletal figure, a Who's Who of cadaverous posture and macabre costume. Hecht's elegant and dryly witty commentaries look beyond the grave by looking at the grave. He must have jumped at the chance to caption such illustrations, the poems have such a show-offy, self-satisfied air, one a little at odds with their subject. Hecht has always been a brooding, melancholy character (sometimes the melancholy has been purchased wholesale), and the pitiless glances of his work have been a stern reminder of a world of violence and holocaust beneath the sweet inconsequentiality of our poetry.

Death abides in life, poets are forever reminding us—we live already swaddled in our burial clothes. Here is "Death the Oxford Don":

Sole heir to a distinguished laureate,
I serve as guardian to his grand estate,
And grudgingly admit the unwashed herds
To the ten-point mausoleum of his words.
Acquiring over years the appetite
And feeding habits of a parasite,
I live off the cold corpus of fine print,
Habited with black robes and heart of flint,
The word made flesh for me and me alone.
I gnaw and gnaw the satisfactory bone.

No poet since Pope has written of scholars with more disdain, and Hecht revels in the ironies of his own long life as an academic (what would humor be without a little self-hatred?). Hecht takes the measure of engravers, too; but Death appears in so many guises (poet, painter, carnival barker, judge, punchinello), the sequence has the festive spirit of a Dance of Death.

There are gorgeously rendered passages throughout this sequence, and two or three poems of fatal, moving eloquence. The longest, "Death the Whore," is an unsparing portrait (like Hecht's haunting poem "The Deodand") of the depravity of the sexual gaze—only Hecht could suffuse *Victoria's Secret* catalogues with the smoke of a crematorium. Hecht's strength as a poet, apart from his easy knowing meter (full of little trysts and elopements), has been this willingness to take the modern on its own terms, to embrace the detritus of popular culture as if it too had secrets to reveal.

The sequence otherwise is disappointingly workmanlike—the verse is professional, artfully crafted, all the sawdust swept out of view; but it is the disinterested labor of a man paid for a job of work. At times Hecht hasn't taken advantage of the subject: "Death the Film Director" might have reminded us how devoted photography has been to death (in the cinema, to the scapegoat death of actors), how all photographs are in the end portraits of the dead. Instead we get shallow ridicule of Hollywood. The worst poems end with cheesy puns or clichés ("Death Riding into Town" compares Death to Clint Eastwood and ends, "Go ahead, make my day!").

The dozen or so poems in the remainder of the book are reminders of Hecht's graces: reworkings of Meleager and Horace, a villanelle, elegies for James Merrill and Joseph Brodsky (so fulsome it might have been written by one of those state poets Brodsky despised), a clutch of poems on classical themes, smelling at times of mildew ("Yet she is wed, in heaven or hell's despite, / To an ignoble, titled troglodyte"). One of these, however, is a devastating picture of a Latin class, with all the pathos of the boys' halting mistranslations and the teacher's undeciphered homoerotic longing.

> *"Thompson," he'd murmur, "please instruct our class."*
> *And Thompson would venture, timidly, much rattled,*
> *"Caesar did withhold his men from battle,*
> *And he did have enough in presentness*
>
> *To prohibit the enemy from further wastings,*
> *From foragings and rapines." And through a long*
> *Winter campaign of floundering, grief, and wrong,*
> *That little army force-marched without resting.*

"That little army" is the class, and you're reminded that many armies have been made of boys not much older. The stumbling, desperate, hopeless march toward learning is nearly heartbreaking (if this were Greek class, you'd wait—in vain!—for them to get to the mountaintop with Xenophon and shout *Thalassa! Thalassa!*), and you can tell Hecht delights in all he implies about classes, and teachers, and learning. "Proust on Skates" doesn't come to much, but it opens with one of those passages that begs to be quoted:

> *The alpine forests, like huddled throngs of mourners,*
> *Black, hooded, silent, resign themselves to wait*
>   *As long as may be required;*
> *A low pneumonia mist covers the glaciers,*
> *Spruces are bathed in a cold sweat, the late*
>   *Sun has long since expired.*

Flight among the Tombs contains little of Hecht's best work, his acidic lines on human nature (nature nature, too), his astringent, moral colloquy with history. But in a long and magnificient career he's written dozens of poems I've nearly read the ink off of, have taught and quoted with pleasure, among them "Third Avenue in Sunlight," "Behold the Lilies of the Field," "The Dover Bitch," "'More Light! More Light!,'" "'It Out-Herods Herod. Pray You, Avoid It,'" "The Cost," "An Autumnal," "The Ghost in the Martini," "The Deodand," "An Overview," "Persistences," "The Book of Yolek." Very few poets have ever handled English words with such devotion, and Hecht has written with extraordinary passion into late age (always dry, dry passion—like a martini mixed with the memory of vermouth). We have had no better poet of war to honor these decades of peace, or what we have chosen to call peace.

chapter 17

Verse Chronicle:
Hardscrabble Country

Charles Wright

Charles Wright's poetry is the last refuge of nineteenth-century oratory—his overwrought syntax is its own religion. In early books he tried on various styles like a man changing hats. He never made any of the hats his own, and the hats never made him their own, either—they were just hats. For the past decade, as middle age has become mortal, his poems have settled into loose, baggy journals heavily influenced by Ezra Pound. The sea-chop of rhythm, the epigrammatic line, the snatch of foreign language—all are the lost property of a great flawed poet.

> *Through language, strict attention—*
> Verona mi fe', disfecemi Verona, *the song goes.*
> *I've hummed it, I've bridged the break*
>
> *To no avail.*
> *April. The year begins beyond words,*
> *Beyond myself and the image of myself, beyond*
> *Moon's ice and summer's thunder. All that.*

The style seems less a homage than a way of avoiding argument.

Black Zodiac opens with an "Apologia pro Vita Sua"—it's not often a poet is drawn to Cardinal Newman these days. If there's a religious crisis here, it is beyond the reach of style. The poems are usually arranged in short, unattached sections with only the most distracted relation to one another; they stop and start, and get mired in metaphysics. When a poet sinks into his attitudes, mortal thoughts are near; and if he writes, "Time is the source of all good, / time the engenderer / Of entropy and decay, / Time the destroyer, our only-begetter and advocate," you know Eliot and Anglo-Catholicism hover in the background.

Wright threatens to open a minimart of metaphysics. His poems are full of vague notions and vaguer discontents. It's not that I'm deaf to metaphysics; it's that these conundrums were old a century ago—the poets they were alive for are the dust of our anthologies. None of them would have let his metaphysics be muddled with Wright's country sentiment and aw-shucks naïveté: "If God hurt the way we hurt, / he, too, would be heart-sore"; "Can we address a blade of grass, the immensity of a snowflake?"; "The meat of the sacrament is invisible meat and a ghostly substance. / I'll say." If this is innocence, give me experience any day.

It's not clear whether the religious vocabulary reaches for redemption or recognizes that in our secular age even the language of religion has been soiled. The sacred overlay isn't particularly convincing—when Wright composes his "Lives of the Saints," the saints seem to be poets, a romantic and self-pitying idea if ever there was one. He has written with bitter fondness of childhood in hardscrabble country (poets of small towns always recall life as a little hardscrabble), but the religion here doesn't rise from clapboard churches and the mysticism of Southern childhood. It has the scent of Gothic cathedrals and poetry anthologies.

Wright is one of the best poets of his generation, the generation born after Black Tuesday and before the end of World War II. Few poets this good write so pointlessly, but line by line he is a master of gorgeous effects. In a haze of vacant meditation, he has not lost his eye for the natural world.

Nothing is flat-lit and tabula rasaed in Charlottesville,
Umbrian sackcloth,
     stigmata and Stabat mater,
A sleep and a death away,

Night, and a sleep and a death away—
Light's frost-fired and Byzantine here,
                              aureate, beehived,
Falling in Heraclitean streams
Through my neighbor's maple trees.

Umbria and the stigmata and Byzantium and Heraclitus aren't really necessary (living in Charlottesville must be a lot more interesting than I'd suspected), but Wright bothers to see the world—or to imagine it, which is almost better. If his nature is always vivid in the same way, the "sky white as raw silk" and the "willows, medusa-hooded and bone-browed" are the small affairs of spirit his Chinese-sage ventures never approach. A poet who can write, "a little wind / whiffles across the back yard like a squall line" and dozens of other lines as redolent and restless ought to be writing poems, not notes for notes for poems. The sketchy descriptions are lovely, but they're lazy. You could churn out such stuff every day (in *Zone Journals* [1988], Wright did exactly that), and it would cost you nothing.

It's hard to care about poems so resolute in their absences, so deft in their mean evasions. Wright seems to make evasion a moral principle, as if it were the only way to capture the transitory. (If Eliot's hollow men wrote poetry, it would be poetry like this.) These poems are like paintings by Seurat. You back away from the colorful dots and a ghostly image appears, but the image is still made of dots. Wright has worked all his life to perfect a way to say the important thing, only to find he has nothing to say.

Michael Lind

Michael Lind's *The Alamo* isn't as awful as you'd think—not nearly as awful as it might have been. This six-thousand-line epic in rhyme royal is one of those silly ideas that possesses young poets, or used to—there haven't been this many bad rhymed stanzas since Vikram Seth's *Golden Gate*. Lind, a defector from conservative political commentary (author of *The Next American Nation* and *Up from Conservatism*), has done his research and had the historian's nightmare—so many anecdotes, so little space. His epic is stuffed with names if not faces, and every defender of the Alamo gets at least a line for his tombstone.

Americans revel in their old defeats: the Alamo, Pearl Harbor, and Custer's Last Stand are commemorated in the national memory more warmly, and more brazenly, than the victories that followed. Given less of a sweet tooth for nobility and martial valor (the poem is dedicated "to the men and women of the Armed Forces of the United States of America and their families"—I like that *and their families*), Lind might have done for William Travis and his men what Evan S. Connell did for Custer. A minutely detailed account of the battle could dispel the myths more brutally than these jingling stanzas.

Lind has a gift for the arresting phrase: his metaphors and epic similes have a precision missing in contemporary poetry. When Sam Houston becomes a snapping turtle, or Santa Anna's cavalry murder the wounded, "wielding their spears as bargemen would use / their staffs to lever flatboats," or Mexican troops attack the Alamo, "adhesive coils of a colossal squid / smothering a whale caught in its weird / embrace," you're startled by how fresh the antique device seems. The backwoods stumpery of Houston and Crockett flaunts its cracker-barrel wit, and other speeches are drily based on classical models (Travis rouses his officers in the voice of Sarpedon speaking to Glaucus). When a woman and her children defend a fort with her underwear, or new rebels ride across the uncovered graveyard of rebels slaughtered twenty years before, the irony could scarcely be more poker-faced.

Unfortunately, Lind's modest poetic gifts are overwhelmed by all the accidental comedy to which a minor poet is subject. His lines galumph along in pentameter, mostly without complaint (though sometimes they lose a foot in battle); but his idea of storytelling comes from supermarket bodice-rippers—with a suitably lurid cover, this might have been called *Tongues of Flame*. His characters are miniature, glossy versions of their historical selves, a TV-movie waxworks of superficial action.

Lind's major negative asset is a hilarious insensitivity to tone. One hopes Travis never said, "Each petty state would be its neigh-

bor's vampire, / till Britain, France, or Russia played the umpire."
A Mexican officer arrives, "his posture stiff, pace brisk, and aspect
worried. / At his approach, gloves blizzarded and flurried." As a
soldier dies, "he tasted sour cud, / his knees went flaccid, and he
slapped the mud." The images are ludicrously up to date. Santa
Anna "scowls, barks, paces like a coach / upon the sidelines in a
frantic game," and later the Alamo becomes the Astrodome: "Far
off, the Alamo looked like a sports / arena, like a stadium by night,
/ where scores are marked by cheering." His vocabulary is some-
times preposterously inflated ("their contumelious suzerain, / a
skewbald stallion") or his imagery comically askew ("Darst, bayo-
neted, left a family / headless in Gonzales"). When children are
bayoneted, "red began to rim / the tiny mouths like mustaches of
jam." Snatches of quotation cannot quite reveal the genial blunder-
ing of the whole martial melodrama:

> *Muskets flamed*
> *and metal swished through flesh. Moaning and maimed,*
> *Bill Blazeby, Captain of the New Orleans Greys,*
> *rolled down the cold dirt rampart in a daze;*

> *his forty-one-year journey from his home*
> *in England through New York and then the port*
> *of New Orleans brought him here, to soak the loam*
> *of Bexar with puddling blood.*

Metal swished through flesh! Soak the loam! We are back in *Ivanhoe.*
The view of battle is so cloyingly naive and piously sentimental,
you expect the dying defenders to break into "The Streets of
Laredo." This version of the Alamo is fit for schoolrooms (you'd
think Texas was born in a manger)—it wears its patriotism on its
sleeve. Lind doesn't do everything wrong (his view of Santa Anna
is remarkably evenhanded); but how, just before battle, can a poet
launch into half-a-dozen stanzas of science fiction to suggest the
Alamo is small in the scheme of things? Davy Crockett and Jim
Bowie, meet "two-legged reptile warriors," "squeaking grubs," and
"leopard-colored slugs."

Mary Oliver

Mary Oliver's bland, consolatory poetry is a favorite of people who don't like poetry (it's a favorite of some poets as well, but then poets often don't like poetry, either). Sometimes in *West Wind* she'll write of small incidents—finding a dead snake or rescuing a field mouse—but mostly she wants to Appreciate Nature. *This is just the way I am,* her poems seem to say; *I love nature to death, why don't you, you pitiful stay-at-home reader of poetry, you?* Reading her poems is like joining a garden club where the members are part of a plant-worshipping cult—no wonder they feel holier than thou. When Oliver looks into her yard, she thinks of the Buddha arising. And herself? She's likely to be lifted into the air by rapture ("as though I had shaken my arms and *lo!* they were wings").

It's one thing for a poet to cultivate a wide-eyed persona capable of saying, "What can we do / but keep on breathing in and out . . . ?" or "How can I hope to be friends / with the hard white stars . . . ?" This is just a version of Little Me poetry that went out with bobbysocks and Shirley Temples. But it's a bit much when such a poet says, "What will ambition do for me that the fox . . . / has not already done?" Oliver has an agent and has not objected to the National Book Award and the Pulitzer Prize. She's not spending all her spare moments working on transcendence. Usually she's writing gimcrack Whitman instead:

Am I not among the early risers
and the long-distance walkers?

Have I not stood, amazed, as I consider
the perfection of the morning star
above the peaks of the houses, and the crowns of the trees blue in
the first light? . . .

Above the modest house and the palace—the same darkness.
Above the evil man and the just, the same stars.
Above the child who will recover and the child who will not re-
cover, the same energies roll forward,
from one tragedy to the next and from one foolishness to the next.

I bow down.

I bow down! There's the humble self-dramatizing touch. Whitman was gimcrack, too, but we forgive him because he was a genius of gimcrack.

Oliver's head is filled with such good-natured mush. You'd love to have her for a next-door neighbor, though you'd worry that she spends too much time in the yard, looking up at the sky. She loves nature (out by her trees she pulls up a pew), but she loves gushing about nature even more: "How the sky flares and grows brighter, all the time! / How time extends!"; "I would touch the faces of the daisies, / and I would bow down / to think about it"; "Snowflakes, coasting into the winter woods, making a very small sound, like this / soooooooooooooooooooooooooooooooooooooooooooo." I begin to long for some sign of six millennia of culture—a fork, say, or a cell phone.

Oliver's poetry is allergic to the interesting word. It's almost always "cold, black fields" or "white skull" or "pure, deep darkness," poetry stripped to its elements, but also stripped of its distinctiveness. When she writes of some black oaks, "I'm pale with longing for their thick bodies ruckled with lichen," at *ruckled* you almost fall over in shock. Perhaps we need plain language and plain sentiment for plain times, but such poetry has all the defects of prose (how Shelley would cringe at what Shelleyesque has become) and none of the virtues of poetry. A poetry so limited in its means and devastated in its imaginings is also deadened to its responsibilities—it's as if poetry meant nothing but a few gestures toward the sentiment of meaning. A baroque revival must be just around the corner. Of course no poet means to be dishonest in her responses; but sometimes language itself is a dishonesty, its responses hardened to cliché. Clichés aren't a neural form of truth; they're truth frozen into fraud.

Robert Bly

When he was a young man, Ezra Pound scribbled a sonnet every morning before breakfast. After a month or two, he had the good sense to throw the whole lot in the fire. A poet doesn't have to believe the Muse keeps appointments to see the virtues of regimen; and yet there's something pillowy and fin de siècle in Robert Bly's self-imposed discipline, to write a poem every morning before rising. *Morning Poems* has a dozy complacency (you feel some of it was written before waking). The book is composed in simple, declarative sentences, full of "wisdom" and "sentiment," as if these were ingredients found in any supermarket; and like a Disney cartoon it's full of talking mice, talking cars, talking cats, talking trees. The poems peter out at sonnet length, the appetite for poetry exhausted where the appetite for breakfast begins.

> *One day a mouse called to me from his curly nest:*
> *"How do you sleep? I love curliness."*
>
> *"Well, I like to be stretched out. I like my bones to be*
> *All lined up. I like to see my toes way off over there."*
>
> *"I suppose that's one way," the mouse said, "but I don't like it.*
> *The planets don't act that way, nor the Milky Way."*
>
> *What could I say? You know you're near the end*
> *Of the century when a sleepy mouse brings in the Milky Way.*

This could hardly be more winsome or sickeningly ingenuous. After a few such trifles, just Aesop without his dentures (I'm especially fond of the talking wheat), a reader feels he has wandered into a children's book by mistake.

In their dotage, poets often go from rage to reason: angry young men rarely become angry old ones. An odd peaceableness falls over them, like a comforter, when they draw Social Security (even Pound grew sorry as a pumpkin and shriveled into silence). Bly was once a critic of captious temper, a scourge of bad poetry who'd have howled at the portentous hush of poems here ("The angels were certain. But we could not / Be certain whether our family was worthy tonight").

Since his days as a devoted *imagiste*, Bly has become the spokesman for New Age manliness; and whenever you hear of men running through the woods half-naked, beating on drums and declaring their manhood, you know he is partly to blame (the author of

Iron John collects a royalty on every drumbeat). Yet something of that earlier poet survives, the poet who wrote reams of anti-war poems, most of them awful, but a few the only lasting poetry to come out of the Vietnam War. Consider this poem of an older war:

> *"The Russians had few doctors on the front line.*
> *My father's job was this: after the battle*
> *Was over, he'd walk among the men hit,*
> *Sit down and ask: 'Would you like to die on your*
> *Own in a few hours, or should I finish it?'*
> *Most said, 'Don't leave me.' The two would have*
> *A cigarette. He'd take out his small notebook—*
> *We had no dogtags, you know—and write the man's*
> *Name down, his wife's, his children, his address, and what*
> *He wanted to say. When the cigarette was done,*
> *The soldier would turn his head to the side. My father*
> *Finished off four hundred men that way during the war.*
> *He never went crazy. They were his people."*

This has the war correspondent's merciless eye, and it's surprising that Bly's mercy elsewhere is just a method of sweet-talking the reader. The sugary seductiveness and mythopoeic posturing spoil poems with Auden's sense of destiny's accident and fate's misadventure: "the wind blows an ash / Into the anarchist's eye, and he pulls / The trigger too soon, and kills the King instead of / The fat factory owner, and then / A lot of men get on motorcycles." When wryness softens into whimsy, we're left with lines like "Some people inside my body last night / Married each other just in order to dance" or "He knew the moon was made of clogged magma, / And volcanic rinsings, and punk and dog poop."

The immanence of nature, the presence of the soul, the farm boy's earned experience come in for hard salesmanship here. When a poet wants to sell you something, you think you're listening to some yarn by a genial man on your doorstep, but soon you own forty acres of Florida swamp.

Les Murray

You can see why the British love Les Murray. He fulfills every British cliché about Australians—rough-mannered, Ur-Other rubes in the wilderness, the bastard progeny of jailer and jailed, they're the empire's loyal second-raters. Australian identity is one of Murray's favorite subjects. He's no joiner, and loathes people who are—gritty, doomed independence is another Australian cliché.

It's too easy to take Murray on his own outsize terms, a great shambling presence presiding over poetry down under (outsize in poetry as well as person—he makes much of being fat). The poetry in *Subhuman Redneck Poems* ranges from oafish social commentary to reminiscences dark with pathos, from simple descriptions of Fabergé-like intensity to gouts of feckless imagery. He can hardly get through a poem without disaster, and part of reading him is waiting for the disaster to happen—the pleasure isn't schadenfreude, it's suspense.

Murray catches the oddity of nature like a blowsy reincarnation of Marianne Moore: "cormorants with musket-hammer necks, plus / the clinician spoonbill, its long pout; // twilight's herons who were almost too lightfoot / to land; pearl galahs in pink-fronted / confederacy." Though he loves to jackhammer his images, he can have the delicate touch of an archeologist:

The impress of a whelk
in hard brown rock,

fluted as a plinth.
Its life gone utterly,

throb, wet and chalk,
left this shape-transmission,

a kin boat of fine brick.
Just off centre is a chip

healed before its death.

This is a series of balanced lines, each just two or three elements in tension; the reader has to read again to be sure *throb* is a noun, not a verb. The intelligence of such tension finds its way into last lines like "For all the death, we also die unrehearsed" or "Beyond choice, we see our loves as indigenes see land," which take poems out of their small rooms and put them in larger ones.

Murray has the scope and restless bearing of Auden—he's not afraid of subject, and will tackle any old thing: a hot-air balloon tragedy, Midas given the gift of metaphor, swearing, a retired lighthouse keeper, a genealogical chart as big as the galaxy, a mall inside Ayers Rock, the suburbs as a tale out of Kafka. His poems about an autistic child and a burned child are full of tenderness, without making the reader regret the sympathies of tenderness— the poems do not plead for the compassion they evoke.

There are other poets in Murray, almost all bad ones. Whole poems collapse in a jumble of messy, ungoverned images. He writes of the poor:

> *Destitution's an antique. The huge-headed*
> *are sad chaff blown by military bohemians.*
> *Their thin metal bowls are filled or not*
>
> *from the sky by deodorised descendants*
> *of a tart-tongued womb-noticing noblesse*
> *in the goffered hair-puddings of God's law*
>
> *who pumped pioneer bouillons with a potstick,*
> *or of dazzled human muesli poured from ships*
> *under the milk of smoke and decades.*

I can make sense of this, more or less (the editorializing is pretty thin), but by the time I get to "human muesli" it hardly seems worth the effort. I find myself rooting for Murray to make his clumsiness a virtue, though it almost never is. If poetry were a primal force, such plenitude would make him an Australian primitive (in poetry, alas, plenitude is a greater vice than parsimony). At times it's hard to tell, especially when he's rhyming, whether Murray's just playing dumb:

> *We are the Australians. Our history is short.*
> *This makes pastry chefs snotty and racehorses snort.*

It makes pride a blood poppy and work an export
and bars our trained minds from original thought.

You could excuse this in any number of ways—satire is a coiled, venomous form, sometimes turning on form. But the rhymes are just as dreadful elsewhere. The subject is schools:

Where humans can't leave and mustn't complain
there some will emerge who enjoy giving pain.

Snide universal testing leads them to each one
who will shrivel reliably, whom the rest will then shun.

Some who might have been chosen, and natural police,
do routine hurt, the catcalling, the giving no peace.

This seems badly translated out of Old Church Slavonic with only a Bulgarian phrase book at hand. Poets of such intelligence can seldom be quoted so plainly against themselves. The loutishness may be calculated; but the more you allow contempt to prove your independence from poetic tradition, the less free you are to invoke that tradition when it suits you. Only by incorporating the unpoetic can the poetic move forward, but bad poetry is no defense against rejection (least of all a revenge for schoolyard rejection). Poetry can give up many things, but when it loses the reader's trust it becomes hostage to its vices.

Edgar Bowers

Not all American poets stopped writing formal poetry after *Life Studies*, though sometimes it seems they did. The second free-verse revolution was more radical than the first, and for decades afterward rhyme and pentameter were as old-fashioned as a whalebone corset. Edgar Bowers was a fifties formalist, the best of the coterie surrounding Yvor Winters (himself still an underrated poet). Bowers's early books, *The Form of Loss* (1956) and *The Astronomers* (1965), were ignored for flashier talents like Wilbur and Merrill and darker ones like Hecht. *Living Together: New and Selected Poems* (1973) added half a dozen poems, but no new book appeared until *For Louis Pasteur* (1989). There was always something fussy and out of date about Bowers—even when pentameter was the fashion his was stuffy and genteel. The ten poems and a long sequence called "Mazes" new to *Collected Poems* show the style not changed but amplified. Bowers has remained a fifties poet, but now that seems a refreshing thing.

Bowers's lines have a weight, a capaciousness, even a resolve not many poets would attempt anymore. It's a pleasure to watch enjambment, the slow elaboration of perception through syntax, so artfully deployed (most poets use a hacksaw rather than a scalpel). His stiltedness has a wary subtlety, the mind moving, as if with armed guards, between the range of its particulars and the ruin of its abstractions. Poets rarely give such serious attention to the form of perception.

> *When Reichenbach treks with Stanley, his white ears*
> *Are tom-tom, labyrinths of chant, dark speech,*
> *Bull elephants, and lions at night; his eyes*
> *Green branch, black feather, antelope thick as dust,*
> *Hyenas at bloody offal thieved from lions;*
> *His skin the fly, the thing that crawls.*

The dense and weedy phrases, unusual in a poet at ease with extinction, crowd the jungle of these lines. Imagery is often the narrative of a syntax, and few poets are as alert to the river-turnings and oxbows a sentence offers up.

Bowers's quiet manner hides a fatalistic humor. In "The Poet Orders His Tomb," the tomb is decorated with a nightmarish menagerie:

> *Dogs in the frozen haloes of their barks,*
> *   A hundred porous arks*
> *Aground and lost, where elephants like quarks*
> *Ape mother mules or imitation sharks—*
>
> *And each of them half-venerated by*
> *   A mob, impartially*
> *Scaled, finned, or feathered, all before a dry*
> *Unable mouth, symmetrically awry.*

This is a little like Michelangelo working his own flayed skin into his painting of the Last Judgment. Even Bowers's best poems, unfortunately, come with defects intimate to the style: phrases stiff-jointed or trite, musty Latin polysyllables, a clutch of Miltonic inversions (*They moped back severe! Books cosmic!*). Without their defects poets often lose their graces—sometimes their defects allow those graces. That doesn't make the defects less irritating.

Bowers has a gift for writing poems withdrawn and a little shy of statement. Many are portraits of young male friends, some just glances out the window. He's never lost a fifties taste for the Greek gods—they elbow their way in even when they're not wanted. At a poetry reading in California, the gods rise within the voice of a minor poet; soon the fatal arrow is aimed at Achilles. I've been to many poetry readings and never seen that.

The god that haunts Bowers is the god of war. His speaker meets a German general on his sickbed:

> *I thought I saw*
> *For him the summer uniforms in snow,*
> *Partisans, savage reprisals, day-long strafing,*
> *Long lines of prisoners never to return,*
> *Comrades armless, legless, and blind. But he,*
> *Clutching my sleeve to pull me closer, whispered,*
> *"It was the SS did it, not my men.*
> *The week before the armistice, they took*
> *Three just-conscripted boys who were afraid*
> *And hanged them, German children, the sky green*
> *Above the uniforms too big for them,*
> *As we saw when we found and cut them down.*
> *It was then that I despaired to live or die."*

The Hanged Man appears twice in these poems, like something out of Madame Sosostris's tarot pack; but the images of war provoke Bowers to passions hidden and unresolved in a life devoted to the cozy truces of academia. In half a dozen poems, in "Clear-seeing," "Clothes" (the splendid ending a view of a mountain, "its double peaks the victory sign"), "Two Poems on the Catholic Bavarians," "The Prince," and "Aix-la-Chapelle, 1945," the fevers of war, and the smudged line between victor and victim, suggest in suffering and sacrifice the Passion of Christ. The late poems of moral existence complete the work of half a century before.

Much of the poetry forgotten in the sea change that followed *Life Studies* was written by poets who were stiffer versions of Auden, less flexible in intellect, less twisted by irony (followers are not more or less; they're always less)—what Pound would have called the bureaucracy organized around genius. At this distance their elaborations look more like an achievement; and it may be the moment, when we are about to have a Lowell revival, to look at the discarded early work of Karl Shapiro, Louis Simpson, Philip Levine, and other poets who came to grief in free verse. Edgar Bowers shows how much could have been accomplished, in a quiet, unassuming way, by keeping the faith.

chapter 18

Richard Wilbur's Civil Tongue

Richard Wilbur is too elegant to be good, and too good to be elegant. The complaints against his work are a litany of old virtue: its sweetness, and its polish, and its cordiality, and its complacence—you'd think he was a peaceable kingdom all by himself, a lamb that has devoured all the lions in sight. His critics have lived within the tensions of his poetry by an ignorant celebration of his faults and a gleeful damning of his perfections. His middle name might as well be Suckling, Lovelace, or Crashaw.

Poets of a silver age bear uneasy relation to the poets before them, though almost any age remembers poets just dead as giants. The critical affinities invented for Pound, or Eliot, or Stevens, or later poets like Lowell have made it that much harder to appreciate poets with a different bearing. Wilbur's complex relation to the moral world of Frost has made matters more and not less difficult. That Wilbur is most of the time a classical poet, a poet secure (some would say *ossified*) in the longer line of tradition and descent, has set him against the Romantic progress of our poetry.

Who but a poet confident in the artifice of tradition would talk so about the potato?

> *Cut open raw, it looses a cool clean stench,*
> *Mineral acid seeping from pores of prest meal;*
> *It is like breaching a strangely refreshing tomb:*
>
> *Therein the taste of first stones, the hands of dead slaves,*
> *Waters men drank in the earliest frightful woods,*
> *Flint chips, and peat, and the cinders of buried camps.*

Scrubbed under faucet water the planet skin
Polishes yellow, but tears to the plain insides;
Parching, the white's blue-hearted like hungry hands.
  ("Potato")

It takes effrontery to treat vegetables like crown jewels. The low subject troubles the high seriousness of the diction; and yet the fine physicality of the writing draws what might have been a Dutch still life, a varnished oil almost alive, almost dead, into the underground of fertility and death: all flesh is the flesh of the potato. A number of Wilbur's early poems make their peace in the aftermath of war, but only when speaking publicly do the lines go false: "Times being hard, the Sikh and the Senegalese, / Hobo and Okie, the body of Jesus the Jew, / Vestigial virtues, are eaten." His familiarity seems a form of contempt.

Robert Bly called Wilbur one of the "jolly intellectual dandies." Certainly other poems in his first book, *The Beautiful Changes* (1947), poems like "&" and "O" and "The Walgh-Vogel" and "The Melongène" ("Natural pomp! Excessive Nightshades' Prince! / Polished potato, you wear / An Egyptian rinse"), gave hostages to his critics. There is something rich and richly excessive, something beyond natural pomp, in such verses. They are too pleased with their own grotesqueness—a dandy dresses for his mirror as much as for his friends, but a poet has to go a long way to seem a greater dandy than Auden.

From the vantage of half a century such coy irrelevance seems less playful and more to the purpose of postwar formalism. Lowell, Nemerov, Wilbur, Moss, Hecht, Simpson, Bowers, Justice, Merrill, Snodgrass, Merwin, Hollander, Howard—these poets with concerns variously classical and variantly formal took modernism at its word, the word wrenched from the terrors of its time. Poetry in the afterthought of war lived on the relief of death averted and the sorrow of death observed. In their early books, many of these poets had a dilettantish, sweetly insouciant air taken from middle Auden. They were so much like boulevardiers you wouldn't have known who had fought overseas and who had been too young to serve—but then our best war poet, Jarrell, never saw combat. Preciousness and purpose often stood side by side, and for Wilbur in sharp conflict with each other. The writers of the Jazz Age were similarly afflicted: this was the source of a privileged torsion. Consider "First Snow in Alsace":

The snow came down last night like moths
Burned on the moon; it fell till dawn,
Covered the town with simple cloths.

Absolute snow lies rumpled on
What shellbursts scattered and deranged,
Entangled railings, crevassed lawn.

As if it did not know they'd changed,
Snow smoothly clasps the roofs of homes
Fear-gutted, trustless and estranged.

The ration stacks are milky domes;
Across the ammunition pile
The snow has climbed in sparkling combs.

You think: beyond the town a mile
Or two, this snowfall fills the eyes
Of soldiers dead a little while.

The snow returns the war to landscape, much as the gorgeous fluency of the terza rima conceals a tetrameter often rigid in design. The mood is vaguely troubling, as if the speaker a little too blissfully welcomed this prettied-up war; but the calmness of the arousing voice seems the proper medium of the voyeur—it convicts the visible. The cost in detachment, in lack of passion, in composure-in-the-face-of, would eat into the art if the camouflage of death, and hence emotion, were not the subject. Nature is the disinterested moral arbiter here, or one assuming a mask of ignorance ("As if it did not know they'd changed"). Beauty temporarily transforms the pitiless, nature effacing the evidence as it conceals the evidence. The cold ironies would scarcely exist without the sentimental touches ("And frost makes marvelous designs"), but the touches cannot subvert the tragedy beneath the snow. Eventually the snow will melt.

The small, bright transfigurations are what a soldier would notice (as if there were many soldiers with the eye of a Wilbur)—the subject bears the condition of its modesty. Compare Lowell's bullying meter and bludgeoning certitudes among the shattered roofs of "The Exile's Return":

> *There mounts in squalls a sort of rusty mire,*
> *Not ice, not snow, to leaguer the Hôtel*
> *De Ville, where braced pig-iron dragons grip*
> *The blizzard to their rigor mortis. A bell*
> *Grumbles when the reverberations strip*
> *The thatching from its spire,*
> *The search-guns click and spit and split up timber*
> *And nick the slate roofs on the Holstenwall*
> *Where torn-up tilestones crown the victor.*

Lowell was a conscientious objector, but the roofs and the meter have been subject to violence still raw. Though *Lord Weary's Castle* was published in the same year as *The Beautiful Changes*, the difference in sensibility is more than a variance in title. If Wilbur's is the better poem, it is not because of the form; it's because the form has a more intimating plan. The plan allows for the excesses that in Lowell seem merely errors of tact (though elsewhere Lowell's tactlessness produced greater poems).

The dangerous insolence of Wilbur's verse courts and fends off such irrelevance. A poem could hardly begin less promisingly than "A Dutch Courtyard": "What wholly blameless fun / To stand and look at pictures" sounds like undergraduate effusion. What saves the poem from being merely another example of postwar ekphrasis (what might be called *ut pictura poesis* with a vengeance) is the dollying at the end out of the frame, out of context.

> *What surprising strict*
> *Propriety! In despair,*
>
> *Consumed with greedy ire,*
> *Old Andrew Mellon glowered at this Dutch*

Courtyard, until it bothered him so much
He bought the thing entire.

Beyond the frame, pictures are a part of commerce (and so they were for the Dutch, as Simon Schama reminds us in *The Embarrassment of Riches*); and yet they retain the capacity to shock the magnate a little, to turn him briefly from material ends, whatever his material means. The wit still lies coiled in wait, for Mellon has bought, not the courtyard itself, only the painted semblance. This semblance is what's disturbing: the courtyard would have been just another courtyard.

Such a slight poem (on a slight painting) is hardly worth lingering over, except for the way Wilbur darkens his concerns by a slight shadow of emphasis. Behind his artifice, when it is more than artifice, is something Greek and sacrificial. Unable to reach into the painting, to take the life while partaking of the likeness, the old banker rouses to a sudden greedy act of possession—he cannot live with the negative capability art requires. The art remains self-possessed, whoever possesses it.

That postwar fondness for the sealed world, a world beyond feeling, cannot conceal in aestheticism the aftershock of a Holocaust witnessed but unavenged. Ten years after the war the antagonism felt by many poets toward the Beats was largely a recognition that the search for a language of feeling had been conducted in the wrong terms. Wilbur's rages are conducted with lecture-hall civility: only in his best work do they threaten the placid comportment of his verse.

A poem like "'A World without Objects Is a Sensible Emptiness'" (from his second book, *Ceremony* [1950]) is remarkable not in the haughty ripeness of technique or the studied texture of allusion—technique and allusion are the peace that never passeth understanding—but in the beautiful withholding of subject.

The tall camels of the spirit
Steer for their deserts, passing the last groves loud
With the sawmill shrill of the locust, to the whole honey of the arid
Sun. They are slow, proud,

And move with a stilted stride
To the land of sheer horizon, hunting Traherne's
Sensible emptiness, *there where the brain's lantern-slide*
Revels in vast returns.

O connoisseurs of thirst,
Beasts of my soul who long to learn to drink
Of pure mirage, those prosperous islands are accurst
That shimmer on the brink

Of absence; auras, lustres,
And all shinings need to be shaped and borne.

The caravan, leaving the lush landscape of grove and locust (we are meant to cast our minds emptily back toward the camels and hard hopes of Eliot's "Journey of the Magi"), nearly refuses its function as metaphor (a metaphor almost as long as a caravan)—it is more alive than what it represents. The mind is in search of its mirages, in search of an emptiness sensible in Traherne's sense—an emptiness less empty, because a matrix of sensation. What are the sensations of the poem but a commentary on the physical world, the sensory employment, of verse itself? The long shimmering of sentences, the tender acoustic variations (how often Wilbur is our poet of timbre), the delicately muted rhymes. Rhyme and syntax cooperate in the small dramas of the quatrain, unshowy in all sorts of showy ways. This is a model of how a poem of great intellectual energy can also be a poem of tact.

Here is the most exacting statement of the rupture between pure philosophy and the duty the poet feels toward the world (Wilbur would rather be a Stevens than a Frost, though he often sounds like Frost). The argument of the poem is counter to the force of its feeling: light must have something to illuminate. And yet how attractive, how delightful, the imagination has made those camels. The languorous metaphor is the imagination's counter-argument: imagination can create its own world, a world often more tactile and less remote than the world outside our windows. However much the poet admonishes his instinct, the "trees arrayed / In bursts of glare," the "country creeks, and the hills' bracken tiaras" have little of the sensuous immediacy of those camels. They live in the action of metaphor; the objects of the world are a still life in comparison.

The poem ends with a vision of the birth of Christ:

> *Wisely watch for the sight*
> *Of the supernova burgeoning over the barn,*
> *Lampshine blurred in the steam of beasts, the spirit's right*
> *Oasis, light incarnate.*

Light made incarnate might be called the terminal case of illumination. Poets of light tend to be religious and classical—the Romantics were haunted by the moon far more than by the sun. (Electric light has forever altered the imaginative tension between them.) Wilbur's moral sunniness is one of his least attractive qualities; but it *is* a quality, and qualities are edged by their opposites. His most striking images are sunlit: "morning's cannonades of brightness," "that lavished sunlight," "lucent as shallows slowed by wading sun," "this chamber furnished only with the sun," "the noon's perfected brilliance." In "After the Last Bulletins," night is the world of trash, unruliness, vandalism, death, and anarchy, while at dawn the words are whole again and the birds sing. Lowell and Wilbur form a naked and correlative pair: the one, emotion reaching upward toward philosophy; the other, philosophy reaching back toward emotion. They are opposed gods. Wilbur understands the tragic—his most luminous poems are shot through with tragic apprehension, but he is no Pluto. He will merely visit the nether regions, like Persephone. (His attempts to write like Pluto sound like playacting, as if he were a boy in a costume beard.)

It is the condition of most poets to write in terms only partly flattering to their talent: much poetry is written against the grain of an author's gifts. In the greatest poets either the gifts rise to meet the crisis of expectation, or failure brings compression and control, a narrowing of the enterprise with a gain of intensity (neither Hardy nor Merrill will be remembered for his epic, but the ambition driven to epic permitted the fluency of poems less ambitious and more lasting). Wilbur's gifts were perfected so early, it's good to remember where they have betrayed, in their very fluency, a poetry that could succeed only despite fluency. His early poems subside eagerly into the merely pictorial, into the plain skin of the writing—he becomes a painter paid for every inch of canvas. Jarrell was right to ridicule the ending of "The Death of a Toad," saying, "you think with a surge of irritation and dismay, 'So it was all only an excuse for some Poetry.'"

> He lies
> As still as if he would return to stone,
> And soundlessly attending, dies
> Toward some deep monotone,
>
> Toward misted and ebullient seas
> And cooling shores, toward lost Amphibia's emperies.
> Day dwindles, drowning, and at length is gone
> In the wide and antique eyes, which still appear
> To watch, across the castrate lawn,
> The haggard daylight steer.

The lines are excruciating, even if posed in greater exaction than Jarrell was willing to admit (excruciating, and yet forlorn and lovely). In irony such talent reaches its greatest excess.

Lines only a little less gilded and inlaid, however, force the beauties to become a moral boundary. Here is "Marché aux Oiseaux":

> Hundreds of birds are singing in the square.
> Their minor voices fountaining in air
> And constant as a fountain, lightly loud,
> Do not drown out the burden of the crowd.
>
> Far from his gold Sudan, the travailleur
> Lends to the noise an intermittent chirr
> Which to his hearers seems more joy than rage.
> He batters softly at his wooden cage.
>
> Here are the silver-bill, the orange-cheek,
> The perroquet, the dainty coral-beak
> Stacked in their cages; and around them move
> The buyers in their termless hunt for love.

Here are the old, the ill, the imperial child;
The lonely people, desperate and mild;
The ugly; past these faces one can read
The tyranny of one outrageous need.

We love the small, said Burke. And if the small
Be not yet small enough, why then by Hell
We'll cramp it till it knows but how to feed,
And we'll provide the water and the seed.

This descends into its knowledge of Hell: Wilbur can be as merciless as Hecht, while seducing the reader with intimations of the beautiful. It isn't merely that culture here is the perversion of nature (the birds present a civil contrast, in their innocence and vain singing, to citizens desperate in their unloveliness for love), but that the moral pollution is only gradually evident beneath the gorgeous vision of the birds. This city square encloses a pastoral of Edenic forest, where Blake's rhyme of *rage* and *cage* (this square is a kind of Heaven) introduces the prison house. In each stanza the last line is the caution or condition of the next. It makes matters worse that the birds don't quite understand their circumstance—their songs are made in dumb pleasure.

The neatness of the rhymed couplets contributes to the daintiness of spirit, a daintiness the images gradually corrupt. The one tainted moment of rhyme, where *small* rhymes with *Hell*, is also the moment of greatest passion and violation. The poem is merciless toward that need for love and that entrapment by love (it isn't difficult to read the moral for marriage here), while not failing to implicate the poet in this human failure. How tempting it would have been to write:

We love the small, said Burke. And if the small
Be not yet small enough for them, by Hell
They'll cramp it till it knows but how to feed,
And they'll provide the water and the seed.

Though dark and chilling, such lines would remove the poet from the precincts of the human. Wilbur's final line is an act of recognition: a more cynical reading might note that this as cleverly evades judgment, that so human an admission makes the inhuman seem inevitable. But in a poet often felt to be impersonal—to be a renderer of surface and a maker of isolated and stylized structures (almost inhuman, however much the talk is of morals and the human)—this embrace of the evil within, this refusal to escape damnation, is as humbling as it is unnerving.

Such attention to the small is the inheritance from Herbert that makes the best of Wilbur's work almost religious. Where Elizabeth Bishop turns that inheritance into clever pathos (thereby risking a glibness only her emotional conflicts avert), Wilbur burns for the philosophy at the heart of example; and in the best poems it is usually a moral, afflicting example. For all their different weights and measures, Wilbur's polished veneer and Bishop's coy reserve, both poets find solace in the trivial and the ordinary. When Wilbur flinches from the mortality of the moral, he collapses into academic draftsmanship, where craft lies short of genius—you feel his ambition is to be a Gray or a Goldsmith. His rhymes seem to tidy matters up (Bishop's poems live in a blur of untidiness, the messy mortality of the world), succumbing to what he calls "a coating of quietudes." (Those rhymes are often dutiful and time-serving— you don't feel he ever sat back in surprise and said, "Now *there's* a rhyme!")

These quietudes, however, are embraced in a different spirit. Wilbur's poetry was the far example of formal elegance much admired in the fifties, and much loathed. The arguments have moved to other quarters, but at this reach the quarrel over rhetoric has been altered by our own expectations—the earlier achievements of line were undermined by *Howl.* Consider the following passage:

> *At Colonus Oedipus complained;*
> *Antigone attended him. He thought*
> *the sun too hot, she shielded him;*
> *his enemies too strong, she fought*
> *for him; his life bitter, she soothed him;*
> *and hope gone, like all things.*
> *His blinded eyes pained him, she bathed them.*

In 1956 a critic called this "a flat near-prose." The poem was by
David Ignatow, and the critic, James Dickey, continued: "Aside
from the flatness, which is only in a very rudimentary sense a tech-
nique, Ignatow does almost completely without the traditional
skills of English versification. He makes no effort to assure his lines
rhetorical effectiveness; the import of each poem is thus far too
dependent upon *what* is said."

The parallelism, the balanced phrasings, the internal rhymes,
the persistent iambs: we'd call this a highly measured rhetoric now,
but then English poetry has gone much further toward prose in
forty years. This ought to leave Wilbur a hideous Louis Quatorze
antique, beyond the rescue of taste. The movement away from for-
mal ornament and classical decoration has instead made him part
of the exemplary perfection of another era. The craft, so easily
managed and so willfully mannered, that once set him apart now
looks ripe for revival, as fresh as a Chippendale pattern book.

The year 1956 was the date of publication of Wilbur's third
book, *Things of This World*, a book ordered between, or disordered
by, the world of transcendence and the world of the human. In the
title poem, "Love Calls Us to the Things of This World," it is the
other world that remains unsoiled:

> *The eyes open to a cry of pulleys,*
> *And spirited from sleep, the astounded soul*
> *Hangs for a moment bodiless and simple*
> *As false dawn.*
> > *Outside the open window*
> *The morning air is all awash with angels.*
>
> *Some are in bed-sheets, some are in blouses,*
> *Some are in smocks: but truly there they are.*
> *Now they are rising together in calm swells*
> *Of halcyon feeling, filling whatever they wear*
> *With the deep joy of their impersonal breathing.*

The language is full of sly entanglement: the soul "spirited" from
sleep (as if a spirit could be bundled off, like laundry) and hanging

bodiless (later the clothesline will be called a gallows), the stinging ambiguity of "simple" (lured from the phrase "simple souls"), the "false dawn" within this real one, the exuberant pun of "awash." A transcendence in meaning prepares the transcendent vision of the angels. The angels are incarnated by their clothes: bed-sheets, blouses, smocks (they are superbly unfashionable). If the laundry were *itself* mistaken for angels (the way sheets are ghosts at Halloween), the poem would be about myopia. Freed from the physical, the soul "shrinks // From all that it is about to remember, / From the punctual rape of every blessèd day." The dark irreligion of the puns (days are "blessèd" more in anger than adoration) suspends the poem between the pure immaterial and the compromised physical world. But in a week the clothes will be dirty again.

The poem never admits that these angels are half-sleepy imaginings. Visionaries must be allowed their visions, however tainted: otherwise the soul too might be an airy nothing. Only when the soul cannot remember the murderous physics of this world do such visions open themselves. But Wilbur refuses to end there, and the poem inverts itself. The vision of supernal order is not an invitation: it is a reminder that love must first be achieved among fallen objects (the title is a line from Augustine). The soul accepts the waking body (surely this is an aspect of love), and the body is "changed" by what it has seen.

> *"Bring them down from their ruddy gallows;*
> *Let there be clean linen for the backs of thieves;*
> *Let lovers go fresh and sweet to be undone,*
> *And the heaviest nuns walk in a pure floating*
> *Of dark habits,*
> *   keeping their difficult balance."*

The clothing is called down from the gallows, as Christ was taken down from the cross. The Gospels have Christ's clothes gambled away—the magic of clothing touched by death extends from the shirt of Nessus to the shroud of Turin (passing through the papyri of Oxyrhynchus: those grave wrappings are the real books of the dead). Thieves, lovers (undone by their love or undone in their clothing), and nuns represent three private societies (crime, eros, and religion) or more abasingly evil, sin, and faith. Even the thieves are to be given the dress of angels, while the nuns (how their heaviness bears both a gravity and a susceptibility to gravity!) walk on in their "dark habits": the wit infringes on organized religion for the sake of the spiritual. It is exactly that difficult balance between the everyday and the unworldly that the poem means to compromise, and keep in compromise. In the misperception of one world the other world is allowed to enter.

It is not just the expectations of line that distance Wilbur's poetry, but what might be called the expectations of spirit. The high formality serves the stately withdrawing of personality. Cool, almost brittle, the formal intelligence preserves its manners with its mannerisms, behind cracked glaze. The being who suffers is rarely present within the one who sees—that is why it is scarcely believable that the man mowing the lawn in "The Death of a Toad" is Wilbur *in propria persona*. But contemplation is, after all, one of the important modes of art. We do not look at paintings to be lectured about the world; we go to be moved by their removals, by their abstract operations upon feeling. We learn of the world through the infidelity of its art. To ask for warmth from poets like Wilbur is a mistake in category. The high logic of his poetry takes place almost entirely within the contemplative. When he asks less of himself, as his later poems make clear, there is almost nothing to give.

For a poet secure in the self, the authorial "I" can be an intrusion, an unforgivable impersonation. The I is what lies behind the words, not in front of them: for such a poet, the personality is incarnate in language, in the intimate operation of the words, not insinuated as a dramatic character. We are still writing in the shadow of postwar poetry, and the difference in assumptions across this half-century is nothing like the change from 1775 to 1825 or 1890 to 1940 (or roughly from the death of Goldsmith to the death of Byron or the death of Whitman to the death of Yeats). We understand the authorial withdrawal in Wilbur in part by the reaction still in place against it.

His argument for the baroque proceeds by meticulous exam-
ination of its virtues. In "A Baroque Wall-Fountain in the Villa
Sciarra" (the subject itself announces certain removed and special
aesthetic concerns), the water

spills
In threads then from the scalloped rim, and makes

A scrim or summery tent
For a faun-ménage and their familiar goose.
Happy in all that ragged, loose
Collapse of water, its effortless descent

And flatteries of spray,
The stocky god upholds the shell with ease,
Watching, about his shaggy knees,
The goatish innocence of his babes at play;

His fauness all the while
Leans forward, slightly, into a clambering mesh
Of water-lights, her sparkling flesh
In a saecular ecstasy, her blinded smile

Bent on the sand floor
Of the trefoil pool, where ripple-shadows come
And go in swift reticulum,
More addling to the eye than wine, and more

Interminable to thought
Than pleasure's calculus.

This tender description, spilling from stanza to stanza, is undone
by the severe, spiritual abstraction of the fountains before St.
Peter's. And yet, the poem argues, the fauns of this bizarre fountain
"are at rest in fulness of desire / For what is given, . . . / Reprov-
ing our disgust and our ennui / With humble insatiety." The
crammed-together, sweatshop artifice is a fulfillment of the urge to
life: the elaborated ground of Wilbur's verse requires an ars poetica
of the spirit. The poem ends with an invocation of St. Francis.

Francis, perhaps, who lay in sister snow

> *Before the wealthy gate*
> *Freezing and praising, might have seen in this*
> *No trifle, but a shade of bliss—*
> *That land of tolerable flowers, that state*

> *As near and far as grass*
> *Where eyes become the sunlight, and the hand*
> *Is worthy of water: the dreamt land*
> *Toward which all hungers leap, all pleasures pass.*

The fine trembling of the unexpected adjective *tolerable* takes root in the Latin for "bearing." The language is part of the learning—a parade of classical, religious, and literary figures crowds the last stanzas of Wilbur's poems to salvage or secure the moral example.

Classical poets draw strength from influence—influence is not merely an aversion. The moral realm so strongly implicated in Wilbur's verse lives with its debts to the physical world of Frost. A poet may absorb an influence, but also be divided against it: the authenticity of feeling may come in resistance. "Sonnet" is a little cast-iron Frost piece about a farmer and a scarecrow.

> *The winter deepening, the hay all in,*
> *The barn fat with cattle, the apple-crop*
> *Conveyed to market or the fragrant bin,*
> *He thinks the time has come to make a stop,*

> *And sinks half-grudging in his firelit seat,*
> *Though with his heavy body's full consent,*
> *In what would be the posture of defeat,*
> *But for that look of rigorous content.*

> *Outside, the night dives down like one great crow*
> *Against his cast-off clothing where it stands*
> *Up to the knees in miles of hustled snow,*

> *Flapping and jumping like a kind of fire,*
> *And floating skyward its abandoned hands*
> *In gestures of invincible desire.*

This is one of Wilbur's many poems about the division of self (he has Cartesian dialogues between milkweed and stone, aspen and stream). His farmer is almost a harvest of himself. The crops are in; but that hard annual victory leaves him in the "posture of defeat," and the "rigorous content" meant to modify what only *seems* defeat bears against a notion of contentment *in* defeat. The clothing has been cast off in a contrary yet collaborative sense: a chrysalis is transforming, a shed skin only outgrown. Out in the snow, the scarecrow is a cold vision of desire, desire forlorn, panicky as a traveler freezing to death, yet "invincible." It is a haunting statement of loss, and of private costs.

Wilbur is tough and unsentimental about the soul (even while romantically indulgent in describing the harvest—he's like Keats when he gets a chance to describe nature). He wears Frost's old clothes here, and amid the debts to Greek and Latin and European literature lie these strange American pastorals. Wilbur can hardly write about nature or compose in quatrains without becoming a version of Frost—the moral strain of his being has been purchased secondhand from our moral New England farmer. His certainties come as Frost's come, from trust in the ordered universe (though Frost is a cynic surprised into gruff serenity and Wilbur an optimist with a dark and troubling stain).

The Frost in Wilbur rescues him from dandified Gongorism— his early poems were loaded with words like "retractility," "periploi," "areté," "rachitic," "bombination," "phlebolith," "informous," "fovea," "noyade," "râle," and phrases like "the ping-pong's optative bop" or "a bell diphthonging in an atmosphere" or "habitude, if not pure // Hebetude" or "now all this proud royaume / Is Veniced." This division is shaped beneath the level of style, since style, if it doesn't accord with division, at least makes certain assumptions about accord. A poet who dissolves himself in influences so little in relation to one another can seem a disjoint presence: not a multiple personality, but a personality that never coheres beneath the ease of style. There is a difference between a classical culture lived (the Horace in Frost) and a classical culture worked up from books.

In *Advice to a Prophet* (1961), how oddly the precious Cartesian dialogues, an allegory about puppets in love, poems titled "Gemini," "Ballade for the Duke of Orléans," "To Ishtar," "Pangloss's Song," and "Eight Riddles from Symphosius," plus translations from Guillén, Quasimodo, de Nerval, and Molière sit next to homely old American subjects like "A Hole in the Floor," "A Fire-Truck," "A Grasshopper," and "In the Smoking-Car." This may suggest the problematic attention of a dandy cum democrat, an arch and academic temper darkened by moral, mortal nature. Those sudden descents into skepticism and mistrust in poems that begin like bright still lifes mark his unease. Wilbur's most beautifully unstable poems are problems of identity.

Saying through others what the self has no language for might be called the state of influence. It seems surprising that Wilbur has not been driven to dramatic monologue, that uneasy formal disguise of the self—but then you realize that in middle career he was driven to, and finally absorbed by, translation instead.

Any critic of Wilbur must face the decline in his original work after about 1960. The variety and intensity of a loyalty to translation comment uneasily on a poet's organization of feeling and display of the substance of feeling. Translation is a tricky medium. It is easy to give up higher imaginative satisfactions for the pleasures of setting right the negotiation between one language and another. A translator becomes the medium or permeable membrane at the cost of his sovereignty. Poets like Lowell or Pound could never fully submit to such a regime: they could translate only by eminent domain. But submission too can be a form of genius. It is to Wilbur's more governed character that we owe his remarkable renderings of Molière and Racine, among the finest translations of our period. Here the formal brilliance, accommodated in the masters because approved by them, becomes a tour de force of faith in and sympathy toward a literature otherwise dead, instead of a force used without sympathy for, because radically unfaithful to, contemporary life. The formality of the plays is no different from the formality that drew criticism to the poems.

Translation provides a pure and alternate world, the raw matter and ready emotion the imagination longs for. Some poets say their piece and retire to gun running, and surely gun running is better than publishing increasingly indecipherable Xeroxes of earlier work. The slight snobbery many writers feel toward translation is not misplaced, if we value the writer over anything he might have translated. We would not have had a Molière or a Racine worthy of their art; but there is about Wilbur's career a sense of incompleteness, of great talent willingly abandoned.

Wilbur's later poems are increasingly occasional. The poems of *Walking to Sleep* (1969) and *The Mind-Reader* (1976) and the new poems gathered in *New and Collected Poems* are the work of a man whose mind is on other matters, often on the matter of translations with which the books are interlarded (so that they seem books by Brodsky, Villon, du Bellay, Voltaire, Borges, and Akhmatova, as much as by Wilbur). Only Auden, among recent poets, was a genius of the occasional: it fired the frivolousness of his imagination. Eliot's occasional verse (not his comic verse) was embarrassing. To take the depths of a writer's imagination, an action usually has to fall on prepared ground. Otherwise a poem is a whim. Wilbur's translations are great monuments to sympathetic imagination—he has made numerous foreign poets as grave and sweet and witty as, well, as Richard Wilbur. His pride in them would be a measure of what he has had to surrender.

Even in elegy, the later poems fall into postures, where the earlier often *were* brilliant postures. Wilbur has lost, not just the careless ease, but even the studied ease that made him more Montaigne than Malvolio. In their perfunctory ends, poems like "On Having Mis-identified a Wild Flower" or "Wyeth's Milk Cans" or "Flippancies" or "A Riddle" or "Two Riddles from Aldheim" or "For the Student Strikers" are starved of substance, unpleasant in their self-satisfactions. Wilbur can be as coquettish as Updike (*"Rillons, Rillettes*, they taste the same, / And would by any other name, / And are, if I may risk a joke, / Alike as two pigs in a poke"), and any poems shorter than a sonnet have been refined past some essential, necessary coarseness: elegance has become a frozen, plump composure. Auden and Merrill were also trivial in their later work: a poet of great instincts in language often becomes a mere collection of instincts. The public voice of Wilbur's cantata, "On Freedom's Ground," shows how far he has strayed from his demons.

Now in our lady's honor
Come dance on freedom's ground,
And do the waltz or polka,
Whatever spins around,

Or let it be the raspa,
The jig or Lindy hop,
Or else the tarantella,
Whatever doesn't stop,

The Highland fling, the hornpipe,
The schottische or the break,
Or, if you like, the cakewalk,
Whatever takes the cake.

This poem on a "national occasion" (the centenary of the Statue of Liberty) reminds us how poets suffer when they speak not for themselves but for their country. Taste is the enemy of patriotic sentiment—we would not have to appoint a poet laureate otherwise.

For all their classical proportion and design, Wilbur's best poems move into uncharted territory. Their ends are not a consequence of their beginnings. We are always at the mercy of our personalities, but at best we become simply the mercy of them. The scholar-farmer, fussily constructed, professional verse had a density, a scalding extremity as rich as a revenge play (something clotted and magisterial by Webster). The glittering surfaces concealed a dangerous undertow: critics rarely recognized that Wilbur's work was more bitter, more severe, more darkly demanded than mere ornament. Even in late poems there are moments of intensity and superb moral resonance.

The horse beneath me seemed
To know what course to steer
Through the horror of snow I dreamed,
And so I had no fear,

Nor was I chilled to death
By the wind's white shudders, thanks
To the veils of his patient breath
And the mist of sweat from his flanks.

It seemed that all night through,
Within my hand no rein
And nothing in my view
But the pillar of his mane,

I rode with magic ease
At a quick, unstumbling trot
Through shattering vacancies
On into what was not,

Till the weave of the storm grew thin,
With a threading of cedar-smoke,
And the ice-blind pane of an inn
Shimmered, and I awoke.

How shall I now get back
To the inn-yard where he stands,
Burdened with every lack,
And waken the stable-hands

To give him, before I think
That there was no horse at all,
Some hay, some water to drink,
A blanket and a stall?

    ("The Ride")

There is almost nothing here not available in Frost. Frost is not so much a particular influence as a sufficient one: a consequence and not a cause of divided nature. To write in Frost's voice is no different from writing in Molière's or Racine's: the echoes of "Stopping by Woods on a Snowy Evening" and "The Draft Horse" are not just beneath the horizon of style, they are mute within the style itself. And yet the unappeasable despair of this sleeper (recall the waking man in "Love Calls Us to the Things of This World") is not for his own loss—his bereavement from dream—but for that horse left unwatered and unfed. Dream, the blind form of memory, is drawn to matters unfinished or acts regretted (as the shades in Homer are drawn to blood)—and yet how selfless and generous this consideration is. When Paradise was lost, Adam didn't worry about feeding the animals. And neither would that farmer-ego Frost. We want our dreams restored for other reasons.

In poetry, the surplus value is whatever is created beyond the direct or intimate need of the poem. This is not merely where the incidental or the incidence of art exceeds the virtue of language, but where something not quite predicted, not quite planned, overtakes the prepared form. The fatal condition of our poetry is that we value authenticity only when it is spelt out or noisily claimed, not where it is implicit in the craft. We have settled for the authentic, but our authentic is a surface value only.

The most obvious (and least oblivious) cast of Wilbur's talent takes seriously the subject—call it broadly the moral function of the visible—that most severely tests the form. The order of form finally has no moral value, though it may have moral suasion (we are all emotion susceptible to rhetoric). Wilbur's poetry must be seen as not just a radical exposition of style, but an uneasy indictment of the limits of style. That his early work had a richness beyond the coy or beautiful exchanges reminds us how impoverished our poems have become. If the world were an abstraction, Wallace Stevens would have written its theology and Richard Wilbur its poetry.

chapter 19

Verse Chronicle:
Betrayals of the Tongue

Geoffrey Hill

Geoffrey Hill's handsome and brutish new poems are fragments of his old covenant with language: in *Canaan* the rough verse measures a private poetry in public themes. The lowlands of Canaan were promised the Israelites before their forty-year diet of manna (how dreadful the stuff must have tasted by the end), the land of redemption Moses could gesture toward but never reach. Redemption is not the subject of Hill's poetry so much as its sin (his difficulty is his greatest conceit): he is one of the last poets to believe language is the proper site of faith, that nothing except language will redeem the betrayals of the tongue.

> *Aspiring Grantham*
> *rises above itself.*
> *Tall churches wade the fen*
> *on their stilts of glass.*
>
> *Crowned Ely stands beset*
> *by winds of straw-burning,*
> *by the crouched run of flame.*
> *Cambridge lies dark, and dead*
>
> *predestined Elstow*
> *where Bunyan struck his fear—*

flint creed, tinder of wrath—
to flagrant mercies.

This bleak vision is called "Dark-Land," and few readers would know the term from *Pilgrim's Progress* if Hill hadn't thoughtfully if perversely used it elsewhere as an epigraph ("I am of Dark-land," said Valiant-for-Truth). The thicket of required facts begins in Grantham, the birthplace of Margaret Thatcher (daughter of a shopkeeper and so rising above her station) as well as site of one of the finest English medieval churches. Ely, in the middle of East Anglian fens (itself an island—eel island—before the fens were drained), the last place of resistance to the Norman conquest, is dominated by its Gothic cathedral. Elstow was Bunyan's birthplace. Through such hints and intimations the poem's drive toward order accumulates; from the darkness of the present, they recall the revivals and religious awakenings of the seventeenth and eighteenth centuries. The modern landscape is scoured and beleaguered, old religion wiped clean for "national heritage," striving mercantile towns more honored than ancient sites of worship. If a preacher like Bunyan strikes a spark in the surrounding night, the mercies are apt to be flagrant; Hill has been a poet for whom a dark pun is a source of light.

The unlikely juxtaposition of terms in the title of the sequence "Mysticism and Democracy" argues, as did the scholar Rufus Jones in a book by that name, that the modern democratic instinct developed in those religious revivals (self-governing churches becoming a microcosm of populist democracy), that democracy was a belief mystical in character. *Canaan* is a series of braided sequences on the body politic, the lines sometimes fragmentary, the sequences divided against themselves: the scattered parts of "To the High Court of Parliament," "Mysticism and Democracy," "Dark-Land," and "Parentalia" are the limbs of Osiris, and the faith (and finicky trust) of readers must restore them to a living whole.

Hill honors those martyred for politics: "De Jure Belli ac Pacis" (the title of Grotius's famous tract, which formed the basis of international law) is dedicated to one of the conspirators in the July plot against Hitler.

The people moves as one spirit unfettered
claim our assessors of stone.
                              When the nations
fall dispossessed such conjurings possess them,
elaborate barren fountains, projected
aqueducts
              where water is no longer found.
Where would one find Grotius for that matter,
the secular justice clamant among psalms,
huge-fisted visionary Comenius . . . ?
Could none predict these haughty degradations
as now your high-strung
                              martyred resistance serves
to consecrate the liberties of Maastricht?

Though the Maastricht treaty, setting terms for European union, is the proper end of the last war, "liberties" is cruelly ambiguous. The merging of Europe is also a loss of identity; and if the resistance of von Haeften and others was "high-strung," they were themselves "high-strung" by piano wire at their executions. Hill finds his faith deep in the phrase, in those assessors of stone that might be gravestone or monument.

I have lingered over the snarled possibility of such lines because Hill's poetry withholds its meanings out of charity, out of respect, as if only the student of the word deserved revelation of the Word. In our lethal time, poetry is the liturgy of a dead language, and Hill's invocation of religious revivals past calls for the resurrection of a tongue now divided by its tongues, even as politicians make louder and lying obeisance to the past (the Bible has become a real-estate map). The damned ambitions of such language have fatal grandeur, most evident in Hill's portrait of the forsaken beauty of English landscape:

                              rain
streams on half-visible clatter of the wind
                    lapsing and rising,
that clouds the pond's green mistletoe of spawn,
seeps among nettlebeds and rust-brown sorrel,

perpetual ivy burrowed by weak light,
makes carved shapes crumble.

Some of these poems were published prematurely in *New & Collected Poems* (1992), and the cunning revisions and additions have sharpened their discontents (a reader may amuse himself at thought of this poet, who so hates to revise in public, revising in public). At times the broken phrasings sink into the fens—Hill is too eager a Valiant-for-Truth, too self-pleased a prophet without honor, as if the difficulty of his poetry were a vengeance on his slack-jawed readers. This is a cost some readers will bear for the barbed wire of such elegies and addresses, such cautious, cautionary verse tangled in Bible and classic, the compact religious ghosts of his first book of short poems in almost two decades.

Rich, quarrelsome (meaning forever contending with meaning), laden with its own soiled pleasures, Hill's poetry is the major achievement of late twentieth-century verse. If it is also at times indrawn, obdurate past reason, sneering at "vacancy's rabble," a public poetry without a public, that is a judgment on our time (Hill is so high-minded, you wish once in a while he'd succumb to low temptations). His sedimentary skills have troubled English poetry for almost half a century, and *Canaan* is one of the few serious books we will have to mark the millennium.

Jorie Graham

The Errancy is Jorie Graham's weakest and most dispiriting book; the tics and fussiness of her recent style have become nothing more than style (many poets praise Graham for her ambition, but ambition is not a classy word for achievement), as if she had forgotten that rendering so minutely her hither-dither, helter-skelter thinking had a point: to call into question the way a poem fixes perception.

And the frontier where the notes pulse, fringe, then fray
the very same stillness we place our outlines
in, the very same one we have to breathe, and flare our tiny nets of
words

into (who's there?) (what do you hear?) (what hear?) (still
there?)—the very same—we listen in there—
the zero glistens—the comma holds—
flames behind where the siren goes off,
where someone is killed but only by accident *so you are free to*
  cross the street now—
I watch the lovers a long time—
they kiss as if trying to massacre difference.

Errancy is the state of error, though it looks like a temp agency for clumsy typists. Here the buttonholing parentheses, the hacked-off line breaks, the italics and breathless dashes all contribute to a taxonomy of emphasis far beyond the requirements (it's just a humdrum day in a city plaza). Half the poems end with a dash, an ellipsis, a question, or nothing at all; some have passages where every line is a new stanza. Her armory of rhetorical and typographical effect also includes the lacuna (her most devious device, for a word that refuses to be called forth), rhetorical questions, little oh's of exclamation, and the long dramatic space.

Punctuation is frustrating and limiting for a poet who wants to take poems beyond the pieties of the past, but Graham's devices (often just housebroken versions of avant-garde tactics) are reminiscent, not of E. E. Cummings, whose effects were joky and painterly, but of the forgotten José Garcia Villa, who wrote countless poems where every word was separated by a comma (as well as a poem consisting of nothing but commas). Graham's major theme is the immanence of the ordinary, but does the ordinary require quite such devout effusion, such faked urgency? She's newly taken with guardian angels—there's a party downstairs, and upstairs an angel is arranging things:

         the honeycombing
thoughts are felt to dialogue, *a form of self-*
congratulation, no?, or is it suffering? I'm a bit
dizzy up here rearranging things,
they will come up here soon, and need a setting for their fears,
and loves, an architecture for their evolutionary
morphic needs.

To *dialogue?* Their *morphic needs?* Suddenly you're watching a version of *It's a Wonderful Life* where Clarence has become a follower of Derrida. Too often Graham's wild means conceal all-too-sentimental ends.

Graham has been one of the most rashly daring contemporary poets (she's the Evel Knievel of odd stunts), but as the praise has gotten louder the poetry has gotten worse. The new poems often begin in trivial domestic experience (being stuck in traffic, say), but soon they're spiraling off into tedious immensities and vacancies, the empty-headed philosophizing that disfigured the verse of James Dickey and Robert Penn Warren. Even by her own standards, the writing is sometimes dreadful: "wielding utter particularity in this pregnant bagfulness," "crustaceous mylar day must nibble at, gum at," "the dogs of perspective gather round me." She seems unable to resist any opportunity for goggle-eyed pretension or gasps of wonder—"Clasp me, trellis of glancings, / delicatest machine—/ body of the absconding *god*," "oh tiny golden spore just filtering in to touch the good idea." Such quotes don't begin to suggest the page-by-page exhaustion of impulse, the near incoherence that makes these poems a kind of mania, as if she were shouting them from street corners, lost in the frenzy and ecstasy of inner monologue.

And yet. And yet. The end of "Le Manteau de Pascal" is a fugue of unreal beauty:

you do understand, don't you, by looking?
a neck like a vase awaiting its cut flower,
filled with the sensation of being suddenly completed,
the moment the prize is lost, the erotic tingling,
the wool-gabardine mix, its grammatical weave
—you do understand, don't you, by looking?—
never never destined to lose its elasticity,
it was this night I believe but possibly the next
I saw clearly the impossibility of staying
filled with the sensation of being suddenly completed,
also of unknown origin, not shade-giving, not chronological
since the normal growth of boughs is radiating.

Earlier in the poem a passage from Hopkins's journals has the hard-edged observation, the sense of the spiritual within seeing, that Graham for all her mugging never approaches. A few of its phrases find their way here, in a moment where the means of her poem do not resist its ends.

Graham can still write lovely lines when she cares to ("when only a bit of wind / litigated in the sycamores"—that series of stresses on the lilting short "i"); and a few religious poems (particularly "In the Pasture" and "Easter Morning Aubade") almost recall the stringency and oddness of her best work, just as a prurient poem about rape recalls her worst. Such gestures are overwhelmed by the uninspired rambling, less and less anchored by subject, of this humorless book. The beauty of Whitman was his I—I—I, but the tragedy of Graham is her me—me—me—me.

J. V. Cunningham

J. V. Cunningham was a poet's poet, which means the appreciation of his peers partly explained the absence of his audience—a poet's poet is sometimes a classic waiting to happen (like Elizabeth Bishop), but often just a minority taste. *The Poems of J. V. Cunningham* is the definitive work of this minor poet, embalming him in a lengthy introduction and seventy pages of notes.

Most of Cunningham's poems were epigrams, which seem a modest ambition now, when art is long and getting longer. A contemporary and sometime friend of Yvor Winters, during the Depression Cunningham was a student of classics at Stanford, eventually writing a doctoral dissertation on Shakespeare. He started as a poet of musty diction and metaphysical torpor: for every phrase like "the wasp in the darkened chamber," there are dozens of lines like "You are the problem I propose, / My dear, the text my musings glose," or passages like

> *More than the ash stays you from nothingness!*
> *Nor here nor there is a consuming pyre!*
> *Your essence is in infinite regress*

That burns with varying consistent fire,
Mythical bird that bears in burying!

Cunningham manages to kill off any taste for metaphysical poetry by such archaizing (his early poems are like those Medieval Faires where people dress up as Vikings and throw axes, then go home and open a Budweiser)—the language had nothing to do with the life lived. It must have been a surprise to learn that Donne and Jonson were never coming back.

In the midst of these ingrown, bookish poems, drab as hotel wallpaper, full of barely recognized rage and sexual tension, "Meditation on Statistical Method" is like Archimedes' shout:

Plato, despair!
We prove by norms
How numbers bear
Empiric forms,

How random wrong
Will average right
If time be long
And error slight;

But in our hearts
Hyperbole
Curves and departs
To infinity.

Error is boundless.
Nor hope nor doubt,
Though both be groundless,
Will average out.

Here the mordant despair finds its medium: the betrayal of the grinding man-in-a-gray-flannel-suit culture is so savage, it's a shock to realize this was written years earlier, during the war. The "Meditation" (almost irreligious in its approach to the ethical) has Empson's oddly intellective passion, his taste for science as ground for the metaphysical—but neither poet could force such tastes to yield much poetry.

This was Cunningham's anthology piece. By his early thirties the poems were over; the next forty years were given mostly to epigrams, when there was anything to give. Epigrams concentrate the mind, and a hangman's gloom hangs over Cunningham's— many are dingy and depressive as his poems (though as he aged the epigrams grew more fluent), but some have the nasty zing of a man with Larkin's misanthropy and considerable neuroses of his own.

Jove courted Danaë with golden love,
But you're not Danaë, and I'm not Jove.
. . . .

God is love. Then by conversion
Love is God, and sex conversion.
. . . .

Naked I came, naked I leave the scene,
And naked was my pastime in between.

The double entendre is an act properly metaphysical: it gives the physical its other name. Cunningham's epigrams are best when sexual; his anxieties serve his self-contempts, while giving them standing in wit. Otherwise this version of a poem from the *Palatine Anthology* would make self-loathing loathsome, cocksure instead of unsteadily comic:

And now you're ready who while she was here
Hung like a flag in a calm. Friend, though you stand
Erect and eager, in your eye a tear,
I will not pity you, or lend a hand.

Timothy Steele's strangely defensive introduction makes quite a sales pitch for the poet, and there's hardly a banality he avoids: "Cunningham is a moving writer," "He well communicates a vivid and respectful appreciation of the precariousness of life," "May living eyes find in this collection delight and profit." No copywriter could have done worse; most would have done better. Steele's notes show scholarly thoroughness and pedantic fussiness (he's the author of an interesting book on meter): though readers under forty may want an introduction to Cunningham's work, Steele assumes they need a history of the epigram and a primer of English meter as well. The notes, occasionally quite helpful, tell us what "Tudor" means and who Freud was ("founded psychoanalysis"). Cunningham would have laughed drily at what idiots his readers have become.

Ted Hughes

It's hard to know what mischievous god (Bacchus, perhaps) lured Ted Hughes into his *Tales from Ovid*. In recent decades the drive to write has found only mediocre expression in Hughes's poetry, though he is still a small industry of poem, criticism, and anthology. The British poet laureate has not found much inspiration in being poet laureate, though that's hardly the fault of the Windsors, who require a satirist with the tragic taste of Swift.

Much of our literature's familiarity with classic myth descends through Ovid, and each generation remakes the myths in its image: these prosy, muscular improvisations attempt to turn Ovid into a version of Ted Hughes, a poet of *passion* ("Not just ordinary passion either, but human passion *in extremis*—passion where it combusts, or levitates, or mutates"). Yet Ovid was a witty bon vivant, pampered and feted when young, risqué enough to have his *Ars Amatoria* banned. His subject may have been the depravity and passion of gods, but he wrote for a society of aesthetes—a lot of lark's tongues must have been devoured during readings of his poetry. We know little about how seriously the Romans took their gods, but the squalid fates of the *Metamorphoses* may have provoked as much laughter as tears—the metamorphoses are often all-too-appropriate punishments for hubris.

Hughes's versions of two dozen tales are in gruff free verse, a no-nonsense style in miner's boots. When he writes that Venus "swirled in the uplift of incense / Like a great fish suddenly bulging / Into a tide-freshened pool," or that Chaos was "A huge agglomeration of upset. / A bolus of everything—but / As if aborted," you think, oh, wicked old Ted Hughes! Though he carts in new metaphors by the barrow load, most of the tales are fairly close to the original; but they lack the deceits and arch torsions of Ovid's verse. If you can't read Latin, the pleasures of that verse have been absent in translation—against Pope's and Chapman's Homer and Dry-

den's Virgil, in English poor Ovid has only Arthur Golding's over-
rated and nearly unreadable fourteeners. Hughes has made his
Ovid mildly up to date, with mention of jujus, gangsters, straitjack-
ets, photons, and spaghetti, though the transformations sound
strained and unlikely. Here is Pentheus on Tiresias:

> *"Dreams," he explained,*
> *"Which this methane-mouth*
> *Tells us are the dark manifesto*
> *Of the corrector,*
> *In fact are corpse-lights, the ignes fatui,*
> *Miasma from the long-drop*
> *And fermenting pit*
> *Of what we don't want, don't need,*
> *And have dumped.*
> *They rise from the lower bowel. And lower."*

Sometimes the metaphors just get in each other's way.

> *You have become sots,*
> *You have dunked it all, like a doughnut,*
> *Into a mugful of junk music—*
> *Which is actually the belly-laugh*
> *Of this androgynous, half-titted witch.*

Hughes can't ruin completely some of Ovid's *tours de force*—
the terror as transformation overtakes Actaeon or the sisters of
Phaëthon, the shame of the raped Callisto or Philomela. But his
handling of minor details is often confused; and, though in his in-
troduction he makes no mention of practice or method, the tales
seem less versions of Ovid than versions of versions of Ovid. En-
glish has startling translations by poets who couldn't read the
originals (Pound's *Cathay*, some of Lowell's *Imitations*, Logue's un-
even *Iliad*). The difficulty in working from another translation
(Mary Innes's stilted fifties prose may have been close at hand) is
not imitation but the phrase-by-phrase aversion from someone
else's words.

Ovid fawned over the Caesars (he too was a poet laureate of
sorts), not that the fawning did him any more good than pandering

to aesthetes with tales of dark love and deadly sex. Men find themselves superior to myth, until they suffer the fate of myth: Ovid died after nine years in exile, still seeking pardon from the emperor for an "indiscretion." To become something original, to be touched by a god—this must have been the sentimental wish of Ovid's audience. You need look no further than the fantasies of the emperors, their cults and faked apotheoses, to know the secret desires of the ruling class. They were so rich they longed to be poor, like Marie Antoinette, who loved to play milkmaid as long as she could go back to playing Marie Antoinette again.

Once or twice in this grim, lifeless book a passage suggests how delightful a Hughes his Ovid might have been.

> *He brushed his hand over a clump of grass,*
> *The blades stayed bent—soft ribbons*
> *Of gold foil. A ripe ear of corn*
> *Was crisp and dry and light as he plucked it*
> *But a heavy slug of gold, intricately braided*
> *As he rolled it between his palms.*
> *It was then that a cold thought seemed to whisper.*

The foreshadowing and the metaphors are pure Hughes—here he's having fun, and you wish he were having fun more often. In *Tales from Ovid* his touch turns everything to lead.

Amy Clampitt

Amy Clampitt died three years ago at seventy-three, barely a decade after publication of her first book. Her poems broke into print in mature form, like Athena from the head of Zeus; and many readers took her for a poet decades younger (for years she was sly about her birth date). It isn't that poetry is a child's game (Chatterton dead at seventeen, Keats at twenty-five, Shelley at twenty-nine) or that many poets write their best work before they turn thirty. Aging poets often suffer arteriosclerosis as awards shower upon them, and even latecomers like Stevens or Frost, whose first books came at or after the cusp of forty, are not immune to an ague of spirit, becoming the great man before they are great men.

Clampitt was a brazen innocent (has any poet starting later started better?), and the poetry never lost that sense of discovery in the landscape as well as the language.

The five books gathered in *The Collected Poems of Amy Clampitt* have been reprinted without editorial interference, a fond and rambling foreword by Mary Jo Salter catching much of Clampitt's wayward spirit—the gawky, birdlike presence; the high-pitched antic voice; the allergy to cars and planes and later even trains (the bus or ship was her preferred mode of travel, and she might have been happier in buggy or dog cart). Her poems spilled down the page with cheerful abandon; and the early poems (in a way her most distinctive) were often single sentences, the syntax artfully deployed in a series of delays and distractions as the thought juddered this way and that. Her long sentences were sometimes a splendor of false climaxes.

> *The poplars gray as a ghost by the creek,*
> *fiddlehead coils still in fuzz, the spruces*
> *tipped fingerling green, tamaracks gauzing*
> *the bog, the aspens translucent, a tremor*
>   *lit from within—oh, and the air*
>
> *here, the sea air an easterly rinsing*
> *of appletrees so decrepit, so crabbed*
> *at the knuckle, it's a wonder they manage*
> *to keep it up, year after year, though*
>   *the fragrance is ageless:*
>
> *carmine love-knots unclenching to a rose-*
> *pink pucker that whitens as it breaks open,*
> *admitting the offices of pollen-combing, nectar-*
> *siphoning bees: all these, at the beginning*
>   *of June, one could count on . . .*

We are still half a dozen lines from the end—she was our Faulkner of gymnastic syntax. Repetition was a form of resistance, of hesitation alive in the form; though her lists often got the better of her, they were reminiscent of Auden in the fecundity of pure imagination.

Inquire what consciousness is made of
with Galen, with Leonardo, Leeuwenhoek
or Dr. Tulp, and you find two hemispheres,
  a walnut in a bath of humors,

a skullcapped wreath of arteries, a weft
of fibrous thoroughfares along the walls
of Plato's cave, the cave walls of Lascaux:
  those shambling herds, this hollow

populous with fissures, declivities,
arboreal thicketings, with pairings
and degrees, this fist-sized flutter,
  mirror-lake of matter,

seat of dolor and jubilee, the law of Moses
and the giggling underneath the bedclothes,
of Bedlam and the Coronation Anthem—all
  these shut up in a nutshell.

Thus, the brain. She could make something from nothing, even of the nothings something was not ("no loom, no spinneret, no forge, no factor, / no process whatsoever, patent / applied or not applied for"). Her poems sidled toward their point, the eye ever caught by some bright flash elsewhere; and sometimes there didn't seem to be much point beyond the piling up of phrases, the hectic disposition of fresh vocabulary, the sentences falling toward an ending cut short, like an amateur singer yanked offstage.

Some poems were too tenuously balanced on a single idea, overloaded with sequins of detail glinting with nothing but the desire to accumulate—Clampitt suffered the Midas touch, without always knowing what to touch. Then the seeing was no longer believing—the richness could become wreckage, the prodigality a selfishness (Clampitt hated to leave anything out, but if a poem includes everything it is just the world—details can be a form of hectoring). Part of her charm was in the danger of being dazzled by local effects—the baroque vocabulary out of a shotgunned page of Roget's, the facts winkled from some encyclopedia: there's nothing like failure thinly skirted to increase the tension of pleasure.

That desperate richness was practiced as if the phrase behind had only just thought of the phrase ahead (the danger was not that a reader couldn't see beyond the particulars, but that there was nothing beyond them to see). It seemed to surprise the author no less than the reader when a poem circled back to its beginning like a benzene ring.

But if Clampitt was content to write the same poems again and again (she was a catalogue of seed plants, a royal aviary), how different she made the best of them—the worst were a dense fabric so similar, poem to poem, a reader had to look at the title to recall if the subject was bird or breviary. Among her contemporaries she was closest to James Merrill—the flamboyant surfaces, the preposterously embroidered lexicon (the inheritance of Auden), the sinuous thought and conversational asides (not as witty, but not as frivolous, either). A longer view might mark a different angle of descent, of association by language and line, from Marianne Moore (born 1887) to Elizabeth Bishop (1911) to Amy Clampitt (1920): their interest in objects, in the humor of the observing eye, created some of the unconscious principles of sensory record in our century. A poet like Clampitt can no longer be dismissed as the best woman poet of her day (in the younger generation the women are more interesting than the men); but if one day we lose our fear of differences between the sexes, something that defines the feminine may reside in these poems. It's not that men can't see this way; it's that behind such observation, so often, stands a woman.

Clampitt's later books were variations on her first, though her range grew more ambitious (and she grew to like shorter sentences): she wrote memorably about a tourist's culture (especially in England and Venice—her poems on classical themes seem just shards from *Bulfinch's*), about writers and public figures she admired (particularly in the brilliant but overlong sequence on Keats—her brief lives were often merely dutiful), about the ignored byways of the natural world. Only the poems about politics or pop culture, from Maytag washers to John Lennon, show an unsure hand. Her later poems became more detached and explanatory—in a way she stopped living her perceptions. Hers was a poetry other in its interests; the few hints of unhappy love dropped in

The Kingfisher, her first book, are never afterwards alluded to, and the recitals of daily events are without inner life. There was not progress so much as profusion. But what lovely and eccentric profusion! We were fortunate to have a poet so excited by the ordinary, who could make out of nothing, or almost nothing, these radiant, unlikely, lasting things.

chapter 20

Verse Chronicle:
Soiled Desires

Ted Hughes

Sylvia Plath would have turned sixty-six this year, and it's hard to imagine that burning, frantic, misshapen talent receiving Social Security. She died unwrinkled as a Romantic, older than Shelley but younger than Byron. Whether her talent would have developed further is that sorry suspicion we have of those who die young—the poems might have continued in angry gouts, or found domestic contentments, or withered up completely. She might have ended a fussy old Wordsworth, blowzy embarrassment to the Plathites who made her a feminist martyr; more likely she'd have reveled in each new award, a grande dame cigarette-waving into her seventh decade, unrepentant as an aging Hollywood star.

Plath is a crucial figure in American poetry. Understudy to confessional poets who were older, even much older, she exceeded their worst nightmares—however darkly Robert Lowell's madness rises into his poems, he sounds like a scholar in slippers compared to her ("My mind's not right" isn't half as scary as "Lady Lazarus," though it's better poetry). *Ariel* (1965) was not just the climax—it was the end of confessional poetry. No matter how shocking the revelation or how steely the revealer, every confessing poet afterward suffered her terms of engagement.

Ted Hughes's *Birthday Letters*, which in January burst unexpected into print, includes three decades of poems written in secret to his dead wife (only a few had appeared in print before). Hughes has been famously silent about Plath's suicide, and just as famously stoic in the face of thirty years of vicious feminist attacks that branded him a murderer (*Hughes* has been repeatedly chiseled from her gravestone). Only rarely has he bothered to defend himself, and then only by dashing off a letter to the editor of an offending publication. His "birthday letters," addressed to Plath, show that keeping silence was a measure of keeping faith.

The faith is much more impressive than the poetry. Though composed over decades, the poems are remarkably similar in their fireside tone and fleshy style (listless at times, at times overstuffed with metaphor). The garrulous free verse is a much toned-down version of Hughes's muscular line. He must get awfully tired of hearing his verse called muscular—the good news is, the verse isn't muscular any more. That's the bad news, too.

In the long battle over Plath's memory, Hughes's reticence has been dignified, his suffering almost magisterial. The early sympathies were hers by right—abandoned by her husband for another woman, raising two babies in a London flat during one of the most bitter British winters of the century, at thirty she squalidly committed suicide, on her knees with her head in a gas oven. Her death grotesquely mimicked the gassing of the Jews at Auschwitz, Jews whose murder she so adroitly appropriated in poems. The biography by Anne Stevenson, among a clutch of others, and the publication of Plath's letters and journals (the journals remain unpublished in Britain) have slowly redressed the balance.

Hughes was no saint (though often saintly in his treatment of her); but the portrait of Plath that has emerged, with some difficulty, is of a young woman with the grinning rictus of ambition, terror to friend and enemy alike, selfish, greedy for attention and willing to use any means to achieve it, vindictive, subject to manic rage and blinding depression. She was also a little gauche and new-minted, mocked by fellow students at Cambridge University (she arrived with a matched set of suitcases). One of her early suicide attempts was over being rejected for Frank O'Connor's summer writing course at Harvard. However much her admirers provide one version after another of incense-laced Sylviolatry, the "misfit self-display" and "dybbuk fury" of the letters and journals shoulder their way in. Memoirs by Dido Merwin and Richard Murphy, appended to Stevenson's biography, are X-rays of a woman at the edge of madness.

These rakings of the past are necessary to criticism of Hughes's poetry, because the past puts him in such an awkward position. He can't blame his own wife without attacking the dead, can't defend his actions without seeming exculpatory or self-righteous. The only moral position is supine, and it helps explain why these awkwardly pious poems (dull when they're not overdramatic) cower before events, why in crisis they excuse themselves in metaphor, or flights of rhetorical fancy, or fairy tale. The poems are a long apologia, but all they can do is prostrate themselves before a memory and clothe themselves in guilt. Any other position would seem monstrous.

There's some revision of Plath's subjects (her earthenware head, her owl), and occasional dry criticism of her ("rhyming yourself into safety"); but mostly this is a shrine, not a star chamber. You need a good biography in order to follow these poems; virtually every incident is better explained in prose. Hughes's version of student life has all the plummy abstractedness of the worst of *The Prelude:*

> *The nursery care of nature's leisurely lift*
> *Towards her fullness, we were careless*
> *Of grave life, three of us, four, five, six—*
> *Playing at friendship. Time in plenty*
> *To test every role—for laughs,*
> *For the experiment, lending our hours*
> *To perversities of impulse, charade-like*
> *Improvisations of the inane,*
> *Like prisoners, our real life*
> *Perforce deferred, with the real*
> *World and self. So, playing at students, we filled*
> *And drunkenly drained, filled and again drained*
> *A boredom, a cornucopia*
> *Of airy emptiness, of the brown*
> *And the yellow ale, of makings and unmakings.*

It's not just badly written, it's badly Wordsworthed—*O the brown and the yellow ale!* Here the lovers' first passion is Donne writ small:

> *How I smuggled myself, wrapped in you,*
> *Into the hotel. There we were.*
> *You were slim and lithe and smooth as a fish.*
> *You were a new world. My new world.*
> *So this is America, I marvelled.*
> *Beautiful, beautiful America!*

The young married couple later visit the Grand Canyon, "America's big red mamma!" Hughes is bold and big and clumsy, like an action painter given gallons of free paint (he's prone to crude foreshadowing and garden-shed mysticism). Plath's death and her afterlife as vengeful spirit and muse have been a vast private canvas for him. He is, after all, the surviving partner in one of the century's great love stories—these are the poems Romeo might have written, or Abelard. But Hughes, a considerable poet when young, has survived to write a poetry of cruel incompetence, with ham-handed allusions to Prufrock's peach and Rupert Brooke and "The Burning Babe."

The poems in *Birthday Letters* have an instinct for the ridiculous. There are touching moments, moments that make you despair for the lives Plath crippled; but the poems collapse in a mumble of metaphor:

> *Your typewriter,*
> *Your alarm clock, your new sentence*
> *Tortured you, a cruelty computer*
> *Of agony niceties, daily afresh—*
> *Every letter a needle, as in Kafka.*
> *While I, like a poltergeist fog,*
> *Hung on you, fed on you—heavy, drugged*
> *With your nightmares and terrors. Inside your Bell Jar*
> *I was like a mannikin in your eyeball.*

Later, Plath's father is "the god with the smoking gun"—there's Freud for you! Sometimes the problem's the dry listing of fact, sometimes the teary sentiment:

Like love forty-nine times magnified,
Like the first thunder cloudburst engulfing
The drought in August
When the whole cracked earth seems to quake
And every leaf trembles
And everything holds up its arms weeping.

No one who has read the biographies will find much new revealed here; indeed, Hughes is strangely closemouthed about their lives together. Plath's final days, like his disastrous affair with Assia Wevill (later to kill herself and their child), dissolve in a cloud of metaphor. The secrets of the marriage, however sane or sordid, are kept secret, largely by making it tiresome as any middle-class marriage. So it may have been; but where the facts might have purchase, the poetry can offer only banal insight—thirty years of brooding and all Hughes will hazard is a moral cliché, that he became the embodiment of her father.

Occasionally, only occasionally, as in a poem about their honeymoon, the mists clear for a few lines:

Spain frightened you. Spain
Where I felt at home. The blood-raw light,
The oiled anchovy faces, the African
Black edges to everything, frightened you.
Your schooling had somehow neglected Spain.
The wrought-iron grille, death and the Arab drum.

On the honeymoon, Plath suffers food poisoning or a fever. She loses all control—shrieks that she's going to die—and Hughes first glimpses the uncontrollable in her, glimpses something a little deranged. The best poem in the book, tellingly, isn't about Plath at all—it's about bats.

Birthday Letters has been welcomed with a pyroclastic flow of praise, more grotesque and misguided compliments than perhaps any poetry has attracted this century. British poets and critics, mostly male, have been nearly unanimous. For Andrew Motion in the *Times*, where the poems were first serialized, "Reading it is like being hit by a thunderbolt. . . . There is nothing like it in literature.

. . . this is his greatest book." For Tom Paulin, "It's a knockout volume, absolutely staggering." Douglas Dunn, in the *Financial Times*: "*Birthday Letters* is of an order that practically places Hughes beyond the ranks of ordinary mortals." Only a few British critics have suggested otherwise.

Something happened to Hughes's poetry after Plath's death. Though his first books look like period pieces now, their wrought-iron language and animal passion deepened the psychology of nature well before Lowell's "Skunk Hour." Later the language flattened into conversation or grew muscle-bound (as if it hadn't been mannered enough already), the poems at times surprisingly glandular and amateur. Plath's Faustian bargain was to die young, writing poetry of scathing brilliance; his was to live into old age, having lost his tongue.

John Ashbery

That old rascal John Ashbery has long passed the grand climacteric (he turns seventy-one this year), and perhaps it's too late to expect the dog to learn new tricks. His softly inflated, discount surrealism looks as easy as ever. Like many poets who settle into the comfort of a style, he's inimitable—if you imitated him you'd not just sound like Ashbery, you'd *be* Ashbery. I don't know why poets don't open Renaissance workshops and have apprentice poets knock off poems in the master's style, but perhaps that's what writing workshops do already.

Wakefulness is like a lot of recent Ashbery (has anyone noticed there's an awful lot of recent Ashbery—over 700 pages this decade?), seamless in its disjunctions, playful in its nonsense or pretend sense, irritatingly elusive, woolly and woolgathering. He's like a vaudeville comedian who doesn't bother to vary his delivery one year to the next: you hear the catchphrases and you laugh, not because he's funny, but because he's not funny. Ashbery's comedy has a tragic edge, though he's now less like Keaton than Beckett—with a lot more words.

His most delicious lines are about language or literature:

> *We thought we had seen a few new*
> *adjectives, but nobody was too sure. They might have been*
> *gerunds, or bunches of breakfast . . .*

The poem drifting off here is titled "Last Night I Dreamed I Was in Bucharest," and the movement toward waking and hunger is something Freud would have understood. It has the dreamy logic that makes so much of Ashbery's poetry a storehouse of half-forgotten phrases, giddy echoes of other poems: Whitman, say ("Once, on Mannahatta's bleak shore, / I trolled for spunkfish"), or Yeats ("Things break. Yes, they fail / or they are anchored up ahead"). One poem is composed entirely of quotations from other poems.

Ashbery's poems revel in their detachments, their refusal of narrative, their refusal of most of the traditional supports of poetry. He proves how little poetry depends on creating meaning—the urge to make meaning is so strong, the reader will supply what the words cannot. Ashbery's poems indefinitely postpone the promise of sense; but, even as they promise, the poems erase their own existence, falling forward rather than leaning back (poetry is one of the arts that usually depend on acknowledging the past)—you can't remember at the end of a poem how or why it started. The poem itself doesn't remember. Ashbery's poems have developed the equivalent of Alzheimer's disease.

> *He took off in a manner that betokened bats*
> *when it was over and they came over. It's time, now, some are good*
> *   and alone,*
> *lost up unto the rest. They can go and cancel*
> *around it's too moot to be played at. They are, for the rest*
> *   unsavory,*
> *thyme in the corral, three jumps from last school*
> *the patio ignited, sworn to safe-conduct, like bread out of a school*
> *conducted at last to here.*

Ashbery isn't often so dreadful (there are few lines like "all over the paisley fields dominoes are braying" or "A diagonal lipstick / chased him across the street"), but when he's bad he's as rotten as poetry gets. The destitution of his phrases is also his strength. His work reminds us that much of contemporary poetry survives on its little narratives, its clumsy emotional urgency: the impertinence of his poems acts most tellingly not in books but one by one in magazines, where they mock little gray-flannel poems (well, poems of any cloth). Ashbery's work looks better the more you forget it (the more you suffer Alzheimer's, perhaps), and he has become a poet of severe importance for what his verse denies rather than what it accepts. There's scarcely a poem worth reading again; but few poets have so cleverly manipulated, or just plain tortured, our soiled desire for meaning. He reminds us that most poets who give us meaning don't know what they're talking about.

Frank Bidart

Frank Bidart's new poems are nightmare fragments, stories that begin so *in medias res* the *res* are never clear. The hidden stories (often elegies) are sexual, but the sex is shamed or confused—the poems of *Desire* live in mystery and withholding. In this world of secret sharers, where the self reaches toward the rejecting Other, the poems are loveless versions of self-hatred because no Other releases their blocked loathing.

Bidart's earlier dramatic monologues by Nijinsky and the anorectic Ellen West carried some of this unlovely passion; but they were preposterous overreadings of character, all too eager to make their points. In *Desire* other texts lie beneath the texts—Dante and Ovid, who understood the dark torsions of love, shadow the poems like learned vultures. Marcus Aurelius contributes a refrain; Tacitus and Plotinus and the Manichaeans make quiet appearances, as if classical authors had the authority of reassurance. When Bidart retells the story of the disappearance of Varus's legions in the Black Forest, that bedtime tale for bad little Roman boys and girls, it's more moving than the surrounding poems but awfully like a history lecture. There's even a prose poem on the author's split personality, a thuggish and self-regarding prose poem deriving from Borges's "Borges and I"—"Frank"'s problems as speaker are a long distance from Proust's idea of *le moi profond*.

The shorter poems here prepare the psychology of "The Second Hour of the Night," a masterwork whose first part is as good as anything Bidart has written, juxtaposing the memoirs of Berlioz, whose wife died slowly and horribly, with the death of the poet's mother. The not-so-subtle merger of Bidart's mother and Berlioz's wife, in the erotics implicitly embraced, is the most important psychological gesture in these poems. The second section, alas, is an overlong rehash of Ovid's tale of Myrrha, whose incestuous love for her father causes disaster all around. The myth doesn't nearly repay the thirty pages it takes to recount (it's only two hundred lines in Ovid), and the thwarted love and doom-laden incest are a textbook parody of homosexual psychology.

As Myrrha is drawn down the dark corridor toward her father

not free not to desire

what draws her forward is neither COMPULSION nor FREE-
  WILL:—

or at least freedom, here choice, *is not to be*
imagined as action upon

preference: no creature is free to choose what
allows it its most powerful, and most secret, release.

This sounds like a speech for the Mattachine Society. The grief that rises so longingly in the first part is here endlessly deferred until we forget that the Ovid was a means rather than an end. After Myrrha is finally turned into a bush, her crime against nature at last become nature itself, she gives birth to Adonis. If Myrrha is a stand-in for the dying mother, that makes the poet . . . well, the answer isn't exactly modest.

Bidart has been a peculiar predatory poet, restricted to techniques more dramatic than recognizably poetic (witness his frequent soapbox typography)—this has given his monologues an unpleasant hysteria. His poems are too often declaimed from the Greek stage, his personae masked as Fates or Furies. My complaint against Bidart's earlier work was the thinness of the fiction: even Browning, the most Jamesian and psychological of poets, could not fully adapt poetry to fiction's grammar of display (though weakness of character accords well with the gestures of satire, as in *Don Juan* or *The Rape of the Lock*). A character like Ellen West can't exceed the drama of her disease—how could she, given a sickness so freighted with meaning, so calculatedly metaphoric? Twenty years before, she would have suffered polio; twenty years later, AIDS. The choice was too easy, easy as the fate of real victims is hard (it takes a Camille to make disease more than its metaphor). Bidart treats homosexual love as a pathology, even a virtuous pathology ("outlaw love," perhaps); but a part of nature can't be against nature—nature is all its instances, not a norm.

Karl Kirchwey

Karl Kirchwey's new poems are soaked in the blood of empire, the history now roped off for the tourist rather than interred by the historian. *The Engrafted Word* follows the grand tour through Italy and the Mediterranean, a Mediterranean still lying under the shattered visage of Rome (a very bookish Rome). Recent American poetry has been so domestic in its harmonies, so commonplace in private quarrels rather than public angers, a passport elsewhere can be an escape. Kirchwey has a sensitive, even soulful manner (a little too soulful at times)—amid dusty ruins, the cruelty and casual blindness of the past make him wary, embarrassed by the culture he enjoys, embarrassed by the privilege of travel. The tourist is the voyeur of old violence.

Even the empire's humble fish contribute to the gory passions of power:

> *a fisherman once surprised Tiberius*
> *on his rugged island of pleasure;*
> *there is blood in the crisscross of scales*
> *where the guards used the gift of the poor*
> *man to rub the skin off his face.*
>
> *Beauty and malignant shame mingle*
> *in a fry of albino gold*
> *and whiskered calico. Witness this hunger,*

flamboyant and utterly normal,
as their poached blindnesses suck the mud
and bask in the sun with a dull glitter.

This calm unfolding of detail has the observant richness of Richard Wilbur, though without the control or taste of meter. Kirchwey dabbles in rhyme (mostly half- or quarter- or eighth-rhyme) and can whisk up pentameter when he wishes; but his flinching from formal responsibilities divorces him from the labored elegance and mannered Europe of so many poets in the fifties. Kirchwey is much more interesting than most of the New Formalists, many of whom write a pentameter so dull it would qualify for workman's compensation (dullness being an occupational hazard).

At times, when the quatrains slacken or rhythm vanishes down a prosy whirlpool, Kirchwey's poems seem secretly to desire a more stringent measure. The beauty of his withholding eye is not always enough—there are passions in this verse still unexplored. That's why his strangled stoicism is so effective—it admits there's something to be stoic about. The strain between guilty pleasure and innocent passion is the heart of a Christian heritage the ancient world is all too willing to attack.

Kirchwey's tone is sometimes unsteady (there's too much of the mock naive for my taste), and the poems of New York are less secure in their habitat than the poems of places thousands of miles away—he has a visa for every country but home. Some poems are precious, and a good many end with an earnest hush, the experience exhausted before the poem is over. There's a villanelle so clumsy it made me want to stop writing villanelles. But just when the defects threaten to overwhelm a poetry otherwise so attractive, the lovely lines or near-perfect stanzas show the richness is not its own reward—richness is the salvation of doubt.

Frederick Seidel

Frederick Seidel treats the high trash of culture with haute serious-ness. No one since Marx (a poet of sorts) has written a poetry so poisoned by capitalism; and you can't read Seidel without feeling sympathy for Lenin, without thinking capitalists really *should* be shot. Seidel is a name-dropper—he rubs shoulders with ambassa-dors and senators ("My friend / The junior senator from Ne-braska"), French film directors, Racine-quoting beauties, louche Euro-trash. The poems in *Going Fast* are a fairyland department store of brand names, always in exquisite taste (so tasteful some-times they're not brands at all, they're addresses). He knows where to get a suit fitted in Milan, how to have a motorcycle custom de-signed, who in London or Paris makes the right bespoke shoes:

> *No one has surpassed*
> *The late George Cleverley's lasts,*
> *The angle in of the heel, the slightly squared-off toe, the line,*
> *Though Suire at Lobb is getting there.*
> *His shoes fit like Paradise by the third pair.*
> *Like they were Eve. The well-dressed man,*
> *The vein of gold that seems inexhaustible,*
> *Is a sunstream of urine on its way to the toilet bowl.*

Such vulgar display, like a closet of Imelda Marcos's pumps, might rouse antipathy in any reader. Seidel began as a Lowell imi-tator; the poems in his first books, *Final Solutions* and *Sunrise* (both of which I admired), repeated the sins and syntax of the master with ironic flair—now Seidel's irony tends to wear jackboots and carry a ball-peen hammer. There's still power in the blunt phras-ings, but the recent books trade in snide juxtapositions (a man "does yoga / High above the homeless") and cheap shock ("I want to date-rape life," "The smell of sperm on the edge of the axe").

The promise (even the premise) of such poetry is its insider knowledge, its view down the nose toward hoi polloi, all the while saying, "But look, I'm a radical, too!" Seidel has a point, if not an important point: the rich suffer as much as anyone, in their way, and their despair has goldplate ironies. But Seidel wants to eat his cake and have it: he wants to flaunt his connections, rub the reader's nose in wealth, and still sneer at privilege. "We're all guilty," he seems to say, but you can't help feeling he wallows smugly in guilt, considering the company he keeps (his Ducati 916 roars into half a dozen poems, but he can't just ride it—he has to "ride to Syria / To President Assad").

It's one thing to repent youthful folly, to see the sickening void of conspicuous consumption, another to long for display while beating your breast like a reformed sinner. This may be his analysis of a condition, the capitalist condition that sells sin and salvation too; but Seidel's jet-set tastes and upmarket sinning get pretty tiresome.

> *Combine a far-seeing industrialist.*
> *With an Islamic fundamentalist.*
> *With an Italian Premier who doesn't take bribes.*
> *With a pharmaceuticals CEO who loves to spread disease.*
> *Put them on a 916.*
>
> *And you get Fred Seidel.*

Only in his retelling of Ovid (like Frank Bidart he chooses the myth of Myrrha) is Seidel distracted into a sordid, knowing art. Though banished in the end, Ovid knew the richness of Rome and used its vanities (religious as well as retail) beneath the raw matter of poetry.

August Kleinzahler

Things happen to August Kleinzahler, any-old-thing kind of things; and you can't see why they should be interesting to someone else when they're not all that interesting to him. The poems in *Green Sees Things in Waves* have a resistant cool, and with his goofy good nature and hip diction Kleinzahler's the nineties version of a poet who hangs out on street corners in a beret and recites poems to passersby.

> *The sopressata fée outside of Calfasso's*
> *with the swept-back 'do and blood on her smock*

grabs a quick smoke on the sidewalk,
tosses it in the gutter then sucks back her lips
till they smack, getting her lipstick right.

Like *wow*, baby! This might be Norman Mailer imitating Norman Mailer, during his white Negro period. Kleinzahler is much taken with the power of the demotic, and when he says, "But still, it was a doozy" or "Oh shit, // there goes the Parcheesi board," it's hard not to smile and wonder what Frank O'Hara would have made of it. At times I expect Kleinzahler to ask for a copy of *New World Writing* to see what the poets in Ghana are up to.

Kleinzahler has a lovely way with landscape:

The oleander on Longitude Lane
flares among the languors and fevers of June
below the south-facing piazzas
the sea breezes find
or don't quite find
along the corridors of ivy-covered brick.

Landscape is never quite enough, however. The fast-talking bebop poet in Kleinzahler likes snappy titles ("Glossolalia All the Way to Buffalo") and impotent fragments (a series of "tankas" called, appallingly, "Tanka-Toys: A Memoir"). His "52 Pick-up" is a scattering of words and phrases that transiently suggest the nonsense ("Irwin Corey"), simulacra ("Frottage"), and brain damage ("Korsakoff's Syndrome") that are part of his technique—his linguistic markers are set as far apart as Chomsky's "Colorless green ideas sleep furiously" and Durante's "Good night, Mrs. Calabash."

Every poet longs to make the language his own, and much of the strutting and fretting here is territorial display: Kleinzahler wants an idiom more adaptable than the one he's inherited, and he has plundered the language to advantage. I like a poet who can use "griseous" and "sintered" and "sphygmology," as well as "pattymelt" and "higgledy-piggledy" and "Victor McLaglen." Unfortunately, as with much avant-garde poetry, these radical methods hide all-too-sentimental secrets. An idiom not yet fouled by the mawkishness of your ancestors is often willing victim to mawkishness of your very own. Too many of these poems descend into vacant longing, weepy regret for dead canaries, for lost chances—even, if I understand him, for pollution ("the aroma / almost comforting by now, like food"). Daily life becomes all too much like religion, every dinner a main course of transcendence and a dessert of revelation:

> because only now, alone in this room
>
> dark and quiet as a chapel
> the garlic has slowly begun to bloom
>
> and the wine in the back of your throat
> will be made sonorous by it
>
> then it is time, after much stirring
> and some contemplation
>
> to find the appropriate tune
> perhaps one of Schubert's final sonatas

Poor Schubert. Here prose meets the death instinct.

I was more taken with Kleinzahler's previous book, *Red Sauce, Whiskey and Snow* (1995), where you had to put up with a lot of triviality to get two or three poems of subversive instinct. He seems to have decided triviality is enough. When he writes love poems, they come in the most peculiar diction imaginable, somewhere between Thomas Wyatt and Elizabeth Barrett Browning: "How well these ladies do contrive, how well, / to keep me in thrall with their sweet neglect." It's a joke, of course. A reader may be forgiven for looking at his watch.

chapter 21

Three Magi

Charles Wright

Charles Wright's rangy metaphysical poetry has the half-drowsy voice of exhaustion. The poems of *Appalachia* may start in the harshly gorgeous landscapes of Virginia, but soon they're dreaming of God and "would-be-saints" and "angel's wings." An American metaphysics may seem a contradiction in terms, so given is our culture to the cruelty of excess (our idea of a floating particular is a decimal point). Our homegrown poet-philosophers have tended to be crackpots like Whitman and Pound—geniuses of the soil, and like Antaeus helpless when they lost touch with the soil.

Wright's early poems still had dirt under their thumbnails. He was born in backcountry Tennessee and couldn't let the reader forget it; worse, he couldn't let himself forget it (in Venice, he seemed a barbarian tribesman sending postcards back to the Visigoths). Those early poems had rustic manners: their awkwardness guaranteed their rude honesty, and his landscapes burned into the eye like gold mosaics. They burn there still:

> *The pollen-colored chestnut blooms*
> > *sweep like a long cloth*
> *Snapped open over the bunched treetops.*

Whether "sunlight showers like sulphur grains across his face" or "the moon rains down its antibiotic light," the radiance of this world never needs excuse.

The tension in Wright between the transcendental and our frac-
tured world used to drag him back to this world's homely, contin-
gent beauty. The bad news is, the other world won. For the last
decade or more, as awards have piled heavily upon him, his poems
have become ghostly versions of their grounded selves, mere
sketches or jottings; and without titles it would be difficult to tell
where one poem ended and another began. What started as an at-
traction to Dante and the *Paradiso* has become high-flown meta-
physical mumbling: "The soul is air, and it maintains us," "Still,
who knows where the soul goes, / Up or down, / after the light
switch is turned off . . . ?"

These new poems are filled with mortal thoughts (even mortal
longings—Prospero couldn't have said goodbye to his magic more
eagerly than Wright to his poems). Their world-weary air has lost
all passion, and the relentless present tense reaches toward a time-
less hereafter, hoping for mystic vision but knowing the mystical is
impossible, that language cannot be abandoned or the self undone
(the self here is the insult of style). That elegantly jaded pose faces
the same failures over and over, until melancholia is just an excuse
for sentiment:

> *Give me the names for things, just give me their real names,*
> *Not what we call them, but what*
> *They call themselves when no one's listening.*

It's hard to think Wright believes such guff (or that he'd know what
to do with those secret names if he got them). There's a lot of
blather about the soul and heaven and saints' hearts here; and it's
insulting when he quotes a real mystic like Simone Weil, who paid
the price of her beliefs.

Edward Hirsch

Edward Hirsch is our Great Sentimentalist: nothing human is
alien to him, and nothing teary is, either. When you read about his
childhood—an ordinary, suburban, knockabout childhood, with
Little League and the rest—you'd hardly believe it could rouse
such gouts of feeling, but Hirsch is shameless. He'll start with a

baseball in hand and by the second inning be deep in the Holocaust. Many of the poems in *On Love* are hardly subtle in their self-flattery: you can't say of yourself at seven that there was a "shadowy, grief-stricken need for freedom / laboring to express itself" and hope to look at the reader with a straight face, not if you mean the freedom of the Jews, all of the Jews.

Even when the poems are compellingly lovelorn, they're creepily lovelorn. His girlfriend in Chicago in 1968 (*Those were the days!* he seems to say) joins the "Sky Church" and he never sees her again. Good riddance, you might think, but no:

> *Days of 1968, sometimes your shutters open*
> *and I glimpse a star gleaming in the constellations.*
>
> *I can almost reach up and snag her by the hand.*
> *I can go to her if I don't look back at the ground.*

You can't be coercively sentimental and reduce the reader to tears; you can only reduce him to laughter.

Love is the major subject of *On Love*, which includes a sequence of two dozen amorous meditations, mostly by European literary figures of the last century or so. Baudelaire and Wilde are there, Brecht and Lawrence, but also odd choices like Margaret Fuller and Tristan Tzara. Each has been invited, at some mythical Convention of Love, to address an assembled audience. It's a delightful premise, as premises go, but the results are hilariously awful. The poet has worn out his fingers taking notes, pored over a dusty cache of biographies, yet the lectures are leaden and monotonous—heavy with abstraction, never a word used with élan, they sink under their musty seriousness. It's hard to know who's the most tedious: Margaret Fuller is dull, Baudelaire duller (Baudelaire!), Valéry dullest of all—but no, Emerson is duller still: "I have been told that in public discourse / my true reverence for intellectual discourse / has made me indifferent to the subject of love, / but I almost shrink at such disparaging words." You can hear the audience snoring away. The lectures lack the verbal risk and sly sidelights on character that make Richard Howard's baroque monologues so preposterous in their invention.

Away from this tedious casting call of literary figures, lost in the sentimental welter of the poems of private life, are two poems so dry-eyed and dark they're unlike anything Hirsch has written. "Hotel Window" is about an incident with the supernatural overtones of James, and "A Painting of Pan" recovers the bleak shock of recognition in a sexual encounter. They don't belong with the soap-opera smarminess or Jaycee after-dinner speeches Hirsch has made his own. They're so good they should be torn out of the book and pinned on the wall.

Henri Cole

The Visible Man is Henri Cole's most brutal and despairing book— what earlier was a dapper young man's mild self-absorption has become self-hatred fit for the burning rain of the *Inferno*. The poems rail against, without being able to free the poet from, the Christianity and homosexuality his by inheritance; and no reference to the "Sodomite's self-loathing" or the "little worn machines of Christ" can protect the victim from torturing himself. These poems have been stripped of the defense of style:

> *sometimes, when I turn to the crucifix,*
> *all I see is a naked man, wounded,*
> *utterly desirable, hanging on my wall.*

Cole's earlier poems were reminiscent of James Merrill and Elizabeth Bishop in their pretty surfaces and sometimes comic touches—the darkness was visible, but not very visible. His poems lived on the edge of formality, sinking under the weight of rhyme, as if rhyme were the anchor to formal poetry he could not abandon. *The Visible Man* retains the ghost of form, but the ghost rarely speaks. That ghost is the final reminder of the life of reason.

Most poets prefer the classical world to the Christian: the life before Christianity speaks more plainly to those who have lost their God. Cole, who has not lost faith ("how can He love me and hate what I am?"), takes the classical world, the world of other gods with other charities, as a necessary solace of the psychological soul

(Freud used the myths, not the gospels). Again and again, Cole has rediscovered myth in the harshness of modern dress:

> *Sunday evening.*
> *Mother is wearing a big cotton shift*
> *and tweezing her eyebrows.*
> *Her head is a thicket of hairpins.*
> *In the round hand-mirror*
> *that parodies her face,*
> *the world looks greater than it is.*

The son is about to bathe in Mother's bath water—a modern Achilles (with the undercurrent of Oedipus)! These poems take homosexual conflict back to the seeping guilts of twenty or thirty years ago (the poet accusing himself of being "womanish, conflicted, subservient"). This unnerving honesty, in a time fawning with self-esteem, has forced his language to suspicion of the coddled self, of the coziness of poetic means. He writes of peonies:

> *Ample creamy heads beaten down vulgarly,*
> *as if by some deeply sado-masochistic impulse,*
> *like the desire to subdue, which is normal and active,*
> *and the desire for suffering, which is not;*
> *papery white featherings stapled to long stalks,*
> *sopped with rain and thrown about violently,*
> *as Paul was from his horse by the voice of Christ.*

Poor peonies! In the epigraph to the ambitious sequence of "sonnets" that closes this book, Ovid's Phaëthon pleads with Apollo: "O let me clean my spirit of all doubt, / Give me the signature of what I am." For Phaëthon the acceptance of who he was meant death. The break with the proprieties of Cole's earlier style, the invention of a self so harrowing in character, will remind readers of Robert Lowell's *Life Studies*, published forty years ago. If Cole's poems are not quite formed, if they are still raw with half-born shouts, most other books would be reduced to ashes by the comparison.

chapter 22

Four or Five Motions
toward a Poetics

Certain experiences in reading poetry don't have a name, and by naming them I want to be obliged less for the taxonomy of a mystery than for a response to what are often unnamed measures. These are not very good names, but name perhaps matters less than extending a forefinger in the right direction. As a name, *objective correlative* is clumsy and ridiculous; but its use is as pointed as saying *aardvark* or *beetle*, and that was Adam's task.

Trust

Violation of the contract between reader and poem is a violation of trust. Trust not merely names the intimate understanding of the terms the poem sets out, or the temporary credit every author is afforded until the language betrays it (minor authors betray us line by line). Trust might be called the quality of significant authority within attending possibility. It is the poem's ability to proceed without distracting the reader with mere clumsiness of technique, while offering benefit to the reader's imagination equal to or exceeding the energy expended in reading. Trust is therefore the inclusive and associating category of aroused interest on the one hand (the excitation of the reader's comprehending sympathies) and controlled momentum on the other (the mere forward drive of the lines, aided by technical supports like meter or enjambment or the imposition of narrative). Trust is that allowance we give to the unsayable as it is said.

Failures of trust must include provision of irrelevant matter, missed opportunities, lapel-pulling, comedies of tone, corruptions of diction, solecism, redundancy, tediousness, inconsistency, sentiment, cliché, pointless obscurity, the whole panoply of which bad poetry is composed and the abyss good poetry struggles to avoid and into which it occasionally descends. What is remarkable about good poetry is how rarely we remember there *are* such disasters: trust is the quality of forgetting disasters can occur, even if the poetry at hand never reaches the highest level of the art. (Bad poetry is not a disaster waiting to happen; it is a disaster reborn every minute in the collapse of trust.)

Where an author has earned the vulnerability of his reader, the reader will risk far more than he would for a writer more expedient (or less skillful) in his authority. And in such intimacy the major author may reach an apprehension beyond that of the minor. In Whitman, the disasters are everywhere sensed even when warded off; though the disasters are just as often fondly embraced. The reader never enjoys trust in his verse (except of a perverse kind)— rather, the reader lives in numbed astonishment at the bad and hapless gratitude for the good. Milton is a different matter.

> *When I consider how my light is spent*
> *Ere half my days, in this dark world and wide,*
> *And that one talent which is death to hide*
> *Lodged with me useless, though my soul more bent*
> *To serve therewith my Maker, and present*
> *My true account, lest he returning chide;*
> *"Doth God exact day-labor, light denied?"*
> *I fondly ask; but Patience to prevent*
> *That murmur, soon replies, "God doth not need*
> *Either man's work or his own gifts; who best*
> *Bear his mild yoke, they serve him best. His state*
> *Is kingly. Thousands at his bidding speed*
> *And post o'er land and ocean without rest:*
> *They also serve who only stand and wait."*

The opening of Sonnet XVI creates a little nest of signification, and our bearing upon its intentions while keeping the exact meaning in suspension is the action of trust. The poem must justify those significances each against the others; and our willingness to permit that slow unfolding (akin in its way to the unveilings of meter, its intricate substitutions and balancings) is the measure and condition of our trust. In a sonnet such trust moves within the language as well as the form, and appropriately Milton's sonnet concerns a matter of trust at the highest reach of faith.

These lines were written in the years before *Paradise Lost*. Milton may have lost his inspiration. He may recently have gone blind. The question is finally undecidable; at least, it has never been decided by critics. The conduct of trust—the conviction in the elaborating character of the language—allows these competing interpretations to exist in mutual apprehension, without the poem deciding on one or the other. Either form of blindness (of sight or insight) is a particular of loss.

The ambiguity of the opening is mirrored by a series of linguistic ambiguities. "Spent" may mean exhausted through overwork or squandered (there is little sense of care here). This is a poem partly about money (the pun informs Wordsworth's "getting and spending"): "that one talent" refers to the parable in Matthew 25 of the man who gives his servants various sums before "traveling into a far country." Two servants invest their talents and double them. The third buries his single talent in fear of losing it. Digging it up for his returning master, he is called wicked and slothful and cast "into outer darkness."

Our modern sense of "talent" derives from the ancient coin, through the medium of this very parable; the language thus divides thematically without forcing the ambiguities into alignment. The specie or medium of exchange exists in a shadowy realm behind the artistry, and vice versa; and whether we take the one as symbol or the other as action makes no difference to the losses the poem was built to confide. That each supports the ambiguities is a provision of trust.

The trust required between poem and reader is partly a fiction of biblical knowledge—the poem will be illegible without the memory of St. Matthew that once could be taken for granted. To that extent trust is a bias threatened by cultural change or cultural error. But the second half of the poem offers revision: its imagery associates more conveniently with the parable of the vineyard in Matthew 20.

A householder hires laborers at a penny a day and through the day continues to hire at the same rate, some workers even about "the eleventh hour." When at evening they're all paid the same penny for toil in the vineyard, those who have sweated through "the heat of the day" protest. The sonnet's "day-labor," its "murmur" darkly echoing the laborers who "murmured against the goodman of the house," the final line's "stand and wait" that finds repose in those "standing idle in the market place"—these are exactions of a richly insinuating language. Christ's vineyard is the visible symbol of the kingdom of heaven, entrance to which must be the unstated longing of the poem—a man who makes nothing of his gifts can hardly guarantee himself access to the God who bestowed them. Milton's answer is that the parable of the talents is mistaken.

The poem like the parable implies a mystery: the mystery of Milton's disorder, as well as the mystery of his anxiety, is subordinate to the mystery of the desire of God. The ambiguities conceal that mystery in one parable in order to reveal it—in sidelong fashion—through another. As Christ, oldest among hermeneutic interpreters, said in Matthew 13, "Therefore speak I to them in parables: because they seeing see not; and hearing they hear not, neither do they understand." The language beneath Milton's disorder is a language of concealment, blindness, outer darkness, and a far country.

When the householder came to the market again late in the day and still found men "standing idle," he said, "Why stand ye here all the day idle?" And they replied, "Because no man hath hired us." It is these men who later received their reward first, received their penny though they had toiled least, and they who became the subject of the lesson: that "the last shall be first," that "many be called, but few chosen."

God does not need the gifts he himself devised—this is a radical

answer to Milton's dilemma. The justice of the poem, the fulfill-
ment of the potential whose exhaustion or squandering the poet
questions, is the *bearing up* under the burden of the mystery (here
sonnet again echoes parable, some laborers having "borne the bur-
den and heat of the day"—but see Christ's words in Matthew 11:
"My yoke is easy, and my burden is light"). Those who stand and
wait also serve their role, a more difficult role because seemingly
an empty one.

Milton's sonnet is a strange act of self-consolation, but the poem
is itself a triumph of trust—its very existence shows the talent has
not been hidden. The poem, as a perfected object, answers the
anxiety about the effect of blindness (imaginative or physical) on
artistry, and is therefore a model of the purposes of trust: to convey
the reader through a series of alternatives without forcing him to
choose alternatives. In this, trust is the reader's account of a nega-
tive capability. Milton's gratitude for the answer was *Paradise Lost*.

Trust is also a matter of assumptions left unquestioned. Part of
the drama of trust is our willingness to listen to a man frame his
analysis in accord with his supernatural beliefs, without being able
to hear the voices of heaven (only the voice of Patience, from
whatever realm Patience inhabits). Trust allows a man to question
his faith, and receive an answer in faith, without our breaking into
nervous laughter; indeed, with our being moved in the process.

Valence

The emotions are affected by matters formal and objective as well
as intimate and subjective. The lyric voice is also the articulation of
a voice, calculated and conditioned by strategies of rhetoric. When
we think of the ways the poet conveys emotion, we think of point
of view, selection of detail, atmosphere, tone—not situation but a
response to situation. When at the end of her villanelle "One Art"
Elizabeth Bishop writes, "It's evident / the art of losing's not too
hard to master / though it may look like (*Write* it!) like disaster,"
the imperative is the final goading toward losses hard to contem-
plate, a way of admitting her hesitation (while overcoming the
hesitation) to write the word most difficult to admit. The sudden

irruption of the author's voice *within* her voice measures the violence of the denial. Here the parenthesis seems very much Coleridge's "drama of reason."

None of these emotional torsions would be as effective had the form not *compelled* that "disaster" be the word written. Valence is the portion of emotion for which the form alone is responsible, and among the armory of valence we may include meter (and the various effects of rhythm), rhyme and all the partial rhymes of assonance and consonance, and the repetitions and returns of form (most significantly, the closure of form), whether ad hoc or traditional. That the contributions of some of these may be arguable does not make them negligible. Emotion in a poem is slippery, often a function of effects of voice barely registered. Valence is where it is a formal matter.

Note, for example, how beautifully Bishop handles the repetition in that final line—this is an example of the plasticity of pentameter. *Like* in the first instance is a down-in-the-mouth, unstressed acknowledgment of the unsaid; when repeated it is like a shout. The stress emphasizes the form of the anxiety as well as the telling shock of the forced comparison. In such cases valence is the emotion that *only* form makes possible.

"Visits to St. Elizabeths" offers a striking instance of the formal contribution to emotional effect. Where the poem is an idea, part of its meaning lies in the particular instance of its form, here in the underlying nursery rhyme: the incremental additions of "The House That Jack Built" constitute a narrative. The poem is partly composed of, partly an editorial about, the reduction of Pound's intelligence to a childlike state (this is surely the madness that Pound built). The house of Bedlam is a grim reminder of *linguistic* contortion, important given Pound's diatribes about Jews—it is the final collapsed and misunderstood pronunciation of what was once the house of Bethlehem, the Hospital of St. Mary of Bethlehem.

This is the house of Bedlam.

This is the man
that lies in the house of Bedlam.

This is the time
of the tragic man
that lies in the house of Bedlam.

This is a wristwatch
telling the time
of the talkative man
that lies in the house of Bedlam.

This is a sailor
wearing the watch
that tells the time
of the honored man
that lies in the house of Bedlam.

This is the roadstead all of board
reached by the sailor
wearing the watch
that tells the time
of the old, brave man
that lies in the house of Bedlam.

The form conducts the meaning in collusive ways. The dozen stanzas, each one line longer that the last, record a succession of visits (the number a timely reminder of time in a poem where a watch is important): at each visit a new perception must be added. The stanzas therefore represent a deepening acquaintance with the condition of madness as well as a failure of consolation in the face of it. The form specifies the repetition, but stanza by stanza Bishop turns against form by slightly varying the prior lines. Pound each time acquires new character, becoming by turns *tragic; talkative; honored; old, brave; cranky; cruel;* and so forth (Pound is never named in the poem, and this extraliterary identification renders him a figure nearly anonymous). These variations lie within the steady monotony of the form, the monotony of the days and years in which Pound is incarcerated (after the opening, every stanza ends with the same flat epitaph: "the ___ man / that lies in the house of Bedlam"—*lies* has an informing ambiguity here). Each adjective adds to the portrait, but some subtract from the humanity—he is finally *tedious* and even *wretched* (the sequence of adjectives is as important as their meaning—the penultimate pair, *the poet, the man*, suggests how divided Pound is as a figure).

> *This is the soldier home from the war.*
> *These are the years and the walls and the door*
> *that shut on a boy that pats the floor*
> *to see if the world is round or flat.*
> *This is a Jew in a newspaper hat*
> *that dances carefully down the ward,*
> *walking the plank of a coffin board*
> *with the crazy sailor*
> *that shows his watch*
> *that tells the time*
> *of the wretched man*
> *that lies in the house of Bedlam.*

Pound's is one tragedy among others. The variations permit Bishop a narrative latitude: a mad boy, a mad Jew, and a mad sailor each has his own story (even the Jews are susceptible to madness—Pound is locked up with the object of his prejudice). These modulations over the stability of form operate like the permissible variations in meter, and not only in their content but in their kind affect the emotional structure of the poem.

The form has at once proposed the monotony that is the character of madness while offering the ground against which character may be construed. Without the form, the madness could not have offered the same descent into the repetitive intensity of the particular (the repetitions almost a form of rage), as well as the variations that invent character and the opposing and critical views of character. The nursery rhyme is a formal as well as tonal restraint, but Bishop takes advantage of the limitations of form: the form admits the accusation as well as the analysis. Each aspect of form contributes to emotion, and the sum of their contributions—what the form itself adds to the emotion—may be called the valence. Such a term is needed as a reminder that emotion is often deeper than what is said, deeper because it exploits the various opportunities form provides.

Gesture and Expression

Gesture is the visual or metaphorical representation of an object—
it may be a description, a characteristic, a color, a posture. Expres-
sion is a gesture to which significance has been added. (Marvell's
vegetable love is an act of expression, *vegetable* compressing and giv-
ing translucence to a number of themes in the poem. It doesn't
particularly matter that Williams's wheelbarrow is red—red is a vi-
sual gesture.) Every expression begins as a gesture, but every ges-
ture is not an expression (poetry is filled with gestures that are not
expressions). All objects in a poem therefore make gestures.

A sufficiently subtle criticism might draw expression from every
gesture, but as readers we are aware that in many poets everything
remains a gesture and nothing becomes expression. An expression
must depend, not just on the underlying flux of meaning the poem
is constructed to convey, but on how each gesture fits the form.
Gesture is the empty form of the visual.

> *Earth has not anything to show more fair:*
> *Dull would he be of soul who could pass by*
> *A sight so touching in its majesty;*
> *This City now doth, like a garment, wear*
> *The beauty of the morning; silent, bare,*
> *Ships, towers, domes, theaters, and temples lie*
> *Open unto the fields, and to the sky;*
> *All bright and glittering in the smokeless air.*
> *Never did sun more beautifully steep*
> *In his first splendor, valley, rock, or hill;*
> *Ne'er saw I, never felt, a calm so deep!*
> *The river glideth at his own sweet will:*
> *Dear God! the very houses seem asleep;*
> *And all that mighty heart is lying still!*

Wordsworth's sonnet is an interesting use of expression because
each object makes such a small visual imprint. The objects are pre-
sented but scarcely described, and so depend to an unusual degree
on the implications in the structure of meaning for their transla-
tion to significance. It is an unusual poem to begin with—for

Wordsworth, at any rate—because in praise of the city. Wordsworth was not like Johnson; he would not have felt a man tired of London was tired of life. The advantage of not being superior to your material, however, is that you are allowed to act innocent.

The poem describes the city in its glory but also notes when the city assumes such glory. Wordsworth is obviously surprised to find the city has any majesty at all, that the civilization of this world can attain the heavenly splendor reserved in his mind for landscape. It is perhaps as a heavenly city that "ships, towers, domes, theaters, and temples" seem almost biblical. The ships of Tarshish (almost ubiquitous in the Old Testament), the towers and temples of Jerusalem (and the domes of Muslim occupation, or the great dome of St. Peter's in Rome)—these are objects more than secular. Those curious temples might be Wren's churches or the Inner and Outer Temple of barristers. Wordsworth specifies *temples*, not *churches*, which would have had the same metrical profile. Even theaters partake of Christian martyrology—and *theater* is mentioned twice in Acts.

Such suggestiveness is not enough to establish those architectural gestures as an expression of meaning, but meaning may be disciplined elsewhere; and here the poet creates his expression by cunning indirection. The religious character of the imagery might not have been a prospect aroused had the poet not conjured "soul" in the second line, followed closely by "majesty." The sun rises "in his first splendor," a dawn that might be the first dawn (one of the small expressions of the poem is the way the list of city sights is itself a landscape, imitating the country of "valley, rock, or hill"). These hints are overwhelmed by the sudden exclamation of the penultimate line—"Dear God!" Wordsworth says. If this is not a city on a hill, it is a city whose splendors are compared to a hill.

The invocation of the deity for so petty a sight, just a city in the stillness of dawn, might seem blasphemous; but it serves two ends, measuring the poet's surprise at his own reaction and delighting in the ways of a Maker for whom civilization might be a final form of glory—He was, after all, a raiser-up of temples. The final line has been prepared in the earlier personification, the city wearing the garment of morning (compare Shakespeare's "morn in russet mantle clad"). The image of houses seemingly asleep might easily close with the city itself asleep, but the line goes a great deal further. The city's heart cannot be lying still unless the city is dead. If our attention has been prepared by the biblical cast to previous lines, we cannot help recalling the tale of Lazarus, a Lazarus who each dawn returns to the living.

The visual gestures are thereby consumed by an expression of meaning not within those gestures alone, but prepared by the intentions of the form, the biblical underpinning to the imagery, and the contrast between this particular poem and all the praise Wordsworth had lavished on landscape. There is a final matter. Wordsworth must remain true to his own nature, a nature out of nature. For this man of the country, there was only one moment the city could be so beautiful—it had to seem empty of people.

Armature

The armature is the technical frame of the poem: the organization of meter, rhyme, or inherited form (the sonnet, for example) and the organic structures of syntax and sentence (rhythm is the organic expression of meter). These organic structures might be called the responsive form—the form not predicated by a formal scaffolding. The logical armature, for example, is the method of argument, the way sentences cohere or fail to cohere in progression.

The available types of argument might be charted from the purely logical (stopping short, perhaps, of mathematical formulae) to the merely associative (where beyond lies the aleatory or dissociative). No doubt many poems have a range of logics, perhaps coexisting at different levels of organization. The deployment of logical armature might be suggested by saying that Shakespeare's sonnets are lyrical and logical but Auden's lyrical and associative, that *The Ring and the Book* is narrative and logical but Browning's monologues, like the border ballads, narrative and associative. The associative is the inductive response to deductive logic; in the associative, steps are left out. Modern poetry depends heavily on the reader's intuition, his ability to bridge gaps of expression—our poetry is now excessively tolerant of the aleatory, not because we are untrained in logic, but because we are no longer willing to dismiss the illogical, or the inautistic, as the inartistic.

Poems once reveled in a different organization, and it is instructive to untangle the cunning logics that exist in narrative even beneath a progression of events. In the first book of *Don Juan*, Byron sets his trap for the reader deeper than narrative. As far back as stanza 79, Julia has been thinking of Platonic love.

113

The sun set, and up rose the yellow moon:
*   The Devil's in the moon for mischief; they*
Who called her CHASTE, methinks, began too soon
*   Their nomenclature; there is not a day,*
The longest, not the twenty-first of June,
*   Sees half the business in a wicked way,*
On which three single hours of moonshine smile—
And then she looks so modest all the while!

114

There is a dangerous silence in that hour,
*   A stillness, which leaves room for the full soul*
To open all itself, without the power
*   Of calling wholly back its self-control;*
The silver light which, hallowing tree and tower,
*   Sheds beauty and deep softness o'er the whole,*
Breathes also to the heart, and o'er it throws
A loving languor, which is not repose.

115

And Julia sate with Juan, half embraced
*   And half retiring from the glowing arm,*
Which trembled like the bosom where 'twas placed;
*   Yet still she must have thought there was no harm,*
Or else 'twere easy to withdraw her waist;
*   But then the situation had its charm,*
And then—God knows what next—I can't go on;
I'm almost sorry that I e'er begun.

116

Oh Plato! Plato! you have paved the way,
  With your confounded fantasies, to more
Immoral conduct by the fancied sway
  Your system feigns o'er the controlless core
Of human hearts, than all the long array
  Of poets and romancers:—You're a bore,
A charlatan, a coxcomb—and have been,
At best, no better than a go-between.

117

And Julia's voice was lost, except in sighs,
  Until too late for useful conversation;
The tears were gushing from her gentle eyes,
  I wish, indeed, they had not had occasion;
But who, alas! can love, and then be wise?
  Not that Remorse did not oppose Temptation;
A little still she strove, and much repented,
And whispering "I will ne'er consent"—consented.

The opening opposition broods over the romantic oppositions be-
low, the moon's chaste exterior having all too symbolic significance
for the woman whose story is slowly exposed. Here, and in the fol-
lowing lines about loss of self-control, we witness the command of
logical form—each action must be prepared in the narrative, and
the otherwise ambiguous modes of character must first be con-
cealed in the argument.

The poem is a series of propositions fulfilled (it is a poem about
propositions, which makes it all the wittier). Julia is the moon-
faced witness to her own chaste undoing: the loss of self-control is
proposed before engaged in meter. (The other way around and ar-
guments would become morals.) The situation through three stan-
zas follows in just such a methodical way—and then Byron over-
throws all expectation. He can't go on—he must—he can't. It's an
old actor's ploy, but with it he has seduced the reader. The reader's
expectation is heightened, as in any seduction, by delay. Byron's

digression, his curse upon philosophers, is as calculated as the chapters on cetology with which Melville retards the action in *Moby-Dick*.

I can't go on is of course exactly what a girl might say—and in seduction what we say and what we do often collaborate in their opposition (it is these contraries of character the initial proposition is composed of, the dark longing that underlies the moon's modest exterior). That philosophers and not poets are responsible for immorality is a charming thing for a poet to say, especially when using his accusations only to intensify a poetic seduction. That the seduction is of the fictional woman as well as the actual reader is not a matter of philosophy. The poor philosopher here *is* only the go-between, between stanzas 115 and 117 (a philosopher might invent lovers who shout *Plato! Plato!* in their ecstasies).

Much wit is self-referential, which is often what we mean by depth. Julia's voice is lost, and once lost is useless—here silence betrays, but by the end of the stanza even language betrays her. When we betray something we reveal it, to use the sense against itself; Julia's betrayal of one nature only reveals another, where love is an ignorance embraced and knowledge an insolence endured. There is a final little flurry of withholding, while the mighty abstractions Remorse and Temptation grapple with each other; and then comes that beautifully poised final line, rhyming significantly with *repented*. Here *never consent* suddenly and irrevocably topples over into *consented*. Desire finally defeats the desire of language: language is only the conscious denial of an unconscious wish. The power of that wish, and the manner by which it has been achieved over a series of obstacles and objections, is largely the power of the logical armature whose propositions the seduction has fulfilled. The seduction is remorseless, at least on the seducer's part. Here we have unconsciously been given a picture, perhaps even consciously become the object, of Byronic seduction.

It is not in nostalgia that one might view the logical armature—as well as gesture and expression, valence, and trust—as offering certain rigors of pleasure beyond those provided by the permissive inductions of our verse. There is, after all, a great deal of seductive power in the mere saying of a name. To name these aspects of a poetics of reading is not to exhaust the complications of reading, but to push toward consciousness various elopements or escapements by which the marriage of reading is often unconsciously consummated. We read as if asleep, but such a poetics is how we dream.

chapter 23

Twentieth-Century American Poetry, Abbreviated

The poems of a new century are forged in the politics and attitudes of the century just discarded. Twentieth-century poetry was made from the scrap metal of the nineteenth. It may seem odd that the first poet in the Library of America's anthology of the past century is Henry Adams, born in 1838 during the Van Buren administration; but an anthology of our new century will have to open with Richard Wilbur, born in 1921 during the Harding administration. Henry Adams was not much of a poet; but he was great-grandson of John Adams and grandson of John Quincy Adams, who didn't die until Henry was ten. Henry would have known men who fought in the Revolution. He survived into the days of "Prufrock" and *Cathay*.

In 1920, a niece published the late historian's "Prayer to the Virgin of Chartres":

> *If then I left you, it was not my crime,*
> *   Or if a crime, it was not mine alone.*
> *All children wander with the truant Time.*
> *   Pardon me too! You pardoned once your Son!*
>
> *For He said to you:—"Wist ye not that I*
> *   Must be about my Father's business?" So,*
> *Seeking his Father he pursued his way*
> *   Straight to the Cross towards which we all must go.*

Wist ye not! Straight to the Cross! "Prayer" was written in 1901, at the cusp of the new century, only a dozen years before the earliest poems Wallace Stevens wrote for *Harmonium* (eventually published in 1923). The possibilities of diction were about to change radically.

Of course you can't go from Adams straight to Stevens, even if they were published at nearly the same hour. The rules of chronology place poets in their graves—or, rather, their cradles. No matter when a poet was writing his best verse, or when it happened to get into print, most anthologies confine him to birth order. Perhaps there's no better procedure, but it deforms the historical circumstances in which poems were written and read (two very different things). James Fenton once proposed an anthology of poems printed in the order they were published. As a study of influence and the development of style (and counterstyle), it would be a revelation to place Dickinson in the 1890s or Hopkins in 1918. Richard Wilbur and Amy Clampitt were born a year apart, but he's a poet of the late forties and she a poet of the late seventies—their diction is divided by thirty years of practice. Many anthologies print, unobtrusively, the date that poems were written or first published; but the Library of America prefers a format unencumbered by history, as if the general reader might be scared off by encouragement of the critical faculty (a common reader's anthology often conceals the things uncommon readers want to know).

Any reader who buys these volumes blindly will soon discover two things. First, they are not an anthology of twentieth-century American poetry—they are premature and incomplete, restricted to poets born before 1914. Just a dozen of the over two hundred poets are still alive—the youngest would have turned eighty-seven this year. We have an anthology that does not include Robert Lowell, John Berryman, Randall Jarrell, Richard Wilbur, Amy Clampitt, Anthony Hecht, Allen Ginsberg, James Merrill, John Ashbery, or Sylvia Plath, much less the generations of poets now in their sixties, fifties, forties, thirties, or twenties. Some of the poetry here was written as late as the 1990s, but much written in the 1930s and 1940s has been excluded because it was by poets too *young*. (You have a poem that alludes to the Mariner spacecraft, but not

Jarrell's about the B-17.) No doubt these volumes are a work in progress; but they are overly generous to early generations, and a similar generosity to later would require at least three more volumes. The recent century of American verse scarcely needs five thousand pages to represent it.

Second, the editors have been kind to bad poets (they have almost set up a charity on their behalf). There were times, in the deserts of Charles Reznikoff or Gertrude Stein, I thought I'd never reach an oasis. An obscure British engineer, Alec Issigonis, once said, "A camel is a horse designed by a committee"—but the camel was a *success*. The Library of America anthology is an animal with one lung and five livers, cauliflower ears and bandy legs—it may have looked like a predator in the blueprints, but on the savannah it looks like prey. The choices of five diverse editors (so diverse one or two have set up minor kingdoms and crowned themselves) have the virtue of breadth but the vice of pandering, the virtue of even-handedness but the vice of absence of discrimination. Their Balkanized tastes create an aesthetic turmoil and political feverishness that might be said to characterize the century itself, but they churn up a lot of mud.

There are six major poets in the period covered here, and two so nearly major it's heartless not to include them. The six are Robert Frost, Wallace Stevens, Ezra Pound, T. S. Eliot, Marianne Moore, and Elizabeth Bishop. The two nearly major are William Carlos Williams and Hart Crane, poets with more than occasional graces, moments of brilliance and depths of mortifying embarrassment, poets whose faults almost outweigh their favors. The treatment of major poets in an anthology is a guide to its treatment of everyone else: we find there the synechdoches of care and attention that have shallower cause elsewhere. Major poets have large appetites, and the editors' decision was to give them dominant and discriminating room. (I wish they'd been given even more—the forty-first best poem by Wallace Stevens is better than the masterpiece of most poets here.) Nine poets in the first volume account for half the space: five of the major poets (Bishop is in the other volume), plus Williams, Edwin Arlington Robinson, H. D., and Gertrude Stein. The order of precedence and pressure of emphasis are arguable (reviews of anthologies, like anthologies, are mostly arguments). Forty pages of Gertrude Stein is cruel and unusual punishment; and almost fifty pages of H. D. kills off any interest in that frothy, undertalented stray of imagism. On the other hand, sixty pages of Frost and more than seventy of Stevens don't fathom their invention; and Eliot can be shoehorned into sixty pages only by throwing out three of the *Four Quartets*.

Robert Frost is a test case for any anthology of American poetry. He was popular, if only a paper-thin populist (scratch most populists and there's an elitist bleeding underneath), beloved for many of his best poems and some of his worst. The critics of Frost had their Temptation and Fall: it took a long while to see beneath the crust of maple sap to the unhappy man below, the one not quite so ready to take advantage of nostalgia toward a rural past already vanishing. An editor of Frost is pulled in two or three directions. Is the anthology to be a catchment of old favorites, the poems any American would know by heart, if he knew any poem by heart? Or should it have, say, aesthetic standards? (Once you know the anthology contains Joyce Kilmer's "Trees," you know it might print anything.)

The editors have offered readers the old warhorses, served up for their tongues, that have been in every anthology for fifty years—"The Death of the Hired Man," "Home Burial," "Mending Wall," "After Apple-Picking," "The Road Not Taken," "Stopping by Woods on a Snowy Evening." Familiarity hasn't ruined them, but they look like the crumbling obelisks of high-school literature (reading a major work in high school can ruin it forever). You get these poems, worn transparent from reading; but you also get thin-blooded, sentimental poems that should have been sent to a retirement home to die in their rockers: "Birches," "'Out, Out—'" (the poem comes to a chilly end, but the accident is Saturday matinee melodrama), "A Star in a Stone-Boat" (Frost wrote worse, but not much worse), "Nothing Gold Can Stay," "Fire and Ice." You get poems even weaker, from Frost's last and most exhausted period.

There's a Frost not often recognized, the one who understood women and the frustrations of love, the poet of "The Silken Tent" and "The Subverted Flower," which are included, and "The

Thatch," which is not. (In some ways Frost was the greatest woman poet of the century.) And there are poems of the more tormented, more disillusioned Frost. "The Witch of Coös" is a poem everyone should know, and I'm surprised how many don't. "Desert Places" is here, "Neither Out Far Nor In Deep," and poems often neglected: "Spring Pools," "The Strong Are Saying Nothing," "The Draft Horse." These poems provide a bleaker view of the Yankee moralist (born, by dry irony, in California). His plain speech, his weather-beaten irony, and his cracker-barrel jawing were clichés when he started; they fostered the illusion that a major poet can be loved in his time (it's easy to love such poets when they're safely dead). Yet how much better the selection could have been. Why must we endure the damp philosophy of "West-Running Brook" (like a love letter from Heraclitus) instead of "The Code" or "A Hundred Collars," poems Melville might have dropped into fiction? Few novelists have Frost's psychological penetration, and few poets his cunning ease with pentameter—in Frost pentameter sounds like a new dialect. With a great poet you can never include enough, and whatever little you include makes surrounding poets look uneasy in their skins.

Stevens was born in 1879, yet might have been born decades earlier or later. After most of a century, his poems remain uncannily fresh—the trappings of the time don't cling to them, as they do to poems by Pound or Eliot (Eliot was a poet of 1915, even thirty years afterward—he's a poet of 1915 still). You get a lot of strange language in Stevens (sometimes strange beyond strange—if Stevens hadn't been a poet, he might have invented a private tongue and gone around *hoo-hooing* on street corners), but also lines in the diction of the twentieth century, not that of King James or Milton. How easily Stevens turned the simplicity of the modern idiom into philosophy—we've had few poets as abstract, as immersed in perception and epistemology, and few who wore philosophy like a three-piece suit.

Stevens's poems come out of nowhere—that is, out of his mysterious and stolid character. Psychologically he seems a relative not of moderns like Eliot and Pound, but of Dickinson and Whitman—you may read musty volumes on the Civil War without understanding the sources of their work, just as you may read the symbolists all day long without seeing how Stevens did what he did. Years as an insurance executive caged up the lightness of being of *Harmonium*—the aged Stevens seems like a pensioned-off civil servant until he balances on a stool, trunk regnant in air. Those who accuse him of being an aesthete (he *was* an aesthete, but so much more than one) can't have read him very closely, because aesthete poets don't have a sense of humor.

Anthologies are usually unjust to Stevens, gathering a few poems easy to read and not easy to dislike, but far from his greatest (I do dislike "The Emperor of Ice-Cream," and I'd pay not to find "Thirteen Ways of Looking at a Blackbird" in the Easter basket of every anthology—yet how can you omit it?). The editors have given Stevens space for grand abstract sequences like "Notes Toward a Supreme Fiction" and "The Auroras of Autumn," and for bulky poems like "Sea Surface Full of Clouds," "To an Old Philosopher in Rome," and "The Rock." I wish "The Comedian as the Letter C" or "The Man with the Blue Guitar" or "Esthétique du Mal" were also included. In his long poems, as elsewhere, Stevens could be too fond of his blather; but it's blather of rigorous intuition and argument, the sort Thomas Aquinas might have liked. It's hard to quarrel with any grab-bag assortment of his short poems. They're so many and so many faceted that any selection, shy of selecting them all, will leave out some loved by some—yet where are "Anecdote of the Jar," "Le Monocle de Mon Oncle," "Frogs Eat Butterflies . . ."?

Frost and Stevens, despite their originality, are purifications of a tradition. Even Eliot, in a quite different way, is heir to tradition (at times, by design, almost a palimpsest of it). Pound started under the thumb of tradition and slowly became something tradition could never have predicted. He was controversial when there were few rewards for it, apart from poverty and notoriety; his generosity to fellow poets (rarely misplaced, if rarely reciprocated) and his critical eye would have made him a crucial, contrary figure even without the poetry. He can be infuriating, not just for his egotism and bullying omniscience (many of those obscure references were taken from ordinary books), but for his pigheadedness, his idiocies in politics and economics, his attempt to make *The Cantos* a lost-and-found department for stray mittens and broken umbrellas.

Pound's early poems are full of perfumed archaizing, the work of an undergraduate who lived in books (his reputation rises when you juxtapose his poems with run-of-the-mill poems of the age). He chose his influences well (or they did well in choosing him), but a member of the class of '05 *should* have read Dante and the troubadours closely. Slowly the influences ground him into something else; his innovations in the metric and method of American poetry, like his refusal to cater to the mob, look a century later like the courage of madness.

Among early poems, "Sestina: Altaforte" and "The Seafarer" (no one has ever translated Old English more artfully or more gruesomely) are delightful party pieces; but they're immature, cluttered, and their diction is preposterous. Including "Ballad of the Goodly Fere," another party piece, would have given the early work a broader range. Too much young Pound is Pound before he dropped the aesthete's mask—being given Fenollosa's rough translations of Chinese verse was one of those happy accidents a lesser poet could have made nothing of. Few young poets have been more romantic than Pound, or more ignorant of how romantic they were (Pound's infatuation with China is the decayed gesture of Coleridge's fantasy of Kubla Khan). In the poems of *Cathay* and the sequence *Hugh Selwyn Mauberley* a different poet emerges, one more humane but more suspicious. *Mauberley* is a handbook on how to remake your past as irony.

Pound's *Cantos* remains a hodgepodge impenetrable without notes, and once you have the notes it's tempting to ignore the poems. (*The Waste Land* doesn't depend on its notes—they're helpful, but can be read afterward.) It's impossible to read Pound without line-by-line explication of his antiquarian sources, his antique gossip, his history-book characters, his scraps of foreign tongues. More readers have fallen asleep over *The Cantos* than over the *Aeneid;* yet his chisel-struck phrases, in the beautiful hesitations and releases of his rhythm (most American poets think they have Pound's music when all they have is the cloth ear of Williams), leave an indelible memory—you can see Pound's landscapes long after you've forgotten any landscape of the eye. Pound invented the best imagist practice and never again required the euphemisms of Victorian parlors. When you feel your language seduced by its idiom, reading the mature Pound will vaccinate you against a number of viruses even as it infects you with its own.

The anthology's sensitive selection of *The Cantos* balances earlier with later, the epic canvases with the humdrum grind (though never the worst of the grind). Only the absence of Canto I is mystifying—Pound's brutal version of the passage in *Odyssey* XI, which has never been bettered (it is full of alien beauty), was critical to the development of meter. Pound was the great master of radical adaptation and imitation, suggestive even in error (his mistakes could be as calculated as his elegance); but unfortunately the anthology gives only cursory attention to translation. Elsewhere you find a poem by Catullus, some lines of Virgil, some appalling versions of Chippewa songs, but little else. The last century thrived on translation, and much of our poetry lives off secondhand knowledge of the foreign. We owe our addiction to translation, as we often forget, to Ezra Pound.

T. S. Eliot is still the dominant poet of the last century. He casts a long shadow, and we are not yet out from under it, though he is very much a poet *of* the twentieth century. We can't calculate how such a poet will seem a century hence. (Who in 1900 would have thought Shelley's reputation would sink so low?) The generation of poets now in their seventies was baptized in Eliot's language, like Achilles in the Styx. Younger generations met him as an exhibit in a museum, already a little dusty (Eliot's lesser poems now look like rotting flags in old armories). Eliot was a benign influence on later poets, once they stopped trying to imitate him; but he was a disaster for contemporaries like Conrad Aiken, who thought Eliot's methods weren't patented—poor Aiken looks like a carbon copy's carbon copy.

Eliot's poetic oeuvre is small, the smallest of any major American poet—two dozen early poems, then *The Waste Land*, three sequences (only one of them long), and a clutch of Ariel poems, unfinished poems, choruses from *The Rock*, and trivia. It's so small that in an anthology this length you'd have an excuse for printing most of it. *Sweeney Agonistes* is included, as it almost never is—it's laggard and uneven (and also hilarious), unlike anything Eliot wrote except the pub scene in *The Waste Land*. But how can we be missing not just three Quartets, but "Burbank with a Baedeker," "Sweeney Erect," "A Cooking Egg," "The Hippopotamus" (why pretend young Eliot wasn't what he was, a skeptic, and a droll one?), "Mr. Eliot's Sunday Morning Service," and "Journey of the Magi"? Eliot's estate is notoriously greedy, yet a complete selection of Eliot could have fit into the eighty pages devoted to Pound. Eliot's notes to *The Waste Land* follow the poem in the text (oddly, since every other poet's notes are consigned to the rear), but they're useless because the anthology doesn't print the poem with line numbers.

You need great gouts of Eliot if you're to represent his variety. His poetry, early to late, is a supersubtle (as he might have said) narrative of aesthetic change as it impinges on philosophic complication. Eliot aged quickly as a man (he was an antique at forty) and slowly as an artist—by thirty most poets, like limpets, fix on a style they refuse to abandon. "He Do the Police in Different Voices" was the draft title of *The Waste Land*, and those voices took Browning's monologues into the Jazz Age. Eliot never seems to be slumming, unlike many poets in love with lower classes. His poetry reveled in street life, as Dickens's novels did—the draft title came from *Our Mutual Friend*. If Eliot later turned austere and religiose, he never lost his resistant emotional passivity: voyeurism was a pleasure nearly erotic (even the voyeurism that might be called religious meditation), and in religion his self-loathing found consolation and anaesthetic oblivion. Most great poets mature, but few have Eliot's prolonged, punctuated maturities—for another example you have to go back to an even greater poet, Dante.

Marianne Moore's poems are daring, frivolous in very deep ways and deep in frivolous ways (and more morally alert than any number of desert fathers), fussy, old-maidish, nearly Faustian at times, and always, always, scientific (yet prudish in their science—she wants to hold things at arm's length, preferably with tweezers or in cages). She finds poetry where there shouldn't be any, and if you looked there yourself you wouldn't find any. No one but Moore could have made those poems up; and who could have made up Marianne Moore except, well, Marianne Moore?

Moore had an unnatural, quirky imagination when young and when older didn't understand that earlier poet at all. Didn't, indeed, like her very much—her occasional hatchetlike revisions are mostly mutilations. She knew she was an odd duck (only a proud odd duck would have worn that tricorn hat), and her subjects—those improbable animals, imprisoned if only in their armor—often mirror a self plummily satisfied in its peculiarity. We read Moore not to find out what we're all like (her humanity is tenuous and strained), but what one individual in her strangeness is like. Her gangly lines and ungainly idiom are an explanation of self; and her lecturelike sentences argue like apologias, their prosy rhetoric broken into a syllabic verse more bewildering than any animal in her bestiary (at times you feel you've been dropped into a report by the commissioner of fish and wildlife). She made poetry from unlikely things, and made the unlikely seem the true subject of poetry, at least *her* poetry.

The anthology includes "The Pangolin," "The Steeple-Jack," "The Fish," "Marriage," and "Poetry," poems no one would exclude (though I've seen anthologies exclude them), and two dozen more, some of them mere trifles. *Most* selections of her work don't do her justice, but "The Paper Nautilus" and "Spenser's Ireland" and "The Hero" and much else should have been included. A little of Moore goes a long way, but it's a long way in a different direction from any other poet. The virtue of modernism, never a movement as much as a catch-all label, was its tolerance. We owe to that tolerance a poetry that fifty years before wouldn't have seemed poetry at all. Of course the best poetry in many periods wouldn't have been poetry half a century before. Poetry advances into the unpoetic, not like a conqueror but like an ignorant man with a club.

Elizabeth Bishop was Moore's protégée, treated for most of her career like a minor poet's minor poet. She was admired for her toy-theater observations, her sleight of hand with metaphor; but she wasn't taken as seriously as poets like Jarrell and Lowell, except by poets like Jarrell and Lowell. So many poets are understood without being loved; it's dangerous to love Bishop while neglecting the sadness and longing and doubt, the wish to be loved (so much like the will to power) concealed by the sympathies of style. Her poems live not just in what they *can* say but in all that they can't.

Bishop never wrote anything with the deadly earnestness of Lowell, who even at his most personal could sound as if he were making a speech—we forgive him for things we'd never forgive a duller poet for. Bishop's lines tremble with the tentative (the tentative is her moral philosophy), and her observations seem—how like a true scientist!—shyly hypothetical. Her lack of rhetorical affectation quarreled with the rhetoric of the time (her rhetorical questions are real questions), and she never tried to impress anyone. Inside her charming cabinet of wonders—an intimate world, but sometimes a chilly, collected world—Bishop never asks for attention, her style so artless and transparent (what hard work to make it seem so) the poems hardly reveal their depths. Like the calm ocean on a clear day, they give no sign of the slaughter below.

Bishop lived in Brazil for twenty years—she had experience of the exotic that Stevens and Pound could only imagine (or, in Moore's case, visit in zoos), yet her poems never *seem* exotic. She wrote about the dailiness of the foreign, which made the foreign even stranger. Her quiet endings, never straining for a big moment like *Downward to darkness, on extended wings*, linger in the provocation of what isn't on the page.

Any selection of Bishop's poetry is bound to get something right—you could pick her poems with a set of darts and do well. She wrote only eighty or so, almost every one precious as a new element, uncanny as a Van Eyck (one day a book of her unfinished poems—only her finicky nature prevented her from knowing some were finished—will add new favorites). *Questions of Travel*, her third book, was one of the most magical books of the century (many wonderful poets never write wonderful books, but Frost did in *North of Boston* and Lowell did in *Life Studies*)—it's hard not to include nearly everything in it. But Bishop isn't treated like a major poet here. Louis Zukofsky and Charles Olson are given as much space, and H. D. and Gertrude Stein considerably more. Hart Crane sprawls across nearly twice as many pages. In thirty pages you can fit "The Man-Moth," "Roosters," "The Fish," "The Bight,"

"The Armadillo," "Sestina," "Crusoe in England," and "One Art," poems it would be absurd to omit. You can include a dozen others, though some of the others are minor, like "The Shampoo" and "Song for the Rainy Season." Yet why waste so much space on "In the Waiting Room," one of her prosiest and least characteristic works, with a moment of self-revelation so actorly it sounds dishonest? Scholars of Bishop love that poem, reason enough to suspect it.

Imagine the ideal anthology, where you didn't have to calculate space or add up permissions fees. Wouldn't you want "Wading at Wellfleet," "A Miracle for Breakfast," "Cirque d'Hiver," "Florida," "Arrival at Santos," "Brazil, January 1, 1502" (so cunning about empire while writing about landscape), "Manuelzinho," "The Riverman," "The Burglar of Babylon," "Manners," "Filling Station," "From Trollope's Journal," "Visits to St. Elizabeths" (if you don't include that poem you're not really in love with Bishop), "Pink Dog," "The Moose," "Poem," and "The End of March"? Wouldn't you want these, and more? They're missing.

Bishop is loved as no major poet has been loved since Frost— loved never for the difficult, self-pitying alcoholic she sometimes was, but for the tender and unsentimental maiden aunt (a maiden aunt of genius) the verse invented. The intimacy of style is always a deft rhetorical construction, even if the poet is honest as a mirror. It was difficult to see Bishop as a major poet—do major poets write so many poems as *lovable* as this? But they do, or at least Bishop did. If in a century or two readers think we overrated her, they will be different readers and our pleasures will be as foreign to them as the pleasures of the eighteenth century are to us. We'll be alien as the readers who once thought James Thomson as imposing as Milton.

I feel unhappy not to like William Carlos Williams better, not to love him, as many do, as the patron saint and Santa Claus of experimental poetry. He was among the most influential poets of the century, responsible for some of the good and much of the awful poetry that followed, poetry that believed an American idiom could make poems by being innocent of everything else. The prose that now passes for poetry learned its manners from him, often at third- or fourth-hand. At his best, Williams has a gawky farm-boy innocence (barely a stone's throw from outright foolishness—if Pound was the village explainer, Williams was sometimes the village idiot). He made minimalism seem a duty to his diction—poems like "so much depends" and "This Is Just to Say" are so tiny they're almost trivial, and if you didn't know what contemporary poetry was like might *be* trivial. They look better next to poems like Carl Sandburg's. (Every museum should hang bad period paintings next to old masters—they provide not competition but range-finding.)

Williams didn't have an instinctive gift of expression—his endings make you wince, they try so hard for nonchalance (or, worse, they smirk so with satisfaction). His early poems seem part of a Buy American campaign. Everything I like about Bishop's simplicity I find arch and self-congratulating in Williams. What Bishop did with ease Williams does with labor, and exclamation marks. I can't imagine why anyone would want to include "Romance Moderne" or "January Morning," full of lines like "the worn, / blue car rails (like the sky!) / gleaming among the cobbles!" They're excruciating in their dimestore revelations and postcard views of the urban sublime, views Calvin Coolidge would have loved.

Williams was like a blind man with a gun—he shot a lot of trees and very few deer. But I love the poem that starts "The pure products of America / go crazy" and some of the later, more considered poems like "The Yachts," "These," "The Descent," and "To Daphne and Virginia." There are no excerpts here from *Paterson* (just a couple of tryout sketches), that overlong and long overrated poem that starts half well and ends in disaster. Williams bore a famous grudge against Pound and Eliot (*The Waste Land* was "the great catastrophe to our letters") and wanted to match them poem for long poem; but he had no notion of architecture and was satisfied with whatever odds and ends came to hand. (Pound is accused of writing *The Cantos* by intuition, but compared to Williams he was as squarely T square as Frank Lloyd Wright.) Williams was not quite a major poet—for long stretches of his collected poems it's hard to believe he'd ever read a poem, much less written one. He paid a high price for his love of plain American, because few of his lines are memorable; but as he grew old he became meditative as Stevens. A more deliberate poet resulted, one still not as admired as the Williams who wrote about the wheelbarrow.

It's hard not to love Hart Crane, but you have to love him in pieces, like a shattered krater dug from a Greek tomb. Even when it's put back together, with exquisite care, there are pieces missing—the result is something part astonishing and part plaster. There were times Crane could hardly write an uninteresting line, though he could never write a plain one. He was seduced by a juvenile relish for obscurity, and brilliant enough at his obscurities it's depressing when he explains them—they're never as bewitching afterward. Crane died so young he didn't have time to write his way out of his defects; though most poets get worse, the older they get—they become slave to their defects. It's difficult not to include many fatuous or embarrassing passages when selecting Crane, as difficult as it is with Whitman—the good passages come glued to the bad.

Crane was a beautiful boy who wrote beautiful-boy poetry, the kind always seeking approval (sometimes he was a boy with a god in him). Often he wrote to a template—many of his best lines fall into the form [Adjective] Noun Preposition [Adjective] Noun (any of Crane's lines ending with adjective and noun has a chance of being wonderful). Williams listened to his patients; Crane listened only to books and had a fatal sense of diction—he wrote English like a foreigner (at times a brilliant foreigner), without concern for the weights of connotation.

> —And yet this great wink of eternity,
> Of rimless floods, unfettered leewardings,
> Samite sheeted and processioned where
> Her undinal vast belly moonward bends,
> Laughing the wrapt inflections of our love.

The smugness of *this great wink*, the vagueness and artificiality of *rimless* and *unfettered* and *leewardings*, the gleeful obscurity of *Samite sheeted*, and then *undinal*! It would be very hard for any poet except Shakespeare to get away with *undinal*. When Crane writes this badly, it's hard not to rue his adolescent ambitions; mourn poems overplanned yet unfocused; mourn his jejune reflections (like Delmore Schwartz, he came to grief in autobiography); mourn the tragic collapse of *The Bridge*, less readable each passing year (it is here more as a tombstone than a monument); and forget what a strange, haunting, unlikely poet he could be.

> *And so, admitted through black swollen gates*
> *That must arrest all distance otherwise,—*
> *Past whirling pillars and lithe pediments,*
> *Light wrestling there incessantly with light,*
> *Star kissing star through wave on wave unto*
> *Your body rocking!*
>   *and where death, if shed,*
> *Presumes no carnage, but this single change,—*
> *Upon the steep floor flung from dawn to dawn*
> *The silken skilled transmemberment of song;*
>
> *Permit me voyage, love, into your hands . . .*

In such passages his flaws no longer seem flaws (or not quite flaws); they've been annealed into something so Miltonic it's modern.

An anthology composed only of major poets is not an anthology. There are many ways to take a cross section of a period, but the achievement of major poets must be shaped and figured by poets whose imaginations never escaped their limitations (major poets are not always the most talented—the muse is whimsical in her pleasures). Among the other poets here, there are ripe reputations gone rotten and decayed reputations still worth a look. There are poets ignored or little known, poets so obscure they've almost been dug from their graves. There are songwriters and blues singers whose claim is sociological rather than aesthetic. There are curiosities—novelists who wrote verses (and poets who should have written novels), light-verse poets who wrote a quatrain more memorable than the dozen volumes of some withered academic, poets who wrote in baby talk or threw syntax on the scrap heap. It's a crowded and clamorous group, and there are too many of them.

In addition to the major poets, there are eight minor ones: Edgar Lee Masters, Edwin Arlington Robinson, John Crowe Ransom, Allen Tate, Yvor Winters, Richard Eberhart, Theodore Roethke, and Delmore Schwartz. Minor poets seem at times, sometimes all their careers, to have the capacity for genius; but at the distance of half a century it's easy to see that what major poets do offhandedly, even carelessly, is never in the range of a minor poet. Minor poets may be memorable as Housman, may be freakish and individual as Clare; but they never write anything a man or woman of dry talent or docile intelligence might not achieve. That is, their poems seem within the capacity of a poet who comes later. A major poet does something slightly beyond the possible. When you read a minor poet, you're not necessarily reminded of someone else (minor poets are often laws unto themselves, though very unhappy laws); yet you're always reminded that someone else is better.

There was a world, once, where Edgar Lee Masters was considered shocking; it's a world we can scarcely imagine, we who are shocked by things quite different (the future won't believe what we were shocked by—or the things we *weren't* shocked by). *Spoon River Anthology* is full of blank-check homilies and morals telegraphed from three states away. Sometimes the characters have names allegorical as the names in *Piers Plowman*. Masters's poems are never satisfactory alone; they remain a morose mixture of the sophisticated and simpleminded, every morality worn like a sandwich board, every irony wrought from iron. When a poem ends, "I thirsted so for love! / I hungered so for life!" there's not much left to be said—it's an advertisement against itself. Yet his midwestern town of quiet pathologies and thwarted ambition *is* a little town. In brief monologues spoken beyond the grave, his characters spill their secrets as if paid by tabloids. Masters caught the subtleties of resentment and desire in towns where people at close quarters make the worst of things. Alone, the poems are soap opera; together, they're a revenge play.

Edwin Arlington Robinson was a tidy, psychologically alert, sometimes slightly obscure poet whose poems move slowly as a glacier. Like Masters, Robinson had some of the gifts for great poetry, but not the imaginative instinct or stoic reserve. He was a professional—that was his virtue and his tragedy. He could handle pentameter with an ease that makes New Formalist poetry look like a Rube Goldberg invention; and yet, compared to Frost's English, Robinson's is stiff-necked and proper as a butler. Like Masters, he loved his homely morals and throat-clearing sentiments; and he was too easily drawn into high Romantic vision (his poems are larded with references to bold warriors and the good old days of Troy). His best poems were private and mysterious, psychologies taken as case studies. "Eros Turannos" is justly admired (I know poets who have it by heart), partly because its drama is implicit; but the editors have also included dark and lesser known poems like "The Unforgiven" and "The Poor Relation." The double suicide in "The Mill" occurs so quietly you're only half aware of it. Robinson was a fine poet when overestimating his reader's intelligence, not when underestimating his taste.

In John Crowe Ransom the archaic strain in Eliot (they were born the same year) was developed into something near paralysis. It's hard to believe a poet who admired the moderns (though he was resistant to *The Waste Land*) could write, except as a joke, a line like "Sweet ladies, long may ye bloom, and toughly I hope ye may thole"; yet Ransom often seems half-joking in his verse. His poems are unlovely things, made by a craftsman with bad tools (sometimes you think Ransom purposely blunted or broke his tools); but his eccentric, counterpointed rhythms and rough-hewn rhymes brought a version of the ballad into the twentieth century. "Captain Carpenter" is a violent masterpiece of irony—the grim men who composed border ballads would have nodded at the homage, then burst into guffaws. If you listen long enough to Ransom's mannered, nightmarish poems you begin to love them for their peculiarities, because no one else ever wanted to be peculiar in that way. The anthology includes the usual favorites, which have every reason to be favorites: "Bells for John Whitesides' Daughter," "Here Lies a Lady," "Piazza Piece," "The Equilibrists," "Painted Head."

Allen Tate is a smoother, less interesting poet than Ransom, who was his teacher at Vanderbilt. Tate was overwrought in a way that made him an influence on later overwrought poets like Robert Lowell and Geoffrey Hill. The style of early poems like "Mr.

Pope" shows how strange the ambitions of the Fugitives were—
they didn't want to turn back the clock just for themselves; they
wanted everyone to live in a world of mules and water power. "Ode
to the Confederate Dead" is the poem Lowell succeeded in ex-
ceeding, though not until he had watered down the alcohol of his
rhetoric. Tate wrote little poetry after forty. A late poem like "The
Swimmers," about a lynching victim seen by the poet in boyhood,
suggests that in autobiography his style might have been less
crippled by bombast more fit for the pulpit.

Yvor Winters was, like Tate and Ransom, more an academic
than a poet; few poets approach their poetry more academically
than Winters. He started as an arch modernist, if not a talented
one, and ended as a devotee of George Gascoigne and Fulke Gre-
ville. His poetry seems a Walter Mitty fantasy of Cavaliers and
Roundheads. Winters believed so hard in the moral imprimatur of
rhyme and meter he doomed himself to write poems in love with
their limitations. The poems have surprising character, however
grim and stoic they can be (like the treatises Luther nailed to the
door at Wittenberg). Winters was an influential teacher and a
critic with a genius for grievance. Only a critic so confirmed in
eccentricity could have failed to see that the poets he trumpeted,
like Elizabeth Daryush and Adelaide Crapsey ("an immortal
poet"), were trivial. When you think the whole world is wrong, it's
usually not the world that's wrong.

Richard Eberhart is cursed always to be anthologized for "The
Groundhog" (as Elizabeth Bishop is for "The Fish"), a poem so
full of gassy phrases you want to poke it with a pin. Eberhart could
never tell his good work from his bad. "The Fury of Aerial Bom-
bardment," which is present here, and "Ode to the Chinese Paper
Snake" and "An Airman Considers His Power," which aren't, show
a poet of rhetorical gifts who could rarely make use of them. He
has been neglected because he so often, and so cheerfully, wrote so
badly—and a few of his worst poems are included, as if to scold
him.

Theodore Roethke was an undeveloped poet stuck in the larval
stage of emotion: his portion of the collective unconscious was
happiest with slugs. He wrote many poems that were small tan-

trums, and (like too many in his generation) he carried Yeats on his back. His coyness made him vulnerable to poems little better than the worst of Ogden Nash, poems that might have been written by Mr. Toad. Preciousness often got the better of him; but his shorter poems sometimes control their Yeatsian gabble long enough for romance to turn edgy: in "Four for Sir John Davies," "I Knew a Woman," "Elegy for Jane," "The Waking" (one of the loveliest villanelles in the language), and "My Papa's Waltz," his sympathies were not overwhelmed by his maudlin nature. The poems of garden and greenhouse seem self-indulgent now, but I miss his drowsy elegy for office life, "Dolor."

Delmore Schwartz started as a boy wonder—very few debuts have been as celebrated as *In Dreams Begin Responsibilities*, and poems like "In the Naked Bed, in Plato's Cave" and "Sonnet: The Beautiful American Word, Sure" bristle with the self-confidence of a brass porcupine. His early poems took their subjects by main force (as Nelson took the Nile), though wildly and pretentiously, as if trying to impress Eliot. His showy metaphysical phrases look like paste jewelry now. Schwartz's decline into forced, empty rhetoric was rapid, and he has fallen so far in reputation he's in danger of being forgotten (his criticism is unhappily neglected). It's unfair to saddle him with a late and humiliating poem like "Lincoln," as if to emphasize the ruin of his talent.

Anthologies often contain the fossils of past critical practice and public regard. Poetic reputations, once achieved, may linger in ghostly limbo, until no one can quite remember why such poets were famous. In this anthology, many linger still, haunting great tracts of space. As long ago as 1930, R. P. Blackmur demolished E. E. Cummings in a famous essay; but that didn't prevent Cummings from enjoying decades of uppercase prominence for lowercase poems, or from occupying some thirty pages with three dozen poems here. The contrived typography of his poems was the most successful attempt, after Herbert, to make poetry a visual art—but between Herbert and Cummings there is an abyss, the abyss between religion and kitsch. Sometimes, by luck, Cummings managed to write a poem as unlikely as "plato told" (heavy-handed though it is); but most of his poems are like Sunday comics, the disordered typography never more than a Dick Tracy code that can't conceal his daffy sentimentality. The anthology includes two poems of more original temper, a crude caricature of gangsters ("Dick Mid's large bluish face without eyebrows"), and a vulgar lyric ("the boys i mean are not refined") that would be more shocking if it didn't end in blue-plate mush.

Vachel Lindsay belongs in the gallery of poetry's oddballs, a poet who took one ingredient of poetry—rhythm—and made it an Olympic event. (At times he seems to out-Hopkins the then un-known Hopkins.) He might have made a sardonic comic poet if he'd had an ounce of cynicism—decency is bad for poetry, and Lindsay had a lot of decency. He provides the most amusing lines in this often accidentally comic anthology:

> *Thus roared the lions:—*
> *"We want Daniel, Daniel, Daniel,*
> *We want Daniel, Daniel, Daniel,*
> *Grrrrrrrrrrrrrrrrrrrrrrrrrrrrrrrrrrrrrrrrrr*
> *Grrrrrrrrrrrrrrrrrrrrrrrrrrrrrrrrrrrrrrrrrrr"*

To their credit, the editors have not excluded the hilariously naive racist vision of "The Congo," with sections titled "Their Basic Savagery" and "Their Irrepressible High Spirits."

Carl Sandburg was a poet on retainer from the Chicago Chamber of Commerce, though his only inheritor, strangely, has been Allen Ginsberg. (Who can read "Chicago" and not think of "Howl"?) When Sandburg writes a line like "These are heroes then —among the plain people—Heroes, did you say? And why not?" a reader can only shake his head at the audience that lapped up such stuff as if it were cream, and at anthologists who act more like anthropologists by including it. And what can be done for a poet of sermonizing niceties like Stephen Vincent Benét?

> *American muse, whose strong and diverse heart*
> *So many men have tried to understand*
> *But only made it smaller with their art,*
> *Because you are as various as your land,*

As mountainous-deep, as flowered with blue rivers,
Thirsty with deserts, buried under snows,
As native as the shape of Navajo quivers,
And native, too, as the sea-voyaged rose.

The verse is finely turned, almost machined; but it reads like propaganda written by real-estate agents for the Oklahoma land rush. This is verse by committee, now chosen by committee.

There are poets who capture momentary strains of attention, but whose poems forever after look like sepia photographs. Amy Lowell's gauzy, sentimental verse once seemed radical because it was free (it was imprisoned in all sorts of ways, mostly by diction). She took what she could from early Eliot and Pound and cheapened it. It's hard to imagine why we need twenty-two pages of Mina Loy, when the selection starts with "Spawn of Fantasies / Silting the appraisable / Pig Cupid his rosy snout / Rooting erotic garbage." She's all shape and no substance, like a circumference; but what sort of circumference writes lines like "The prig of passion— — — — / To your professional paucity // Proto-plasm was raving mad"? H. D. was fond of vague description, mystic love, and trances. She had a confident sense of line and imagist precision; but her poems natter on, scattering raptures and passions as if the banal were not banal enough already. Her lines are so gilded you think they'll come to something sooner or later, though they never do. It's hard to imagine what would have followed her marriage to Ezra Pound, had they made good their engagement.

Poets like Don Marquis and Ogden Nash must have seemed sidesplitting once, but when the humor of humor is lost there's no digging it up again (Elizabethan joke books present the same problem). As poets they're so winsome you can't read them without grinding your teeth. Didn't the editors grind their teeth, just a little? At times the historical imperative of this anthology is to present whatever America once thought was poetry, as well, alas, as what Americans *should* think is poetry—there's a bossy, didactic intent to some selections. You might as well include, in a physics textbook, every crackpot theory that ever troubled physicists.

One of the duties of any anthology is to turn a cold eye on current reputation. The past must be reread each generation, some poets degraded and others rescued; and among those rescued are those we once held prejudices against. Such poets wrote in the spirit of the times, and when the times were outworn the poetry seemed outworn, too. Certain poets, like Edna St. Vincent Millay, have long provoked a nearly reflexive response—pure loathing. Her early poetry was scandalous in a Shirley Temple way, and her late poetry patriotic in a Shirley Temple way. She was a hedonist with a prissy streak and tended to gush unpleasantly. We are distant enough from her language, and the fashionable bohemia and titillated suburbs to which she catered, to see her virtues more clearly.

> *If I should learn, in some quite casual way,*
> *That you were gone, not to return again—*
> *Read from the back-page of a paper, say,*
> *Held by a neighbor in a subway train,*
> *How at the corner of this avenue*
> *And such a street (so are the papers filled)*
> *A hurrying man—who happened to be you—*
> *At noon to-day had happened to be killed,*
> *I should not cry aloud—I could not cry*
> *Aloud, or wring my hands in such a place—*
> *I should but watch the station lights rush by*
> *With a more careful interest on my face,*
> *Or raise my eyes and read with greater care*
> *Where to store furs and how to treat the hair.*

The casual, carnal irony is self-mocking at heart. If you didn't know the lines were by Millay, they might remind you of the gentle wryness of Elizabeth Bishop. And consider the ending of a sonnet that would have amused Frost:

> *I would indeed that love were longer-lived,*
> *And vows were not so brittle as they are,*
> *But so it is, and nature has contrived*
> *To struggle on without a break thus far,—*

Whether or not we find what we are seeking
Is idle, biologically speaking.

Biologically! Millay dealt more honestly with sex, if also more romantically and wearisomely, than many poets who followed (she was Olds before her time). Her tomboy nature is an unconvincing disguise—she was less faux innocent than faux experienced.

Elinor Wylie has for decades been dismissed as a minor talent for summer tea parties, and so she was. She can be prim and proud in a way that makes you cringe, more teary than Millay; but her language, at the distance of most of a century, has the hazy clarity of old windows. She could almost never protect a whole poem from the waves of bathos that threatened it, but "Village Mystery" could slip into a Hardy anthology with no one the wiser.

To her back door-step came a ghost,
A girl who had been ten years dead,
She stood by the granite hitching-post
And begged for a piece of bread.

Now why should I, who walk alone,
Who am ironical and proud,
Turn, when a woman casts a stone
At a beggar in a shroud?

I saw the dead girl cringe and whine,
And cower in the weeping air—
But, oh, she was no kin of mine,
And so I did not care!

Archibald MacLeish often managed to make himself look ridiculous; and, when he didn't, parodists like Edmund Wilson were there to help him. He adored grand themes and grander pretensions, but for a few lines he can sound like a version of young Eliot:

He sits in the rue St. Jacques at the iron table
It is dusk it is growing cold the roof stone glitters on the gable
The taxies turn in the rue du Pot de Fer
The gas jets brighten one by one behind the windows of the stair

Any adult forced to read *J. B.* in high school loves to see MacLeish lost in a gale of sententiousness (even Polonius might have shied from saying, "A poem should not mean / But be"). Lines like those above are a reminder of the poet he might have been, given more prussic acid in his blood.

Robinson Jeffers is another poet who often looks ridiculous— his blowsy self-righteousness, by Whitman out of Woolworth's, worked better for Woolworth's than Whitman. Every time I see lines that tempt me, they're followed by rhetorical phrases so grandiose, it's as if he had heathens to convert, and a deadline. And yet, though spoiled by battery-operated verbs and adjectives fingered from wholesale bins, the better lines have a stormy vividness.

> *The days shorten, the south blows wide for showers now,*
> *The south wind shouts to the rivers,*
> *The rivers open their mouths and the salt salmon*
> *Race up into the freshet.*
> *In Christmas month against the smoulder and menace*
> *Of a long angry sundown,*
> *Red ash of the dark solstice, you see the anglers,*
> *Pitiful, cruel, primeval,*
> *Like the priests of the people that built Stonehenge.*

Laura Riding gave up poetry for obscure philosophical reasons and, given long enough, a century or two, might have returned to poetry for reasons equally obscure. She and Robert Graves had a permanent grudge against Auden (they felt he'd filched his early style from them), but they had grudges against nearly everyone. Her poems show a delightful off-kilter way with argument, and her oblique perceptions hide the complications beneath:

> *The map of places passes.*
> *The reality of paper tears.*
> *Land and water where they are*
> *Are only where they were*
> *When words read* here *and* here
> *Before ships happened there.*

Most of Riding's poems threaten to shift, at any instant, into analytical philosophy; but "Chloe or . . ." has the giddy awkwardness of Ransom. As with so many poets, her best lines read like might-have-beens.

Such reconsiderations may seem few and partial. In this over-long anthology many poets contribute a poem, or even a few lines, that bring the dozing reader up short. Who would have thought Harriet Monroe capable of an odd poetic dialogue like "Radio"? It's just a ham-radio operator talking about talking to a distant freighter, but with disturbing comic psychology. H. P. Lovecraft could write a spooky little poem, "The Well," like an abbreviation of Frost's "The Witch of Coös." Wilbert Snow is capable of stained-glass passages of natural description, if little else:

> *Marvels undreamed of suddenly unfold*
> *The secrets they have kept concealed so long;*
> *The rancid mud-clams whose white shells betray*
> *A worthlessness within, like beggar's gold,*
> *Or empty conkles farther up the beach;*
> *The iridescent clam-worms blue and green*
> *With escalading red and yellow fringes,*
> *Like Chinese dragons whose soft tentacles*
> *Expand, contract, and writhe in oozy slime;*
> *Long-buried whore's eggs; razor-fish with shells*
> *Brown as old ivory and smooth as glass.*

This is Milton after a day at the beach. What you appreciate, in the longueurs of these volumes, are poets who weren't trapped by period diction, who didn't try to out-Keats Keats or out-Tennyson Tennyson (the early century overdosed on them). Poets like Djuna Barnes and John Peale Bishop didn't produce lasting verse; but compared to the poets around them their lines are still readable, fresh with an instinct of language that hasn't gone rotten decades later.

Like MacLeish, Maxwell Bodenheim can ape the young Eliot, though once Eliot had been the young Eliot there wasn't much reason for anyone else to be. Donald Davidson's "Sanctuary" holds up well for the first half (how aromatically Southern the minor Fugitives could be!), then turns to sentimental guff. Rolfe Humphries's comic and nightmarish "Europa" works too hard for its effects; but his myth has a lovely, skewed, understated ending. H. Phelps Putnam hit too many lines with a sledgehammer; but *his* nightmarish poem, "Bill Gets Burned," is even more of a nightmare. Robert Francis lives in the shadow of Frost; yet some of his shorter poems, like "By Night," have Frost's vulnerability:

> *After midnight I heard a scream.*
> *I was awake. It was no dream.*
> *But whether it was bird of prey*
> *Or prey of bird I could not say.*
> *I never heard that sound by day.*

There are other poets worth looking at, if only to see how strong the influence of better poets was, or how far out of the way a poet had to go to escape such influence. Elder Olson, Edwin Rolfe, Winfield Townley Scott, and a few others get less space than many poets made of nothing but cornbread. An anthology like this can't neglect hardworking journeymen like Robert Penn Warren, Karl Shapiro, and J. V. Cunningham (though his best poem, "Meditation on Statistical Method," is missing), who are given their due, or a little better than their due. But why include ten pages of an airless academic like Robert Fitzgerald, or twenty pages (including four very long poems) of doctrinaire, stiff-jointed verse by Muriel Rukeyser ("Whoever despises the clitoris despises the penis / Whoever despises the penis despises the cunt")? Such are the mysteries of taste.

Of course there are many poets much worse. The dreadful are here in their dozens and scores. It's pointless to quote bad poetry, except as amusement; but a reader should know that someone (indeed, the majority of a committee!) thought the past century of American verse couldn't do without Walter Conrad Arensberg (later an important art collector): "Ing? Is it possible to mean ing? / Suppose / for the termination in *g* / a disoriented / series / of the simple fractures / in sleep. / Soporific / has accordingly a value for soap." Or Anna Hempstead Branch, who wrote

> *It took me ten days*
> *To read the Bible through.*
> *Then I saw what I saw,*
> *And I knew what I knew.*

And the reader, too, will see what he sees and know what he knows.

What *is* poetry, except whatever people choose to call poems? The anthology opens with a cluster of ballads—the ballad is one of the few forms of song to retain the status of poetry. Ballads can be difficult to date, so the editors limit their subjects to twentieth-century newspaper headlines, like the sinking of the *Titanic* or the train wreck behind "Casey Jones." They're not good ballads, though the assassination of McKinley provokes a fiery bit of political raillery.

Ballads are one thing, song lyrics another. Lyrics, like oral poetry, depend on something denied to the page—on paper they suffer curious flattening. The poet has to work with different and narrower means than the songwriter—the poem must satisfy the intelligence of the eye. The editors aren't seriously committed to paying tribute to American song; otherwise there'd be more of it. We get Ma Rainey, Bessie Smith, Blind Lemon Jefferson, and Robert Johnson on the one hand, and Cole Porter, Oscar Hammerstein, Ira Gershwin, and Frank Loesser on the other (the editors never get beyond their bias toward the blues and Broadway). Irving Berlin is the lonely representative of old-fashioned Tin Pan Alley songwriting and Woody Guthrie almost the sole example of a folk singer.

However prolific or popular they were, few of these songwriters are allowed more than one song. I can see the temptation to include lyrics; but a few pages should have convinced the editors that what makes songs memorable isn't the lyrics alone. Look what happens on the page to a Cole Porter song that lights up the stage.

> *I get no kick from champagne.*
> *Mere alcohol doesn't thrill me at all,*

So tell me why should it be true
That I get a kick out of you?
Some get a kick from cocaine.
I'm sure that if I took even one sniff
That would bore me terrific'ly too
Yet I get a kick out of you.

Even if you know the tune, the lines lie there like a corpse. It doesn't help the lyrics that they're nowhere identified as lyrics— and yet a reader almost always knows they *are* lyrics, because the rhythms are awkward and something seems to be missing. It's condescending to treat song this way, and I can't imagine what the editors will do for the later twentieth century. Give us Paul Simon and rap music?

The avant-garde creates more problems than song lyrics. Perhaps it's time to admit that experimental poetry is just that—experimental. Most scientific experiments end in failure, and literary experiments are rarely more successful (experimental poetry ends in failure, traditional verse in mediocrity). Experimental poetry ought to be treated like genre fiction, a bastard form with its own rules (even having no rules is a rule), ones that tend to produce poetry as quickly passé as sci-fi. Many of the poets are included only because they contributed their failures to someone else's success. Or merely contributed their failures. The babble of Eugene Jolas ("illa mala rulidala / singa rusta prilanala / buina ruli astara") or Abraham Lincoln Gillespie ("punziplaze karmasokist DecoYen Pompieraeian / scaruscatracery timmedigets") or Elsa von Freytag-Loringhoven ("Ildrich mitzdonja—astatootch / Ninj—iffe kniek —/ Ninj—iffe kniek! / Arr—karr—/ Arrkarr—barr") must have looked embarrassing even in the twenties, just as the poems by John Cage, if they *are* poems, look embarrassing now.

I can't be alone in finding Gertrude Stein unreadable, a mixture of the nursery and the lecture hall. Every line sounds as if it had been translated into French and then out of it, by Germans. Deranging our easy comprehensions of language has moral and philosophical purpose, but isn't the purpose obvious after a page or two? A child could never write like Stein, because a child would feel more obliged to be interesting. Forty pages of Stein is just torture by another name.

Experimental poetry is various as the languages of Babel, but much of it is composed of different doses of Pound, Williams, St. John of the Cross, and the Yellow Pages. Why waste more than thirty pages on Louis Zukofsky, whose poems are what Pound would have written if he'd had no talent? There are thirty-two anemic pages of Charles Olson, twenty-six of George Oppen, twenty of Lorine Niedecker, nineteen of Kenneth Rexroth—lavish allotments for poets of such dull, didactic execution. Olson's crisp descriptions, typical of many poets influenced by Pound, descend into ranting sentimentality ("o mother, if you had once touched me // o mother, if I had once touched you"). He writes like a Habakkuk of the junkyard:

> *O souls, in life and in death,*
> *awake, even as you sleep, even in sleep*
> *know what wind*
> *even under the crankcase of the ugly automobile*
> *lifts it away.*

George Oppen's small poems got smaller the longer he wrote, and owe heart and soul (and their lungs and livers) to better poems by William Carlos Williams. Lorine Niedecker's poems are babyish and tinted with sentiment ("Remember my little granite pail? / The handle of it was blue. / Think what's got away in my life—/ Was enough to carry me thru"). If I say that Niedecker's "Darwin" is better than dozens of poems here in the main tradition (the editors have a taste for sincere, dull mainstream poets), and that on occasion a line by Olson or Oppen or Rexroth glows like radium, it won't satisfy the critics who treat them as the hallowed forebears (Pilgrims and pioneers wrapped up into one) of new American poetry.

The exception is William Everson, a poet beloved of the avant-garde though not really *of* the avant-garde (he's avant-garde only by forced adoption). Sometimes he sounds like a west coast Whitman, though the poems pay homage, less attractively, to Robinson Jeffers, the Yeats of Carmel. Everson's poems are overwritten; but

"A Canticle to the Waterbirds," as dotty and obsessive as Smart or Clare, shows off his mad observant eye in a form that almost forgives his overwriting.

> *And you freshwater egrets east in the flooded marshlands skirting*
> *   the sea-level rivers, white one-legged watchers of shallows;*
> *Broad-headed kingfishers minnow-hunting from willow stems on*
> *   meandering valley sloughs;*
> *You too, you herons, blue and supple-throated, stately, taking the*
> *   air majestical in the sunflooded San Joaquin,*
> *Grading down on your belted wings from the upper lights of sun-*
> *   set,*
> *Mating over the willow clumps or where the flatwater rice fields*
> *   shimmer.*

Black poets present difficulties more profound than those of the avant-garde. Until the current generation, black poets, like women, labored under disadvantages easy for later readers to ignore, disadvantages psychological as well as social, with harsh aesthetic consequence. The forerunners of modern black poetry are very difficult to read now. W. E. B. Dubois, for example, is a more embarrassing version of Vachel Lindsay:

> *I am the Smoke King*
> *I am black!*
> *I am swinging in the sky,*
> *I am wringing worlds awry;*
> *   I am the thought of the throbbing mills,*
> *   I am the soul of the soul-toil kills,*
> *   Wraith of the ripple of trading rills.*

The Harlem Renaissance has received more critical attention than its achievements deserve. James Weldon Johnson wrote hardworking, spiritual poems of crude and heartfelt simplicity, and an occasional poem in the excruciating dialect of Uncle Remus (dialect may have seemed an act of liberation, but now it reads like an act of submission).

Dis caused a great confusion 'mongst de animals,
Ev'y critter claimed dat he had won de prize;
Dey 'sputed an' dey arg'ed, dey growled an' dey roared,
Den putty soon de dus' begin to rise.
Brer Rabbit he jes' stood aside an' urged 'em on to fight.

However much you know the reason such poetry assumed the form it did, reason doesn't make the poems any better. The poems of many of the Harlem poets are disfigured by the need to make the case for black poetry—make the case merely for being black. Sterling A. Brown's dialect poems are relics of another era, and not interesting even as relics:

I laks yo' kin' of lovin',
  Ain't never caught you wrong,
But it jes' ain' nachal
  Fo' to stay here long;

It jes' ain' nachal
  Fo' a railroad man,
With a itch fo' travelin'
  He cain't understan'.

This is faux naivete at its worst. Langston Hughes is a more conventional poet, but he had a taste for high-flown rhetoric and morality tales dreary as advertising slogans:

I, too, sing America.

I am the darker brother.
They send me to eat in the kitchen
When company comes,
But I laugh,
And eat well,
And grow strong.

He rarely wrote the sly social observation of which he was capable ("Be-Bop Boys": "Imploring Mecca / to achieve / six discs / with Decca"). For too many black poets, poetry was meant to prove a point, and always the same point—that a black man was human. It's a dispiriting point to make, to believe you have to make; and it explains why such poetry was corrupted (like anti-war poetry) by the corruptions it exposed.

There are black poets far better, given less space because they took their influences from more traditional sources. Jean Toomer, for example, could write with the moral sufficiency of Frost:

> *Black reapers with the sound of steel on stones*
> *Are sharpening scythes. I see them place the hones*
> *In their hip-pockets as a thing that's done,*
> *And start their silent swinging, one by one.*
> *Black horses drive a mower through the weeds,*
> *And there, a field rat, startled, squealing bleeds,*
> *His belly close to ground. I see the blade,*
> *Blood-stained, continue cutting weeds and shade.*

Sometimes the syntax only awkwardly accommodates his rhymes. On city life, Toomer was a bad journalist, full of city-hall good works; but his country poems have a scathing, suspicious eye at ground level (oddly, he became a gullible follower of Gurdjieff). Arna Bontemps was an unaffected romantic poet whose language suddenly darkened to stark ambiguities:

> *Yet what I sowed and what the orchard yields*
> *my brother's sons are gathering stalk and root;*
> *small wonder then my children glean in fields*
> *they have not sown, and feed on bitter fruit.*

Claude McKay wrote sonnets—proud, angry, and overwrought sonnets—but the end of "The Lynching" shows what even second-hand rhetoric could rise to, given passion and contempt enough:

> *Day dawned, and soon the mixed crowds came to view*
> *The ghastly body swaying in the sun:*
> *The women thronged to look, but never a one*
> *Showed sorrow in her eyes of steely blue;*
> *And little lads, lynchers that were to be,*
> *Danced round the dreadful thing in fiendish glee.*

It's almost a scene from Hogarth. The blue eyes remind us, subtly and not so subtly, that the women are white. And those children! They should have been strangled at birth. Countee Cullen suffered the defensiveness black poetry is heir to; but his marriage of Christian and Greek myth has clumsy, peculiar beauty:

> *I doubt not that God is good, well-meaning, kind,*
> *And did He stoop to quibble could tell why*
> *The little buried mole continues blind,*
> *Why flesh that mirrors Him must some day die,*
> *Make plain the reason tortured Tantalus*
> *Is baited by the fickle fruit, declare*
> *If merely brute caprice dooms Sisyphus*
> *To struggle up a never-ending stair.*

The notion that a poetry indebted to spirituals or the blues is more essentially black condescends to what it pretends to honor. (That the blues and hymns are partly rooted in white music is conveniently forgotten.) Cullen showed promise in forms not thought his to possess, and might have been considered a modernist in reverse. He fled his inheritance without abandoning its lessons.

Experimental poetry and black poetry have been given special dispensation in this anthology, in a way other poetry has not. Once poems are chosen not for their aesthetic but their social character, an anthology turns merely polemical. The Library of America is not the worst offender. The poet most lavishly represented in Oxford's new *Anthology of Modern American Poetry* is Melvin B. Tolson. Melvin B. Tolson? His *Libretto for the Republic of Liberia*, a ludicrous pastiche of modernist practice, *The Waste Land* imitated by a shelf of reference books, is printed in its entirety. Here are Oxford's top two-dozen poets, with the pages they're allotted:

Melvin B. Tolson	58
William Carlos Williams	37
Muriel Rukeyser	35
T. S. Eliot	34
Gertrude Stein	29
Ezra Pound	28

Allen Ginsberg	27
Ron Silliman	27
Marianne Moore	26
Hart Crane	24
Langston Hughes	23
Robert Frost	22
Adrienne Rich	21
Wallace Stevens	20
Theodore Roethke	18
Sylvia Plath	17
Elizabeth Bishop	17
Adrian C. Louis	17
Gwendolyn Brooks	16
Charles Reznikoff	16
Robert Hayden	15
Robert Lowell	15
Sterling A. Brown	13
Kenneth Rexroth	13

It takes an editor without fear of God to favor Muriel Rukeyser over T. S. Eliot, Gertrude Stein over Ezra Pound, Ron Silliman over Marianne Moore and Hart Crane, Langston Hughes over Robert Frost, Adrienne Rich over Wallace Stevens, Adrian C. Louis over Robert Lowell. Far down the list are poor Walt Whitman and Emily Dickinson, who, though they open the anthology, receive eight and nine pages respectively. The editor, Cary Nelson, has idiosyncratic taste and isn't always taken in by the darlings of the avant-garde (Charles Olson receives only six pages, George Oppen five). He neglects song lyrics but has included poems by Chinese immigrants and haiku by Japanese internees in west coast concentration camps—these have haunting historical presence, as would tombstone rhymes from New England cemeteries or Boot Hill.

Nelson's disgraceful selection of poets born after World War II uses academe's current standard for admission: the young must be any race but white, unless they are any gender but male. Following Ron Silliman (born in 1946 and given more pages, recall, than

Moore, Crane, Frost, Stevens, Roethke, Bishop, or Lowell), the youngest poets consist of six American Indian, five black, five Asian, and four Hispanic poets, as well as two white women and a gay white man. This peculiar but now common practice might have been testimonial to our oddly various (and proudly various) society. Alas, most are examples of how "representation" becomes unrepresentative—poetry makes an unhappy bedfellow to the self-esteem industry. It is all too easy to confine poets (for all sorts of high-minded reasons) to the accidents of birth—that is just another way of refusing to take them at their word. One day such restricted readings will seem strange and old-fashioned. Meanwhile, all a critic can do is blink in disbelief and plead with readers that contemporary poetry, for all its faults, is not nearly as boring as this, that some of the most talented poets have been excluded, strangely, because of the color of their skin. The Oxford anthology will be out of date tomorrow, and the day after tomorrow will be reissued by its happy publisher with the politics updated. Politics are poetics, I'm sure someone will say.

The Library of America volumes pretend to a permanence no anthology can claim: in a few years even our plain speech may no longer be plain. Many poems of the last century already require annotation to be read—not just for brand names and historical figures now forgotten, but for lines whose obscurity can be pierced only by a homely fact. The editors state that "No note is made for material included in standard desk-reference books, such as *Webster's Ninth New Collegiate Dictionary* or *Webster's Biographical Dictionary*," which falls short of promising that anything not in such books will be explained. The scanty notes are neighborly and thorough—allusions are pinned, newspaper stories retrieved from the morgue, phrases parsed, songbirds identified—but any reader who's not an encyclopedia will be lost. Pound's belligerent knowledge is the final exam for any anthology's notes (usually the work of graduate students or gypsy scholars). To take a single page from the selection of *The Cantos*, why are we not told where Pergusa, or Gargaphia, or Gourdon are? Which passage of Ovid is being muttered? What was the "Tree of the Visages"? What does "Hymenæus Io! / Hymen, Io Hymenæe! Aurunculeia!" mean? Who was

So-Gioku? Who was Ran-ti? All are glossed in Carroll F. Terrell's *A Companion to the Cantos of Ezra Pound* (Ran-ti under the name Hsiang, a correction), so the knowledge isn't common.

As you page through other poems, other poets, you begin to think there's a conspiracy of silence. I don't know what Frost meant by a "Cyb'laean avenue," though I assume he's referring to Cybele. In one of Carl Sandburg's poems, I know that Dazzy is Dazzy Vance, but not who the football player Foozly was. Who were Tom Dines, Art Fitzgerald, and Platt (all from one poem by Vachel Lindsay)? We're told what Nujol was, but not, in the same Cummings poem, what a Cluett shirt might be or how to untangle lines like "land of the Arrow Ide / and Earl & / Wilson / Collars." Or that "comes out like a ribbon lies flat on the brush" was an advertising slogan (but for which toothpaste?). There are far too many places where the curious reader will simply be left curious. These are the petty difficulties—more complex ones, such as what Hart Crane meant by "Thomas // a Ediford" (some interstate merger between Edison and Ford?) are simply overlooked. Wouldn't a reader want to know the learning, or mock learning, behind Charles Olson's "Tartarian-Erojan, Gaean-Ouranian"? And why is the allusion to Wordsworth in Elizabeth Bishop's "Crusoe in England" ignored, when the point of the poem is that Crusoe can't remember the key word *solitude*?

Editors have long sought the Holy Grail of textual authority—final manuscript draft, first book-publication, last publication under author's control (some editors would accept revisions tendered through a Ouija board). This anthology chooses the "earliest book edition prepared with the author's participation," a rule not always, as it admits, followed consistently and one that solves fewer problems than it causes. Are the editors such companions to error they don't want to save the authors from their printers and proofreaders, save them even from themselves? It was long known that *The Cantos* was pockmarked with mistakes, caused by Pound's inadequate library, his trust in memory, and the problems of producing poems difficult lexically and typographically when the author lived in Europe and banged out lines on a balky typewriter. The 1970 edition, still in Pound's lifetime, corrected a score or more errors left uncorrected here (including typos as obvious as a pair of *theys* that should be *thys*). Even if the anthology had printed line numbers to *The Waste Land*, the text it follows would be confusing— from the middle of "What the Thunder Said," the notes are one line off, and a note at the end of "The Fire Sermon" is three lines off. (These are old errors often repeated. And why not let Eliot correct, as he later did, the Latin at the end of "What the Thunder Said"?) Frost died wanting the poem "Choose Something Like a Star" called "Take Something Like a Star"—shouldn't he be allowed to have his way?

Any reader loves to find slips and misdemeanors (if the errors are rare in a long anthology it's a miracle), and here are a few of them. I don't think the Sioux Control in Frost's "The Witch of Coös" is a "U.S. agent in charge of the affairs of the Sioux Indian tribe"—surely it's the witch medium's "control," her contact in the supernatural world. A line in Wallace Stevens's "A Postcard from the Volcano" should read "with our bones," not "with out bones." Pound's "Women of Trachis" is almost everywhere misspelled "Women of Trakis." In his Canto XIII, the two lines before "And Kung said, 'Without character . . .'" are falsely interpolated. (I think the volume of *The Cantos* listed in the acknowledgments doesn't exist.) St. Elizabeths is at least twice misspelled St. Elizabeth's. In Elizabeth Bishop's "The Man-Moth," the phrase should be "as a disease," not "as disease" (a typo corrected in later books). In the biographies, Anne Spencer's death date and Claude McKay's birth date don't agree with the dates in the text.

The biographies are often more fascinating than the poems, as biographies usually are (one reason readers prefer biographies of poets to their poetry is that the lives are more poetic, and more unlikely, than the poems). A West Point graduate, Charles Erskine Scott Wood campaigned in the 1870s against the Nez Percé, the Bannock, and the Paiute, but sixty years later served on the Committee for the Defense of Trotsky. (It's like reading that the old gunfighter Bat Masterson died—in the newsroom—as a sports reporter for the *New York Morning Telegraph*.) I'm delighted to know that Hart Crane's father, a candy maker, invented the Life Saver. And that Elsa von Freytag-Loringhoven went through three husbands before she found a baron, and that after marrying him they "settled at the Ritz." And that William Carlos Williams had her arrested for assault. There's a perverse pleasure in learning that Vachel Lindsay drank Lysol, and Orrick Johns poison; that George Sterling ate cyanide, and Sara Teasdale and Edwin Denby sleeping pills; that Emanuel Carnevali choked on a piece of bread; that Harry Crosby murdered his lover before committing suicide; that Maxwell Bodenheim and his wife were murdered by a "former mental patient who believed they were Communists." But do we really need to know which high school Robert Frost attended?

What makes an American poet American? Eliot left his country at twenty-six, wrote all but a few early poems in England, and became a British citizen at thirty-nine. Yet, despite fifty years in Oxford and London, and raging cases of Anglophilia, Anglicanism, and monarchism, he was rarely mistaken for anything but an uprooted American. Pound was stateless, though a stateless American—he fled in his early twenties and never returned long except for the sad decade of incarceration in St. Elizabeths. On the other hand, Auden arrived in America at thirty-one and stayed nearly to the end of his life (*he* became an American citizen at thirty-nine). You end up feeling he's not in this anthology because the British claim him as part of the empire; yet Auden's mature poetry revels in American scene and American idiom ("I sit in one of the dives / On Fifty-Second Street"). Was Vladimir Nabokov included because, though he didn't arrive in America until he was over forty, no other English-speaking country has a right to him? No simple algorithm defines nationality for the anthologist, but if we're denied Auden why is the minor Scottish poet Helen Adam included? She didn't immigrate until she was thirty, when she had already published three collections in Britain. If you accept her weak imitation of the border ballads ("Sing doun the mune. / When a' seas are motionless, / Then will she droon"), you ought to demand in compensation

Nobody I know would like to be buried
  with a silver cocktail shaker,
a transistor radio and a strangled
  daily help, or keep his word because

of a great-great-grandmother who got laid
  by a sacred beast.

All anthologies are founded on the punishment of sins. What will the future say of our anthologies, our attempt to rescue the past by laying waste to it? That we were idiots for including most poets and that we should have worshiped someone we now ignore. That we, we who lacked the exquisite taste and moral sensibility of that future, loved the wrong poems by the right poets, the right poems for the wrong reasons, and that our wrong reasons defined the taste of the age (it's always taste, rather than tastes—the future thinks the taste of the past homogenous). Much of the past is propaganda, and our selection of the past another sort of propaganda—a selection of the past is an explanation of the present. The Library of America has produced a version of American poetry that is myopic, biased, sometimes infuriating—in short, everything an anthology *should* be, except selective enough. There are few tools for analysis and far too many poems only a poet's mother could love—the tattered revenants look like Marley's ghost, loaded with the chains of old poetic sins.

Most poetry has designs on us, which means it asks for a species of pity—and pity requires a denaturing of language. When Degas groused to Mallarmé that he couldn't seem to write a sonnet, though he was full of ideas, Mallarmé responded, "But, Degas, it's not with ideas that you make verses. It's with words." In the long run, it's the words that last, not the ideas. The poetry of a country is the history of its idiom—diction is the devil; but the devil dies each generation, not to be revived. (If we think our diction transparent, as most generations do, we are only as ignorant as most generations are.) An American poetry becomes American not in its differences from itself but in its differences from poetry beyond its borders—and these are differences of premise and assumption as well as differences of diction (the reason real translation is not so much difficult as impossible). The anthology of our poetry cannot define those differences so much as gesture emptily toward them.

The twentieth century is not just the most important century of American verse; it is the only century of American verse—the poetic tradition in previous centuries was English. American poetry was no more than a colony until Whitman and Dickinson (the way out, oddly, was prepared in Poe's criticism), but their independence had nothing to do with what followed half a century later. They established no tradition and without modernism would have seemed isolated and eccentric accidents. William Carlos Williams was wrong—*The Waste Land* made it easier for American poets to challenge Europe on home ground (such a poem could never have been written by an Englishman). Modernism was not just the major movement of the last hundred years, but the movement that shifted the attention of English poetry away from England. Poets have spent the rest of a century, on both sides of the Atlantic, coming to terms with that. Much of this was plain to Randall Jarrell fifty years ago—it is plainer now.

It would have been fitting to end this anthology with Robert Lowell, the last major American poet. He was the most significant poet after World War II; he created a high formal style and then killed it with a glance (how many American poets fled formal verse within months of reading *Life Studies*?); and he continues to haunt our idea of poets and poetry. We may be living in the decaying manner of free verse a long while yet, but our poetry is now as frozen in its customs as the Augustan mode after Pope. This anthology shows, like the most pitiless of X-rays, how soon the diction that leaves readers breathless leaves a later generation faint with laughter, how swiftly bad poets are drowned in the wake of good, and how rare, mysterious, and lacking in conscience good poets are.

Books under Review

Abroad and at Home

Ted Hughes, *Wolfwatching*. Farrar, Straus, and Giroux, 1991.
Eavan Boland, *Outside History: Selected Poems, 1980–1990.* New York: W. W. Norton, 1990.
John Ashbery, *Flow Chart*. Alfred A. Knopf, 1991.
Paul Muldoon, *Madoc: A Mystery*. Farrar, Straus, and Giroux, 1991.

The Fallen World of Geoffrey Hill

Geoffrey Hill, *New and Collected Poems, 1952–1992*. Houghton Mifflin, 1994.

Dreams of an Uncommon Tongue

Gjertrud Schnackenberg, *A Gilded Lapse of Time*. Farrar, Straus, and Giroux, 1992.
C. K. Williams, *A Dream of Mind*. Farrar, Straus, and Giroux, 1992.
Thom Gunn, *The Man with Night Sweats*. Farrar, Straus, and Giroux, 1992.

A Material World

Jorie Graham, *Materialism*. Ecco Press, 1993.
Richard Kenney, *The Invention of the Zero*. Alfred A. Knopf, 1993.
James Fenton, *Out of Danger*. Farrar, Straus, and Giroux, 1994.

Old Faithfuls

W. S. Merwin, *Travels*. Alfred A. Knopf, 1993.
Mona Van Duyn, *If It Be Not I: Collected Poems, 1959–1982*. Alfred A. Knopf, 1993.
———, *Firefall*. Alfred A. Knopf, 1993.
John Ashbery, *Hotel Lautréamont*. Alfred A. Knopf, 1992.

Pound at the Post Office

Ezra Pound, *The Letters of Ezra Pound, 1907–1941*. Ed. D. D. Paige. Preface by Mark Van Doren. Harcourt, Brace, 1950 (out of print). New Directions, 1971.

———, *Pound/Joyce: The Letters of Ezra Pound to James Joyce, with Pound's Essays on Joyce*. Ed. Forrest Read. New Directions, 1967.

———, *Pound/Ford: The Story of a Literary Friendship*. Ed. Brita Lindberg-Seyersted. New Directions, 1982.

———, *Ezra Pound and Dorothy Shakespear: Their Letters, 1909–1914*. Eds. Omar Pound and A. Walton Litz. New Directions, 1984.

———, *Pound/Lewis: The Letters of Ezra Pound and Wyndham Lewis*. Ed. Timothy Materer. New Directions, 1985.

———, *Pound/Zukofsky: Selected Letters of Ezra Pound and Louis Zukofsky*. Ed. Barry Ahearn. New Directions, 1987.

———, *Pound/The Little Review: The Letters of Ezra Pound to Margaret Anderson*. Eds. Thomas L. Scott and Melvin J. Friedman with the assistance of Jackson R. Bryer. New Directions, 1988.

———, *Ezra Pound and Margaret Cravens: A Tragic Friendship, 1910–1912*. Eds. Omar Pound and Robert Spoo. Duke University Press, 1988.

———, *The Selected Letters of Ezra Pound to John Quinn, 1915–1924*. Ed. Timothy Materer. Duke University Press, 1991.

———, *Ezra Pound and James Laughlin: Selected Letters*. Ed. David M. Gordon. W. W. Norton, 1994.

Eliot among the Metaphysicals

T. S. Eliot, *The Varieties of Metaphysical Poetry: The Clark Lectures at Trinity College, Cambridge, 1926, and The Turnbull Lectures at The Johns Hopkins University, 1933*. Ed. and intro. Ronald Schuchard. Faber and Faber, 1993.

Classics and Commercials

Christopher Logue, *The Husbands: An Account of Books Three and Four of Homer's Iliad*. Farrar, Straus, and Giroux, 1995.
Alice Fulton, *Sensual Math*. W. W. Norton, 1995.

In the Lectureship of Verse

Seamus Heaney, *The Redress of Poetry*. Farrar, Straus, and Giroux, 1995.
Helen Vendler, *The Breaking of Style: Hopkins, Heaney, Graham*. Harvard University Press, 1995.
———, *The Given and the Made: Strategies of Poetic Redefinition*. Harvard University Press, 1995.

Anthony Hecht, *On the Laws of the Poetic Art.* Princeton University Press, 1995.

The Bounty of Derek Walcott

Derek Walcott, *The Bounty.* Farrar, Straus, and Giroux, 1997.

Martyrs to Language

John Ashbery, *Can You Hear, Bird.* Farrar, Straus, and Giroux, 1995.

Adrienne Rich, *Dark Fields of the Republic: Poems 1991–1995.* W. W. Norton, 1995.

August Kleinzahler, *Red Sauce, Whiskey and Snow.* Farrar, Straus, and Giroux, 1995.

Billy Collins, *The Art of Drowning.* University of Pittsburgh Press, 1995.

Rita Dove, *Mother Love.* W. W. Norton, 1995.

Stanley Kunitz, *Passing Through: The Later Poems, New and Selected.* W. W. Norton, 1995.

Elizabeth Spires, *Worldling.* W. W. Norton, 1995.

Gravel on the Tongue

W. S. Merwin, *The Vixen.* Alfred A. Knopf, 1995.

Sharon Olds, *The Wellspring.* Alfred A. Knopf, 1996.

Virginia Hamilton Adair, *Ants on the Melon.* Random House, 1996.

Mark Doty, *Atlantis.* HarperCollins, 1995.

Louise Glück, *Meadowlands.* Ecco Press, 1996.

Seamus Heaney, *The Spirit Level.* Farrar, Straus, and Giroux, 1996.

Lowell in the Shadows

Paul Mariani, *Lost Puritan: A Life of Robert Lowell.* W. W. Norton, 1994.

Old Guys

Charles Simic, *Walking the Black Cat.* Harcourt Brace, 1996.

A. R. Ammons, *Brink Road.* W. W. Norton, 1996.

Robert Hass, *Sun under Wood.* Ecco Press, 1996.

C. K. Williams, *The Vigil.* Farrar, Straus, and Giroux, 1997.

Joseph Brodsky, *So Forth.* Farrar, Straus, and Giroux, 1996.

Anthony Hecht, *Flight among the Tombs.* Alfred A. Knopf, 1996.

Hardscrabble Country

Charles Wright, *Black Zodiac.* Farrar, Straus, and Giroux, 1997.

Michael Lind, *The Alamo: An Epic*. Houghton Mifflin, 1997.
Mary Oliver, *West Wind*. Houghton Mifflin, 1997.
Robert Bly, *Morning Poems*. HarperCollins, 1997.
Les Murray, *Subhuman Redneck Poems*. Farrar, Straus, and Giroux, 1997.
Edgar Bowers, *Collected Poems*. Alfred A. Knopf, 1997.

Richard Wilbur's Civil Tongue

Richard Wilbur, *New and Collected Poems*. Harcourt Brace Jovanovich, 1988.

Betrayals of the Tongue

Geoffrey Hill, *Canaan*. Houghton Mifflin, 1997.
Jorie Graham, *The Errancy*. Ecco Press, 1997.
J. V. Cunningham, *The Poems of J. V. Cunningham*. Ed. and intro. by Timothy
  Steele. Swallow Press/Ohio University Press, 1997.
Ted Hughes, *Tales from Ovid*. Farrar, Straus, and Giroux, 1997.
Amy Clampitt, *The Collected Poems of Amy Clampitt*. Foreword by Mary Jo
  Salter. Alfred A. Knopf, 1997.

Soiled Desires

Ted Hughes, *Birthday Letters*. Farrar, Straus, and Giroux, 1998.
John Ashbery, *Wakefulness*. Farrar, Straus, and Giroux, 1998.
Frank Bidart, *Desire*. Farrar, Straus, and Giroux, 1997.
Karl Kirchwey, *The Engrafted Word*. Henry Holt, 1998.
Frederick Seidel, *Going Fast*. Farrar, Straus, and Giroux, 1998.
August Kleinzahler, *Green Sees Things in Waves*. Farrar, Straus, and Giroux,
  1998.

Three Magi

Charles Wright, *Appalachia*. Farrar, Straus, and Giroux, 1998.
Edward Hirsch, *On Love*. Alfred A. Knopf, 1998.
Henri Cole, *The Visible Man*. Alfred A. Knopf, 1998.

Twentieth-Century American Poetry, Abbreviated

*American Poetry: The Twentieth Century. Volume 1: Henry Adams to Dorothy
  Parker*. Library of America, 2000.
*American Poetry: The Twentieth Century. Volume 2: E. E. Cummings to May
  Swenson*. Library of America, 2000.

Credits

The year these pieces were written is in parentheses following the chapter titles.

"The Other Other Frost" (1994): *New Criterion*, June 1995.
"Abroad and at Home" (1991): (Ted Hughes and Eavan Boland) *New York Times Book Review*, April 21, 1991. Copyright 1991 by the New York Times Company. Reprinted by permission. (John Ashbery and Paul Muldoon) *Chicago Tribune*, September 8, 1991.
"The Fallen World of Geoffrey Hill" (1993): *New Criterion*, March 1994.
"Dreams of an Uncommon Tongue" (1992): *New York Times Book Review*, November 15, 1992. Copyright 1992 by the New York Times Company. Reprinted by permission.
"A Material World" (1994): *New York Times Book Review*, July 31, 1994. Copyright 1994 by the New York Times Company. Reprinted by permission.
"Old Faithfuls" (1993): (W. S. Merwin) *Times Literary Supplement*, January 14, 1994. (Mona Van Duyn and John Ashbery) *Parnassus: Poetry in Review* 18, no. 2, and 19, no. 1 (1994).
"Pound at the Post Office" (1993): *Parnassus: Poetry in Review* 20, nos. 1 and 2 (1995).
"Eliot among the Metaphysicals" (1994): *Essays in Criticism* 44, no. 2 (April 1994).
"Classics and Commercials" (1995): (Christopher Logue) *New York Times Book Review*, October 8, 1995. (Alice Fulton) *New York Times Book Review*, December 10, 1995. Both copyright 1995 by the New York Times Company. Reprinted by permission.
"In the Lectureship of Verse" (1995): *Washington Post Book World*, February 25, 1996.
"The Bounty of Derek Walcott" (1996): *New York Times Book Review*, June 29, 1997. Copyright 1997 by the New York Times Company. Reprinted by permission.

"Martyrs to Language" (1995): *New Criterion*, December 1995.

"Gravel on the Tongue" (1996): *New Criterion*, June 1996.

"The Unbearable Lightness of Elizabeth Bishop" (1993): *Southwest Review*, Winter 1994.

"Lowell in the Shadows" (1994): *New Criterion*, December 1994.

"Old Guys" (1996): *New Criterion*, December 1996.

"Hardscrabble Country" (1997): *New Criterion*, June 1997.

"Richard Wilbur's Civil Tongue" (1995): *Parnassus: Poetry in Review* 21, nos. 1 and 2 (1996).

"Betrayals of the Tongue" (1997): *New Criterion*, November 1997.

"Soiled Desires" (1998): *New Criterion*, June 1998.

"Three Magi" (1998): *Washington Post Book World*, January 10, 1999.

"Four or Five Motions toward a Poetics" (1995): *Sewanee Review*, Spring 1999.

"Twentieth-Century American Poetry, Abbreviated" (2000): *Parnassus: Poetry in Review* 25, nos. 1 and 2 (2001).

William Logan is the author of five books of poems, *Sad-faced Men* (1982), *Difficulty* (1985), *Sullen Weedy Lakes* (1988), *Vain Empires* (1998), and *Night Battle* (1999). He is also author of two books of criticism, *All the Rage* (1998) and *Reputations of the Tongue* (UPF, 1999). He lives in Florida and in Cambridge, England.